Apache Struts 2
Web Application Development

Design, develop, test, and deploy your web applications using the Struts 2 framework

Dave Newton

PUBLISHING

BIRMINGHAM - MUMBAI

Apache Struts 2 Web Application Development

First published: June 2009

Production Reference: 2040609

Published by Packt Publishing Ltd.
32 Lincoln Road
Olton
Birmingham, B27 6PA, UK.

ISBN 978-1-847193-39-1

www.packtpub.com

Cover Image by Vinayak Chittar (vinayak.chittar@gmail.com)

Credits

Author
Dave Newton

Reviewers
Sandeep Jadav
Dale Newfield
Michael Minella
Sharad Sharma

Acquisition Editor
Viraj Joshi

Development Editor
Ved Prakash Jha

Technical Editor
Gaurav Datar

Copy Editors
Sumathi Sridhar
Leonard D'Silva

Indexer
Monica Ajmera

Editorial Team Leader
Akshara Aware

Project Team Leader
Lata Basantani

Project Coordinator
Abhijeet Deobhakta

Proofreader
Joel T. Johnson

Production Coordinators
Shantanu Zagade
Adline Swetha Jesuthas

Cover Work
Shantanu Zagade

About the author

Dave has been programming for as long as he can remember, and probably a bit longer than that. He began by playing a Star Trek game on a library computer, and quickly graduated to educating his grade school teachers about computers and the BASIC language. Receiving a TRS-80 Model 1 was pretty much the end of his social life, and he's never looked back.

A diverse background in both programming languages and problem spaces has provided him with a wide range of experience. Using a diverse set of languages, which includes Pascal, Forth, Fortran, Lisp, Smalltalk, assembly, C/C++, Java, and Ruby, brings an appreciation for many programming paradigms. Working on AI, embedded systems, device drivers, and both desktop and web application programming, has brought him an appreciation for the problems and solutions that each environment offers.

Even after thirty years of typing in his first infinite loop, he's still entertained by the process of programming. He never tires of looking for ways to do less work, and is convinced that he should never have to repeat himself to a computer. He still occasionally writes an infinite loop.

Acknowledgement

I'd like to thank Packt for providing me an opportunity to share what I hope is some useful information about my favorite Java web application framework, Struts 2, and along the way, throw in some techniques I've found my clients appreciate (and many of them mean I get to do less work, so it's a win-win!)

My parents, of course, deserve far more thanks than I could ever hope to express. From them, I received a robust sense of exploration and curiosity, which are traits that have served me well during my personal and professional career. They, and the rest of my family, have prodded me along by continually asking, "How's the book coming?", which was surprisingly motivating. They have also provided, along with my friends, much needed moral support during recent months.

I'd like to thank my co-workers, who have zero compunction about telling me when I'm completely wrong, and who provide me with a constant stream of ideas about programming, the associated processes, and how to make programming easier and more flexible.

The creators of the frameworks and libraries we use every day deserve more than they usually receive. Putting one's code out there for everyone to see and use is a brave step. They're under-appreciated when everything works, and unfairly punished when it doesn't. I hope this book pays homage to them in some small way, and contributes back to the various communities that have made my programming work easier.

Finally, the open source and Java communities deserve a hearty "Huzzah!" It includes places like the Struts 2 mailing lists, where all types of developers contribute by asking and answering questions, making suggestions, and politely reminding those involved with the framework that our documentation could be better. It also includes JavaRanch, where "No question is too simple", and sometimes the "simplest" questions turn out to be surprisingly interesting. Finally, the Apache Foundation and fellow Struts developers, who have made Struts possible in all its incarnations. All those people who write the code that we use, contribute to discussions, and try to help others out know who they are. I can't possibly begin to list all of them, but thanks.

About the reviewers

Sandeep Jadav has been in the IT industry for three years and is currently working as a Software Engineer for an IT firm. Sandeep is an MCA qualified professional and is well-versed with Java technologies. He empowers people around him to work and play better, by helping them resolve complex issues with the simplest and most durable solutions.

In addition to reviewing, Sandeep has a history of using his technical skills for more practical purposes — providing technical leadership to past companies. He has an experience in developing on a large scale, n-tier and Web applications, for business and engineering uses.

Sandeep has a large network of friends and makes frequent contributions to a variety of content areas in many online IT communities.

I would first like to thank Packt Publishing, and the author Dave Newton, for spearheading this edition of Apache Struts 2 Web Application Development, and giving me an opportunity to revisit and improve upon the first efforts.

I am deeply grateful to my family for allowing me to encroach on many months of what should have been my family's quality time.

I extend my deepest appreciation to my friends, for all their support, encouragement, and guidance throughout my work.

I appreciate Packt Publishing for allowing me to gain a very new and delighting experience of reviewing the book.

While reviewing may seem a solitary pursuit, it is actually very much a collaborative effort, and as such, I extend my thanks and appreciation to my author, editor, and the staff at Packt Publishing for their support throughout this project.

Finally, I especially thank Payal for providing great support on each and every step of my life.

Dale Newfield is a computer scientist trained at Carnegie Mellon and the University of Virginia (ABD). Mr. Newfield has designed, built, and maintained a wide variety of systems in many languages. He has vertical knowledge in fields as disparate as graphics, user interfaces, virtual environments, networking, network technology design, network modeling, distributed and disconnected computation, bioinformatics, along with both web and POS systems requiring tight integration of hardware and software. Having built scalable web applications using both Struts1 and Struts2, his input was helpful in keeping this text focused on teaching best practices.

Michael T Minella has been working with, and teaching about, open source software and agile methodologies for over seven years. He holds degrees from Northern Illinois University and DePaul University in Computer Science and E-Commerce Technologies respectively.

Michael lives just outside Chicago, IL, and works at a major financial exchange there. In addition to his day job, Michael currently teaches at DeVry University, has authored a Refcard on JUnit and EasyMock (`http://refcardz.dzone.com/refcardz/junit-and-easymock`), and maintains the site `http://www.michaelminella.com`.

Michael would like to thank his wife Erica for her continued support in all the ways he expands his career.

Sharad Sharma is working as a Software Engineer with a reputed MNC. He completed his Bachelors in Technology (B.Tech) from Sikkim Manipal University, Sikkim, and has a passion to learn and teach new technologies. He has successfully completed many projects based on Java/J2EE technology. In spite of having less experience, due to his dedication and hard work, he was able to achieve the top position among all the developers of the organization. This is the first book he has worked upon and wishes to work on many more in future.

I would like to thank my family and friends for the support they have provided me in all the areas.

Table of Contents

Preface

Struts 2.1 is a modern, extensible, agile web application framework, which is suitable for both small- and large-scale web applications.

The book begins with a comprehensive look at the basics of Struts 2.1, interspersed with detours into more advanced development topics. You'll learn about configuring Struts 2.1 actions, results, and interceptors via both XML and Java annotations. You'll get an introduction to most of the Struts 2.1 custom tags, and also learn how they can assist in rapid application prototyping and development.

From there, you'll make your way into Struts 2.1's strong support for form validation and type conversion, which allows you to treat your form values as domain objects without cluttering your code. A look at Struts 2.1's interceptors is the final piece of the Struts 2.1 puzzle, which allows you to leverage the standard Struts 2 interceptors, as well as implement your own custom behavior.

After covering Struts 2.1, you'll journey into the world of JavaScript (a surprisingly capable language), the Document Object Model (DOM), and CSS, and learn how to create clean and concise client-side behavior. You'll leverage that knowledge as you move on to Struts 2 themes and templates, which give you a powerful way to encapsulate site-wide user interface behavior.

The book closes with a look at some tools that make the application development life cycle easier to manage, particularly in a team environment, and more automatic.

What this book covers

Chapter 1 gives us a bird's-eye view of Struts 2 and examines some useful techniques of lightweight, agile development.

Chapter 2 gives an introduction to Struts 2 application configuration, using both XML and annotations. It also covers the beginning of our sample application, RecipeBox.

Chapter 3 covers some of the functionality provided by Struts 2's ActionSupport class, including I18N, and a first look at form validation. It also covers some basic RecipeBox functionality after gathering some user stories.

Chapter 4 examines several common, standard Struts 2 result types. It also covers how to write our own custom result types.

Chapter 5 gives an in-depth look at the generic Struts 2 custom tags. These include tags for iteration, list generation, conditionals, and internationalization (I18N).

Chapter 6 continues our exploration of Struts 2 custom tags, focusing especially on its form tags.

Chapter 7 examines Struts 2 form validation, including both XML and annotation-driven validation. It also teaches more about how Struts 2 converts our form values into domain objects, and shows how to create our own type converters to handle custom data types.

Chapter 8 finishes our comprehensive introduction to Struts 2, by checking out the included Struts 2 interceptors. It also discusses how to write and configure our own interceptors.

Chapter 9 looks at how to handle errors in Struts 2, as well as discusses error and exception handling in general. It also covers some general Java logging topics, focusing on using Apache Commons Logging and Log4J.

Chapter 10 explores how to best leverage JavaScript and how to keep it modular.

Chapter 11 covers the client-side functionality, which depends on more than JavaScript. By using CSS and the DOM effectively, we can accomplish a lot with a minimal amount of code.

Chapter 12 covers Struts 2 themes and templates. The themes and templates in Struts 2 allow for application-wide functionality on the client side, keeping our JSP pages lightweight and adaptable. Rather than writing boilerplate HTML on our pages, we can separate it into themes and templates.

Chapter 13 takes a look at some of Struts 2's built-in support for Ajax using the Dojo tags. It also covers the Struts 2 REST plug-in that furthers our "convention over configuration" path.

Chapter 14 covers how to apply the TDD concepts to several testing aspects, including unit, functional, and acceptance tests.

Chapter 15 looks at many aspects of documentation, including "self-documenting" code, Javadocs, generators, methodologies, and so on, with a focus on automating as much documentation as possible.

What you need for this book

You'll need all the typical Java web application development tools. An IDE is very handy, but it doesn't matter which one you use. Almost any modern application server can be used to run the sample application.

Having an Internet connection while reading is *extremely* useful. The Struts 2 download includes the documentation wiki, along with the XWork and Struts 2 API Javadocs. However, we may also need to reference the Servlet API, various library APIs, and so on. Having access to the Struts 2 user mailing list can also be very beneficial, as sometimes searching the web for a question is the quickest way to get it answered.

The most important requirements aren't dependent on a particular Java version or specification. Curiosity, willingness to experiment, and patience will never be written up as a JSR, but they're critical qualities in a developer. It's perfectly fine to never learn the ins and outs of a framework. However, by digging into the documentation, and *especially* the source, we gain a much better understanding of *why* things happen the way they do. This increases our efficiency, our usefulness, and our value.

Who this book is for

This book is for Java developers who are interested in developing web applications using Struts. If you need a comprehensive introduction to Struts 2.1, along with the most important aspects of additional web application development technologies, agile programming practices, tool creation, and application life cycle management, this book is for you. You needn't know JavaScript and CSS to use this book, as the author will teach you the required basics.

If you are a Struts 1 or WebWork user, and wish to go ahead and migrate to Struts 2, this is a perfectly practical guide for you.

Conventions

In this book, you will find a number of styles of text that distinguish between different kinds of information. Here are some examples of these styles, and an explanation of their meaning.

Code words in text are shown as follows: "ActionSupport is an XWork class that provides validation and default implementations of several common interfaces needed for I18N."

A block of code will be set as follows:

```
package com.packt.s2wad.ch03.actions.i18n;
public class TextExamplesAction extends ActionSupport
                                implements TextInterface {
    private static Log log =
        LogFactory.getLog(TextExamplesAction.class);
    public String execute() throws Exception {
        log.debug(getText("from.class.props"));
        return SUCCESS;
    }
}
```

When we wish to draw your attention to a particular part of a code block, the relevant lines or items will be shown in bold:

```
<!-- Incorrect "validation" interceptor configuration. -->
<action name="brokenConfiguration"
```

Any command-line input or output is written as follows:

```
$ find . -name "*.java" | xargs grep -l "public interface"
./com/opensymphony/xwork2/Action.java
```

New terms and **important words** are shown in bold.

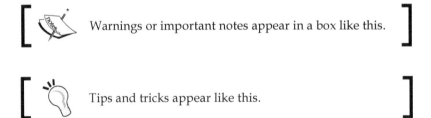

Warnings or important notes appear in a box like this.

Tips and tricks appear like this.

Reader feedback

Feedback from our readers is always welcome. Let us know what you think about this book — what you liked or may have disliked. Reader feedback is important for us to develop titles that you really get the most out of.

To send us general feedback, simply drop an email to feedback@packtpub.com, and mention the book title in the subject of your message.

If there is a book that you need and would like to see us publish, please send us a note in the **SUGGEST A TITLE** form on www.packtpub.com or email suggest@packtpub.com.

If there is a topic that you have expertise in and you are interested in either writing or contributing to a book, see our author guide on www.packtpub.com/authors.

Customer support

Now that you are the proud owner of a Packt book, we have a number of things to help you to get the most from your purchase.

Downloading the example code for the book

Visit http://www.packtpub.com/files/code/3391_Code.zip to directly download the example code.

The downloadable files contain instructions on how to use them.

Errata

Although we have taken every care to ensure the accuracy of our contents, mistakes do happen. If you find a mistake in one of our books—maybe a mistake in text or code—we would be grateful if you would report this to us. By doing so, you can save other readers from frustration, and help us improve subsequent versions of this book. If you find any errata, please report them by visiting http://www.packtpub.com/support, selecting your book, clicking on the **let us know** link, and entering the details of your errata. Once your errata are verified, your submission will be accepted and the errata added to any list of existing errata. Any existing errata can be viewed by selecting your title from http://www.packtpub.com/support.

Piracy

Piracy of copyright material on the Internet is an ongoing problem across all media. At Packt, we take the protection of our copyright and licenses very seriously. If you come across any illegal copies of our works in any form on the Internet, please provide us with the location address or website name immediately so that we can pursue a remedy.

Please contact us at copyright@packtpub.com with a link to the suspected pirated material.

We appreciate your help in protecting our authors, and our ability to bring you valuable content.

Questions

You can contact us at questions@packtpub.com if you are having a problem with any aspect of the book, and we will do our best to address it.

Struts and Agile Development

Congratulations! Our team has been airdropped into brand-new Java web application with a non-existent specification and a ridiculous deadline. Thought it couldn't happen? Many factors can conspire to create development nightmares. Staying light on our feet allows us to outmaneuver changes.

We've chosen Struts 2 for our framework. Our deliverables not only include the application and its associated industry-standard buzzwords, but also include complete testing (including unit, functional, and acceptance tests), along with full documentation.

Fortunately for our team (and the client), this is possible and enjoyable! Struts 2 not only meets the requirements of a modern web application development, but it exceeds them. Struts 2 fits nicely into the world of Web 2.0, and allows a rapid development cycle, necessary for both the client and developer to remain competitive.

Struts 2 in a nutshell

Struts 2 began as WebWork. It was an answer to some of the perceived deficiencies in Struts 1—arguably the most popular and long-lived Java web application framework. Struts 1 was tied closely to the servlet specification and contained several Struts 1-specific constructs. This made testing difficult. In addition, because the constructs were Struts 1-specific, using them in non-Struts applications was more difficult than necessary.

Struts 2 reduces (and in most cases eliminates) ties to the servlet specification, making the testing process substantially easier. Struts 2 also allows Dependency Injection (DI) at many levels, meaning that both testability and re-usability are enhanced.

Dependency Injection (DI) or Inversion of Control (IoC) will be covered throughout the book, from several angles. In a nutshell, this means that rather than a class deciding which implementation it wants to use, it is told which implementation to use through one of several mechanisms. If you're familiar with Spring or an equivalent, then it is probable that you're already quite comfortable with the idea.

Architecturally, S2 is conceptually simple, if somewhat more complex in practice. The request cycle process can be summarized as: "Requests are filtered through interceptors and are implemented by actions. The actions return results, which are executed and returned to the browser."

The filter dispatcher

Under standard configuration, Struts 2 gets a chance to process every incoming request. It is implemented as a filter (Struts 1 used a servlet) and mapped to all of the requests (Struts 1 was generally mapped to an extension such as `*.do`). The reason Struts 2 (usually) needs to examine all of the requests will be discussed later. However, for now, it's enough to know that the filter is the first step in processing a Struts 2 request.

Interceptors

Interceptors are similar to Servlet Filters, but specific to Struts 2. Interceptors are configurable for an entire application, groups of Struts 2 actions, a single action, or any combination thereof. Interceptors provide the bulk of the core framework functionality of Struts 2. Most of the "cool stuff" lives in the interceptors!

Validation, page setup, access to session and request parameters, and so on, are all provided by interceptors. They're great for providing wide-ranging functionality that cuts across an entire web application or parts thereof.

For those of us familiar with Struts 1, the (somewhat close) corollary is the Struts 1 request processor. Once, where we might have extended the request processor, we might now configure or implement an interceptor.

Many application will need only the interceptors provided by Struts 2, although we might need to configure them differently. However, many applications can benefit from even very simple custom interceptors. We'll cover details of the most useful and common Struts 2 interceptors as we go along. We will also cover (in Chapter 8) detailed interceptor configuration and implementation to add impressive and quick-to-implement functionality.

Actions

"Struts 2's actions are POJOs! Struts 2's actions are POJOs!". You'll hear that a lot. Note the following things about Struts 2's actions:

- Struts 2's actions are not (generally) tied to the servlet spec.
- They are not required to use any Struts 2-specific constructs.
- The actions handle form data more elegantly than Struts 1's `ActionForm` and return simple strings instead of the `ActionForward` used in Struts 1.

Every Struts 2 action could be a POJO. Unless we want the cool built-in functionality of Struts 2 such as form validation, I18N, and little things like that.

Let's put it this way: Struts 2's actions are more like POJO than ever before and aren't tied to the servlet spec (unless we specifically tie them to it, which is necessary on some occasions). The non-POJO aspects are wrapped up in the `ActionSupport` superclass, which provides a default implementation of the most useful non-POJO functionality.

This makes testing and reusing actions much easier, and eliminates one of the biggest Struts 1 headaches (we'll cover actions in depth in Chapter 3).

Results

Results determine what will be sent back to the browser, typically a JSP that produces HTML. Struts 2 has several other result types defined in addition to the standard dispatch to a JSP. These include redirection, redirection to actions, action chaining, FreeMarker templates, file streaming, JasperReports, and more.

We can also create and configure our own result types to provide additional application functionality that is not available in the standard Struts 2 distribution. We'll cover results, configuration, and creation of custom result types in Chapter 4.

Plug-ins

Struts 2 is extensible using its plug-in mechanism. Plug-ins can be used to provide additional functionality such as the JasperReports result. They could also be used to completely change the way we use Struts 2. An example of this is the REST plug-in, which provides Ruby on Rails-like URL handling and lessens our XML configuration. Plug-ins are a neat way to encapsulate functionality that can be used across our own applications, or even released into the wild for others to use.

Agile in a nutshell

Extreme Programming (**XP**) was the buzzword several years ago. It involves test-first development, pair programming, on-site customers, and more. Compare and contrast this with the **waterfall method** (or **BDUF: Big Design Up Front**), where detailed requirements are built upfront, followed by the application design. Finally, comes the implementation, verification, and maintenance part. It's still (arguably) the most common development model, despite repeated failures.

Many companies are pretty firmly entrenched in the waterfall method (XP or anything like it borders on heresy). The problem is that as soon as the toner on the specification has cooled, it's probably already incomplete or incorrect. As soon as development begins, the unanticipated will almost certainly appear.

At this point, either the original spec (or more likely, an emailed copy of a Word document with a date appended to the filename) might be updated to reflect the new reality, or the software will continue developing until it barely resembles the original design document. Generally, there will either be a formal change management process, or a customer that doesn't end up with what they wanted. (Or ends up with what they thought they wanted, but they were wrong.).

If the application and specification are significantly out-of-sync, the specification is no longer a useful document. A developer being introduced to the project for the first time needs to either ignore the specification and look only at the code, or reconcile differences between the two.

Whether or not a client buys in to a full-blown agile methodology may not be up to us (the consultant). However, by picking and choosing components typically associated with the agile development, we can get many of the benefits.

User stories

One of the more useful XP concepts is the "user story". **User stories** capture system interaction at a fairly high level. Details that are unable to be determined without testing, or that are not as important as the basic functionality, may be omitted during the design phase (and may never be formally specified). We'll cover user stories as we develop the sample application.

Testing

One of the most important aspects of agile development is testing and testability. It allows for both minor and localized changes, as well as sweeping application changes, while ensuring that the functionality isn't broken.

Applications can be tested at various levels. At one end of the spectrum is **unit testing**, focusing on small units of functionality, and preferably not involving any of the other system's components.

Functional testing focuses on the overall system, and can consist of testing the application by using a browser driven by any of several methods. We'll discuss several types of testing in depth in Chapter 14. However, we will touch upon testing issues throughout the book.

Refactoring

Refactoring includes the process of identifying and consolidating similar functionality at any level in the application. Consistent and correct refactoring is made possible (or at least made much easier and more reliable) by the presence of tests. Without the ability to test easily, refactoring becomes an error-prone, hit-or-miss proposition.

Aggressive refactoring at all levels in the application (Java, JSP, HTML, CSS, and so on) can significantly reduce absolute code size, along with the cognitive overhead needed to understand the application.

Short iterations

Which one of the following options would you choose:

1. Design and code an application, present it to the client, and be presented with a list of changes that necessitate changing the internals of the application itself.
2. Present small chunks of functionality, so that changes in design or implementation are identified early, and hence the impact is as minimal as possible.

Yes, the first option gives us a chance to do the mythical "complete rewrite". However, clients rarely seem willing to fund the development of the same application twice. Moreover, refactoring is, in essence, a chance to rewrite early and often.

XP's take on this (and it *is* extreme) is that there should be a client on site during much of the development, providing immediate feedback on the direction of application development. This gives the developers a chance to nip problems in the bud, whether they're issues with the domain model, user interface, documentation, and so on.

While an on-site client might not be possible (or desirable!) it's easy to give clients access to the work-in-progress. This allows the client to review functionality and provide feedback early in the process. Both functionality and design can be addressed in parallel. This can help identify usability issues, application flow changes, functional requirement changes, and so on.

However, along with shorter iterations comes a responsibility to keep the client informed about the real cost of change, both now and in the future. Big changes (or lots of little ones) may require a change in the schedule, the deliverable, or both.

Real applications in a nutshell

Real-world web applications are much more than just the underlying web framework. Database access, CSS, Ajax, reporting, testing, the build and deploy cycle, documentation, and administration, all factor in to deliver a complete application that can be handed off to a client.

Making it pretty

We'll cover some of the most basic aspects of making our application look good, using CSS and Struts 2's themes and templates. These offload the bulk of "prettification" to FreeMarker templates and keep our JSP (or FreeMarker) pages fairly clean.

We'll include some CSS basics, while focusing on separating content from presentation. We will also see how we can use CSS, along with JavaScript, to provide us with easy ways to enhance functionality, usability, and testability. Along with making our applications look nice, markup that is intelligent and semantic also gives us more ways to manipulate our pages with JavaScript and Ajax.

JavaScript

We'll spend some time looking at JavaScript, which is the dominant player in the browser. While this isn't a complete JavaScript book, it's very important to understand how to use it to good effect, as it's a remarkably powerful language.

Grasping some of the more advanced topics makes working with existing libraries (for example, jQuery, which is used later in the book) much easier. It also makes our own JavaScript much cleaner, safer, and easier to maintain. Like any other language, using JavaScript effectively takes time, but the time it saves over using it poorly is well worth the effort.

Documentation

Documentation, perhaps one of the least entertaining aspects of application development, can be made to be a relatively automated process by using a combination of existing tools and custom tools. A small amount of effort throughout the life of a project can make a big difference and enhance our final deliverable.

All of the rest

Scattered throughout the book will be tips and tricks that can be used to ease our development process, facilitate the creation of useful tools, and open the development process for automation. These tips and tricks enhance our "bag of tricks", making our lives easier, and our clients happier.

Getting started

At the time of writing this book, the most recent version of Struts is 2.1.6. Downloading a release is straightforward, just follow the links on the Struts website. There are currently five downloads: "all", "apps", "lib", "docs", and "src". The "all" download, of course, includes everything. The "apps" download includes all of the Struts 2 sample applications, including the "blank" application (which isn't totally blank, but close).

The "lib" download includes all of the libraries required by Struts 2. This includes Struts 2 core libraries, Struts 2 plug-in libraries, and all of their dependencies. The "docs" download contains...wait for it...the documentation, including the API JavaDocs for both Struts 2 and XWork, as well as the entire Struts 2 documentation wiki. Finally, the "src" download contains the source for Struts 2, but not for XWork.

Creating our own applications

There are several ways in which we can create a Struts 2 application:

1. By copying the "blank" sample application
2. By manually using the libraries download
3. By using a Maven archetype

AppFuse also allows the use of Struts 2 for the backend.

Again, we're assuming some general familiarity with JEE web application development, and comfort with whatever development environment we're using.

Doing it "by hand"

We could just grab the necessary libraries from the "lib" distribution and do things completely by hand. It works, and it's simple (in a way). Determining which libraries are necessary can be surprisingly irritating. However, poking inside the blank sample application tells us that we really only need a few.

Getting that list of libraries is left as an exercise for the reader. This seems unnecessarily cruel. However, I really want to foster an attitude of exploration, discovery, and familiarization, with the framework and the tools we can use to expand our own knowledge and skills. Yes, I'm a little mean. By poking around we learn much more than having all the answers handed to us on a silver platter. (Especially, as it's a simple matter of looking inside the blank application WAR file. That's a hint for the future.)

The biggest drawback to this approach, despite its simplicity, is that as soon as we start adding libraries (which we do in the next chapter), we don't necessarily understand the relationships between required libraries. In other words, we may not understand which libraries depend on which other libraries.

Using Maven

One of the tasks Maven was created to tackle is transitive dependencies. Simply put, Maven allows us to say: "I want to use so-and-so library", and Maven will respond with: "Oh, okay, you also need these other libraries in order to do that, and here they are for you." (Maven is actually capable of much more.)

When we look at the source for the blank sample application, we start getting a handle on how Maven works (sort of), so that we can declare a project's dependencies. However, some of the magic is hidden, as the blank application relies on a non-local resource that declares the bulk of the dependencies.

Another option is to use a Maven "archetype". In this case, it would be a representative Struts 2 application that includes everything necessary to get started. There are a few Struts 2 Maven archetypes, including a generic blank application, a RESTful application (discussed later), and so on. The Struts 2 documentation wiki explains the process of using Maven archetypes. However, you are encouraged to read the Maven documentation if that's the chosen path.

This book takes a non-committal approach to its source. The apps are available as Maven projects, or as complete non-Maven bundles. If you're interested in using Maven archetypes and typing the code yourself (or copying the source into a Maven project), then that's fine. For the most part, I will completely ignore environmental issues to focus solely on the issue(s) at hand.

Summary

Struts 2 is a flexible web application framework that can be used to create highly-functional applications very quickly. The features provided by Struts 2 give developers many ways to increase functionality, while keeping the development cost low and the client happy. By leveraging the power of standard browser technologies, along with a combination of existing and custom tools, Struts 2 can be used as an integral part of an agile development process, which eases the creation of complete applications, satisfies the client, and helps the consultant look good in the process.

2
Basic Configuration

There are several ways we can configure our Struts 2 applications. These include using everybody's favorite, XML, annotations, and some agile convention-over-configuration methods.

In this chapter we'll cover the minimum necessary to get an application up and running, deferring more complex topics until they're necessary. We'll also begin our journey into lightweight application specification capture by introducing the "user story" concept. Along the way, we'll also begin coding our sample application.

Setting up our environment

Our first task is to get a minimal Struts 2 application running. We're not concerned with application functionality at this point. Our goal is to make sure our builds and deploys are working properly, and to sanity-check our Struts 2 configuration.

We won't cover any IDE-specific setup requirements, or discuss application-server-specific deployment issues. We'll assume an environment including Java 1.5, Servlet 2.4, and JSP 2+.0.

Struts 2.0 is shipped with a set of JAR files usable under Java 1.4. Struts 2.1 no longer ships those libraries. The build process, however, still supports their creation. Struts 2 states a requirement of Servlet 2.4; however, full applications have been run under Servlet 2.3. Again, this capability may not always exist.

The sample applications are available in both a Maven-based distribution and a typical non-Maven directory layout. When we refer to source code, it will almost always be obvious where the directories and files belong (if you're not very familiar with Maven and wish to do things the "Maven way", there's an introduction to the Maven directory layout on the Maven website). The book text assumes that we're already able to get a Java web application compiled and deployed.

Being dependent on an IDE's build process is, in general, a bad idea. Creating a build file allows our build process to be replicated across developers, IDEs, and tools. For example, a build file might be used by a Continuous Integration server to automate compilation, testing, and deployment. We won't delve deeply into the various build process options. Therefor, you may build the book source code in whatever manner you're most accustomed to, including relying on only an IDE.

A sanity-checking application

Our sanity-checking application will be as simple as possible. It will consist of only the minimum libraries necessary to get:

- A Struts 2 application running
- The Struts 2 Configuration Browser Plug-in
- Apache Log4J for logging

The Struts 2 Configuration Browser Plug-in lets us check out what Struts 2 thinks our configuration is. (Believe it or not, we do occasionally make mistakes. And ultimately it's the framework that decides what works, not us!)

Log4J is the ubiquitous logging framework. We'll discuss logging later in the book; however, we will use logging before then. Logging statements in the code can be safely ignored until then. The following is the table listing the minimum jar files to get a Struts 2 application running:

Required JAR file(s)	The Struts 2 application
struts2-core-2.1.6.jar	Struts 2 framework.
xwork-2.1.2.jar	XWork framework.
ognl-2.6.11.jar	OGNL, an expression language similar to JSP's EL, used by the Struts 2 tags.
freemarker-2.3.13.jar	FreeMarker, a templating library used to implement Struts 2's UI custom tags.
commons-fileupload-1.2.1.jar commons-io-1.3.2.jar commons-logging-1.1.1.jar	FileUpload and IO are used for Struts 2's file uploading capabilities. Logging is used as a logging library wrapper.
struts2-config-browser-Plug-in-2.1.6.jar	Struts 2 Config Browser Plug-in, used to examine application configuration.
log4j-1.2.14.jar	Ubiquitous logging library.

The dependency on the Commons FileUpload package and IO libraries is required, even if we're not uploading files in our application (not having them will cause the application to fail on startup). Note that we can decide to use other file upload libraries.

 Including a Struts 2 plug-in may introduce additional dependencies. For example, if we were using the Spring or JasperReports plug-ins, we would need to include their dependencies as well. Otherwise, our application may fail on startup. This is one area in which Maven is particularly handy. (There are dependency managers for Apache Ant as well. However, if we're gluttons for punishment, we can figure out the dependencies on our own.)

Configuring web.xml for Struts 2

Struts 2 dispatches requests with a filter (Struts 1 used a servlet). By default, Struts 2 expects to have a look at all requests. This allows Struts 2 to serve static content from the classpath. This includes JavaScript files for Dojo/Ajax support and FreeMarker templates for Struts 2's custom tags.

The default filter configuration defines the filter and its mapping.

```
<filter>
  <filter-name>struts2</filter-name>
  <filter-class>
org.apache.struts2.dispatcher.ng.filter.StrutsPrepareAndExecuteFilter
  </filter-class>
</filter>
<filter-mapping>
  <filter-name>struts2</filter-name>
  <url-pattern>/*</url-pattern>
</filter-mapping>
```

Note that we map the Struts 2 filter to /*, and not to /*.action (the default Struts 2 extension). We can check whether our server and environment are correctly configured or not. If we visit any URL ending with .action, such as /sanity/foo.action, we should see an error message along the lines of: **There is no Action mapped for namespace / and action name foo**. This lets us know that Struts 2 at least attempted to process our request, but it couldn't.

If we don't see a similar error message, we have to troubleshoot our build and deploy environment. We can place a simple JSP file in our web context root to determine if we're able to process *any* request, and to determine whether we're processing JSP files correctly. (The URLs shown in the text won't include host or port information, and assume the root context.)

The specifics of troubleshooting are environment, IDE, and server-specific. These won't be covered here. The usual suspects include classpath and deployment issues.

Writing our first action

We'll start by writing one of the simplest actions possible:

```
package com.packt.s2wad.ch02.sanity;
public class VerySimpleAction {
    public String execute() {
        return "success";
    }
}
```

As could be seen from above, the action doesn't extend or implement anything — it just has a method named execute() that returns a String. The execute() method is the method Struts 2 will call by default (we'll see how to call others a bit later on).

Configuring our first action with XML

Struts 2 configuration files are expected to be on the classpath (in Struts 1 they were typically located under /WEB-INF). By default, Struts 2 will look for a file named struts.xml in the root of the classpath. The top-level elements of our Struts 2 configuration file are shown here:

```
<struts>
  <constant name="struts.devMode" value="true"/>
  <package name="default" namespace="/" extends="struts-default">
    <!-- Action configurations... -->
  </package>
</struts>
```

The constant element defining struts.devMode puts Struts 2 into "developer mode", increasing the variety and quantity of error messages, reloading Struts 2 configuration files when they change, and so on.

It's also possible to define constants in our web.xml file; this is useful when we don't need an XML-based configuration. Either is acceptable: which is used depends on our needs and preferences. We can also define constants in a file named struts.properties, also on the classpath, but this is not preferred.

The <package> element defines a unit of configuration that our actions will live in. We'll learn more about packages later on. For now, it's enough to know that Struts 2 packages are a way of dividing up an application's functionality and configuration. The namespace attribute defines the URL prefix used for all actions in the package, and should begin with a slash (/).

We configure our simple action by placing an action element inside our package and giving our action a result—a JSP in this case.

```
<action name="verysimple"
        class="com.packt.s2wad.ch02.sanity.VerySimpleAction">
  <result>/WEB-INF/jsps/verysimple.jsp</result>
</action>
```

For the most part, every action will have name and class attributes. The name attribute is used to map a URL to the action class, specified by the class attribute.

Visiting /verysimple.action should display the contents of our JSP file. If it doesn't, we need to troubleshoot our deployment.

Configuring our result

Results determine what gets returned to the browser after an action is executed. The string returned from the action should be the name of a result. Results are configured per-action as above, or as a "global" result, available to every action in a package.

Results have optional name and type attributes. The default name value is success. In the previous example, we didn't give our result a name. This is because we're returning success from the execute() method, so we don't need to provide the name explicitly.

We also did not define the type attribute of the result. However, we can surmise that as we provided the pathname of a JSP file and we end up seeing the JSP contents in the browser, it's some sort of dispatching process. In fact, the default result type is dispatcher, which dispatches to our JSP using the normal JEE mechanism.

We could have specified both the `name` and the `type` attributes as seen here:

```
<action name="verysimple"
        class="com.packt.s2wad.ch02.sanity.VerySimpleAction">
  <result name="success" type="dispatcher">
    /WEB-INF/jsps/verysimple.jsp
  </result>
</action>
```

If we have a JSP that needs no additional processing, we can omit the action's `class` attribute. Struts 2 will forward to the JSP (similar to Struts 1's `ForwardAction`).

```
<action name="verysimple">
  <result>/WEB-INF/jsps/verysimple.jsp</result>
</action>
```

This keeps our JSP files hidden from direct access, and normalizes our application to use only action-based URLs. If we later modified the action to use an action class, the URL wouldn't need to be changed.

Choosing an action method

Our very simple action had a single method, `execute()`, which will be called by default. Consider an action with multiple action methods:

```
package com.packt.s2wad.ch02.sanity;
public class MethodSelectionAction {
    public String method1() { return "success"; }
    public String method2() { return "success"; }
}
```

We can define which method to call using the `method` attribute as seen here:

```
<action name="method1" method="method1"
        class="com.packt.s2wad.ch02.sanity.MethodSelectionAction">
  <result>/WEB-INF/jsps/method1.jsp</result>
</action>

<action name="method2" method="method2"
        class="com.packt.s2wad.ch02.sanity.MethodSelectionAction">
  <result>/WEB-INF/jsps/method2.jsp</result>
</action>
```

Some people prefer creating separate classes for every action, rather than filling an action with several methods. Which route to take can depend on several factors, including personal preference. In some cases it makes perfect sense to keep related functionality in a single class, in other cases it may not.

This last example seems repetitive—the method and result names are the same and the JSPs have similar naming conventions. Struts 2 allows wildcard mapping in several ways, which we'll use now to help lay out our application flow.

Getting started with our application

The traditional model of application development generally starts with the gathering of requirements, followed by separate design, implementation, verification, and maintenance phases. This is called the **waterfall method** and has been around for many years.

In contrast, more agile models of development focus on the user experience, rapid turnaround of functionalities, and iterative development. This allows our clients to provide feedback in parallel with development, requesting changes in functionality, detecting usability and application flow issues, and so on, early in the process. In many circumstances, this lightweight development cycle can greatly speed up the development time, and deliver an application that more accurately meets the client's needs.

Gathering user stories—defining our application

Our client is building a recipe swapping website, which allows us to build a shopping list from a set of selected recipes. Even without any further requirements, we know we'll need at least five pages—home, recipe search, recipe list, recipe entry, and shopping list.

The first tool we'll explore for capturing application functionality are user stories. User stories are very short descriptions of functionalities (often captured on index cards) that represent a user experience.

User stories do not contain implementation or specification details. A simple example might be: "A user can search for recipes." This might even be expanded to read: "A user can search for recipes by name, ingredients, and so on." Anything significantly more detailed than that is (usually) better expressed as additional, equally short stories.

At this stage in our application requirements gathering, we have five user stories; a couple of them with some minor reminders of expected functionality:

- Users see an informational homepage
- Users can enter recipes to share
- Users can list recipes
  - ° Users can list either their own recipes or recipes from all users
  - ° Users can mark recipes to create a shopping list
- Users can search recipes
  - ° Users can search by the recipe's name, ethnicity, ingredients, and so on
- Users can see a shopping list of ingredients needed for their selected recipes

Obviously, this isn't a complete application specification. However, it is enough to get started on coding the most basic website pages, organizing our development effort, and defining a tangible set of deliverables for the client. Even at this stage, the client might identify some missing functionalities, poor application flow, and so on.

We already know enough to define our action mappings to create skeletons of these pages, although they're a bit heavy considering our simple needs. Struts 2 provides handy wildcard configuration mechanisms making early prototyping really simple.

Building skeletal applications using wildcards

Wildcard action definitions are a quick way to create the skeleton of an application. The following configuration, along with the required JSP files, is enough:

```
<action name="*">
  <result>/WEB-INF/jsps/{1}.jsp</result>
</action>
```

The {1} refers to the first (in this case only) wildcard in the action's `name` attribute. In this case, visiting `/foo.action` would return the `/WEB-INF/jsps/foo.jsp` file.

Supplying a JSP page for each story creates an outline of the application. We might use the previously shown wildcard technique and create `home.jsp`, `recipesearch.jsp`, `recipelist.jsp`, `recipenew.jsp`, and `shoppinglist.jsp`. Visiting `/home.action` would give us `/WEB-INF/jsps/home.jsp`. We're not actually going to do it this way: the URLs are ugly, and we suspect there must be a better way.

Matching multiple wildcards

We have at least two different major divisions in our application—recipes and shopping lists. In the examples above we had pages such as `/recipenew.action`, rather than the more natural and hierarchical `/recipe/new.action`.

One solution would be to use multiple wildcards. Multiple wildcards allow us to map individual portions of the URL to action names, JSPs, directories, and so on. For example, see the following:

```
<action name="*/*">
  <result>/WEB-INF/jsps/{1}/{2}.jsp</result>
</action>
```

Here, we use the first wildcard as a directory (like `/WEB-INF/jsps/recipe`). The second defines the page (JSP) to be shown, such as `list.jsp`, `new.jsp`, and so on. Now the cleaner `/recipe/list.action` URL would return `/WEB-INF/jsps/recipe/list.jsp`.

 Using this method means that we have a slash (/) in our action name. To do this, we must set the `struts.enable.SlashesInActionNames` in our `struts.xml` file (shown next), our `web.xml`, or (not preferred) our `struts.properties` file.

```
<constant name="struts.enable.SlashesInActionNames"
          value="true"/>
```

More wildcard tricks

We can also use wildcards to define action methods and/or action classes. Class names, of course, must still be legal Java class names. If we're using a wildcard to create a Java class name, we'll have mixed-case URLs, and they are case-sensitive. The following definition demonstrates a possible configuration that differentiates between class names and methods within those classes:

```
<action name="*/*"
        class="com.packt.s2wad.ch02.examples.{1}Action"
        method="{2}">
  <result>/WEB-INF/jsps/{1}/{2}.jsp</result>
</action>
```

Assume `UserAction` and `GroupAction` classes, both with `list()` and `create()` methods. Visiting `/User/list.action` would call the `UserAction.list()` method then dispatch to `/WEB-INF/jsps/User/list.jsp` as the result.

Just to reiterate, the case of the word User in the URL is significant. The class name created by appending the wildcard contents to the package name is the class that Struts 2 will attempt to instantiate.

Using wildcards is a flexible way to break up our application. However, for large and complex applications, it can lead to a brittle configuration, bizarre URLs, and more trouble than they're worth. Naturally, there's another way, which can be used alone or in combination with wildcards.

Packages and namespaces

Packages and namespaces help group and classify various configuration elements, delineate areas of responsibility, provide package-specific resources, and so on. In our recipe application, we do not yet have much functionality. However, we can still draw a "line in the sand" between our two obvious sections, recipes and shopping, and intuit that each of these might deserve their own package.

Packages can declare a namespace, which is effectively a portion of the URL. Adding to our original default package, our first look at defining some packages looks like this:

```
<package name="default" namespace="/" extends="struts-default">
  <action name="*">
    <result>/WEB-INF/jsps/{1}.jsp</result>
  </action>
</package>

<package name="recipe" namespace="/recipe" extends="struts-default">
  <action name="*">
    <result>/WEB-INF/jsps/recipe/{1}.jsp</result>
  </action>
</package>
```

Visiting /recipe/list.action puts us in the recipe package, whereas visiting /home.action leads us to our default package.

Creating site navigation

We'll use <jsp:include> tags as our templating mechanism to keep things simple. Our pages will have a navigation bar at the top, and contents underneath.

We'll peek ahead at our first Struts 2 custom tag—<s:url>. This tag is used to create URLs. We could also use JSTL's <c:url> tag, but we'll discover some reasons for sticking with <s:url> in a bit.

Full documentation for the `<s:url>` tag (and all the other tags) is available on the Struts 2 wiki, which is also exported in the distribution. For now we'll only concern ourselves with the `action` and the `namespace` attributes. However, I always encourage people to read the documentation and consider it a necessary resource.

The `action` attribute specifies the Struts 2 action of the link (without the `.action` suffix, which is added by the tag). The `namespace` attribute defines the namespace the action is in. Our simple navigation page, `/WEB-INF/jsps/shared/nav.jsp`, contains links to each of our story pages:

```
<%@ taglib prefix="s" uri="/struts-tags" %>
<a href="<s:url namespace="/" action="home"/>">Home</a>
<a href="<s:url namespace="/recipe" action="list"/>">
  List Recipes</a>
<a href="<s:url namespace="/recipe" action="search"/>">
  Search Recipes</a>
<a href="<s:url namespace="/recipe" action="new"/>">
  Create Recipe</a>
<a href="<s:url namespace="/shopping" action="list"/>">
  Shopping List</a>
```

Why specify the namespace as a separate attribute as opposed to just including it in the action name or URL? The `<s:url>` tag is namespace-aware: creating links within a namespace doesn't require the `namespace` attribute. Actions within other namespaces require the `namespace` to be specified. Navigation links, which must work no matter what namespace we're in, can just use it all the time.

The slash (`/`) in a namespace is not optional. Without it, Struts 2 will not know that we're in a namespace and will prefix an additional namespace to the URL, thereby breaking it.

Namespaces allow us to use common sense links within a package. For example, if we were administering a large number of simple data models (users, groups, and so on), we could split them in to packages, each getting a `namespace`, and each with a `list` action.

On a page in the "users" package, `<s:url action="list"/>` would refer to the "users" package's `list` action. To link to the "groups" package `list` action, we specify the namespace: `<s:url action="list" namespace="groups"/>`.

Including external configuration files

Struts 2 configuration files can include additional configuration files with the `<include>` element. For example, we might configure our shopping list package in its own file and include it after our other packages were defined as seen here.

```
    <!-- ... existing config file ... -->
  </package>
  <include file="com/packt/s2wad/ch02/shopping/shopping.xml"/>
</struts>
```

The `shopping.xml` file is placed in our shopping package and referred to by a classpath-relative path, like any other classpath resource. We can put the configuration files wherever we want—we could just as easily keep it at the root level.

This is a simple way to break up areas of responsibility, delineate application functionality, reduce potential edit conflicts, and keep configuration as local to the implementation as possible.

Our application so far

To complete our wireframe application, which is just enough to show our user stories, we need to create several JSP files to match our story URLs. The / namespace holds the home action, so we create `/WEB-INF/jsps/home.jsp`. The `/recipe` namespace holds the recipe list, new recipes, and recipe search pages. Each JSP is named as we'd expect, and in `/WEB-INF/jsps/recipe/`. The `/shopping` namespace contains only the shopping list action with its JSP in `/WEB-INF/jsps/shopping/list.jsp`.

Each of these skeletal JSP files contains our navigation JSP and a header letting us know which page we're on. For example, our `home.jsp` file is mostly HTML.

```
<html>
  <head>
    <title>Home</title>
  </head>
  <body>
    <div id="nav">
      <jsp:include page="/WEB-INF/jsps/shared/nav.jsp"/>
    </div>
    <div id="content">
      <h1>Home</h1>
      <p>Home page.</p>
    </div>
  </body>
</html>
```

When we visit /home.action, we'll see the navigation links at the top and a big "Home" headline. Visiting /recipe/list.action is the same, but with a big "Recipes" headline. Not terribly exciting, but we already see the beginnings of the functionality.

Examining our configuration

We can use the **Configuration Browser Plug-in** to examine what Struts 2 believes our configuration is. (Struts 2 doesn't always agree with us, but is nice enough to tell us when we're wrong.) We just add the library to our classpath.

To browse our configuration, we visit /config-browser/index.action, where we'll see something similar to the following:

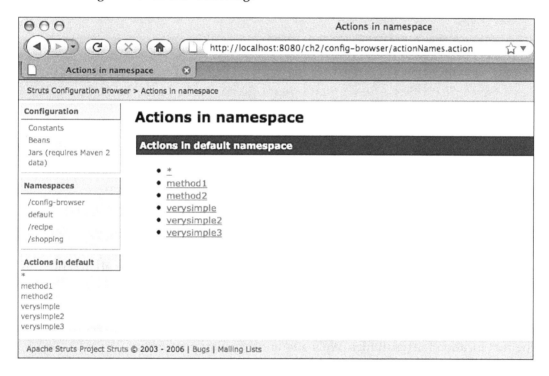

From here, we can examine our action configurations, result attributes, and so on. It's a handy way to compare what we think our configuration is with what Struts 2 thinks it is. Struts 2 is running the show, and its version wins even if we think it's wrong.

Configuration via convention and annotations

Hate XML? The **Convention Plug-in** allows us to operate completely configuration-free, and to use annotations when the defaults aren't quite what we need. The Convention Plug-in is also used by the **REST Plug-in** (discussed later in the book).

Using the plug-in is almost as simple as dropping its JAR file into our classpath, but not quite easy. The Convention Plug-in has its own library dependencies. Maven makes this trivial. Without Maven, it's easiest to grab the libraries from the REST Plug-in showcase application.

In this example, we won't use a Struts 2 configuration file. We'll set all of our constants in our `web.xml` file. For example, we'll still set `struts.devMode` to `true`.

```
<filter>
  <filter-name>struts2</filter-name>
  <filter-class>
org.apache.struts2.dispatcher.ng.filter.StrutsPrepareAndExecuteFilter
  </filter-class>
  <init-param>
    <param-name>struts.devMode</param-name>
    <param-value>true</param-value>
  </init-param>
</filter>
```

The Convention Plug-in and action-less actions

When we make a request for which there is no mapping and no action, the Convention Plug-in will attempt to locate a reasonable result. For example, if we request `/sanity` or `/sanity.action` (the ".action" extension is optional), the plug-in will look for a result in `/WEB-INF/content/sanity.*`, checking for `.jsp`, `.ftl`, and `.vm` files.

The Convention Plug-in has many configuration parameters, including one to set the root location for result files. We'll add another filter parameter:

```
<init-param>
  <param-name>struts.convention.result.path</param-name>
  <param-value>/WEB-INF/jsps</param-value>
</init-param>
```

Now the Convention Plug-in will search for files under `/WEB-INF/jsps`. Our previous request would look for `/WEB-INF/jsps/sanity.jsp` (and `.ftl` and `.vm`). If no file is found, we'll get an error message in our browser (or a 404 if development mode isn't activated) saying that there's no action mapped for our request.

The Convention Plug-in allows us to create a skeletal application with no XML configuration whatsoever — we need only create the necessary JSP files.

The Convention Plug-in and action configuration

The Convention Plug-in can detect and configure our action classes on application startup as well. The plug-in will scan for implementations of com.opensymphony. xwork2.Action (as the ActionSupport superclass does) in Java packages whose names contain "struts", "struts2", "action", and "actions", and whose classname ends in "Action".

 There are several parameters we can set to fine-tune the Convention Plug-in. Set the packages to scan via the struts.convention. package.locators constant. Set struts.convention.package. locators.disable to true to disable scanning. Exclude a list of packages from scanning with the struts.convention.exclude. packages constant. However, be aware that the Convention Plug-in already sets this to a default value. We must set the default, as well as our own value, for this to work well. To change the suffix of action classnames, set the struts.convention.action.suffix constant (for example, the REST Plug-in changes the suffix to Controller).

Our first Convention-based action has an execute() method returning success — that's it. The Convention Plug-in will search for results in the same way as with action-less requests, but will use the action class name as part of the file name to search for. Our first result test action contains the following (imports elided):

```
package com.packt.s2wad.ch02.convention.actions;
public class SanityAction extends ActionSupport {
    public String execute() {
        System.out.println("***** Hello from SanityAction!");
        return "success";
    }
}
```

We're getting a sneak peek at the ActionSupport class. If we request /sanity, we'll see our println() call on the console, and our JSP displayed in the browser.

The Convention plug-in will also search for action-named JSPs with the result string appended; we could also have named our sanity.jsp file sanity-success.jsp. The Convention Plug-in will use files with appended result codes first. In other words, if our action returns success, the file named sanity-success.jsp will be rendered, even if there's a file named sanity.jsp.

To demonstrate, consider an action returning `odd` or `even` based on the current time:

```
package com.packt.s2wad.ch02.convention.actions;
public class WhichresultAction extends ActionSupport {
    private long ctm;
    public String execute() {
        ctm = System.currentTimeMillis();
        return ((ctm & 1L) == 1L) ? "odd" : "even";
    }
    public long getCtm() { return ctm; }
}
```

We'll create two JSP files under `/WEB-INF/jsps`—`whichresult-odd.jsp` and `whichresult-even.jsp`. Here's the meat of `whichresult-odd.jsp`:

```
<h1><s:property value="ctm"/> is odd!</h1>
```

It's not a coincidence that our action class has a property named `ctm` and we're using the `<s:property>` tag to access something named `ctm` in the JSP. Remember setting values into request scope, or `ActionForm`? No more of that! We'll get to this magic soon!

When we request `/whichresult`, we'll see either the odd or the even page. After a few clicks, we'll likely see both results, letting us know the magic of Convention is working.

Configuring the Convention Plug-in with annotations

If Convention's defaults don't suit us, we can use its annotations to configure the action. For example, the `@Action` annotation can change or add action mappings beyond what Convention automatically provides. Complete documentation, along with many examples, is available on the Struts 2 documentation wiki.

We can also configure results with Convention's annotations. We don't have to rely on the Convention plug-in's idea of what our result JSP files should be named. We can define results manually using the `@Result` annotation, and the `@Results` annotation if we need multiple results. (We can use the `@Results` annotation only at the class level, while the `@Action` and `@Actions` annotations are available at the method level. We can define multiple results at the action level via the `@Action` annotation's `results` property.)

We'll create `MoreresultsAction` to demonstrate some of this. Its `execute()` method is the same as in `WhichresultAction`, and accessible through `/moreresults`. We'll add a `tristate()` method and configure it to respond to the `/tristate` URL:

```
@Action(value = "/tristate")
public String tristate() {
    ctm = System.currentTimeMillis();
    long tmp = ctm - ((ctm / 10L) * 10L);
    if (tmp <= 3) return "three";
    if (tmp <= 6) return "six";
    return "nine";
}
```

The JSP pages are located under `/WEB-INF/jsps`, and are named `tristate-three.jsp`, `tristate-six.jsp`, and `tristate-nine.jsp`. Let's say we want the JSPs to live under `/WEB-INF/jsps/tristate`, we can add to the following to the `tristate()`'s `@Action` annotation:

```
@Action(value = "/tristate",
    results = {
        @Result(name="three",
            location="/WEB-INF/jsps/tristate/tristate-three.jsp"),
        @Result(name="six",
            location="/WEB-INF/jsps/tristate/tristate-six.jsp"),
        @Result(name="nine",
            location="/WEB-INF/jsps/tristate/tristate-nine.jsp")
    })
```

We can also configure results at the class level. We'll modify `MoreresultsAction`, so both `execute()` and `tristate()` use a result defined at the action level.

```
@Results({
    @Result(name="nine",
            location="/WEB-INF/jsps/tristate/tristate-nine.jsp")
})
public class MoreresultsAction extends ActionSupport {
    @Action(value = "/tristate",
        results = {
            @Result(name="three",
                location="/WEB-INF/jsps/tristate/tristate-three.jsp"),
            @Result(name="six",
                location="/WEB-INF/jsps/tristate/tristate-six.jsp")
        })
    public String tristate() {
        // ...
    }
}
```

The `nine` result is now defined at the class level, and is accessible to both `execute()` and `tristate()`. Only `tristate()` may use the `three` and `six` results.

If we stick with Convention's naming patterns, we can remove a fair amount of annotations, but we know we can override the defaults if they don't work for us.

There are a few more games we can play with Convention's annotations—set an action's namespace using the `@Namespace` annotation (only at the class level), define an action's parent package, configure interceptors, and more.

Summary

This chapter gives us an overview of Struts 2 configuration, covering the very basics of action configuration, and a bit about the Convention Plug-in. The chapter introduces some basic Struts 2 concepts at a foundational level, along with certain ways to break up application functionalities into logical or functional portions. We also see our first Struts 2 custom tag.

The chapter quickly covers user stories as a way to capture functional requirements in a high-level, abstract way. Even with minimal specifications, we can create enough functionality to begin creating the code, design, layout, and flow.

In the next chapter, we'll explore Struts 2 actions in more depth and discover some of the functionalities that Struts 2 gives us for free through the `ActionSupport` class.

References

A reader can refer to the following:

- XML-based configuration elements:
  http://struts.apache.org/2.x/docs/configuration-elements.html

- Struts 2 and XWork API Javadocs:
  http://struts.apache.org/2.x/struts2-core/apidocs/index.html

- Convention Plug-in (and its annotations):
  http://struts.apache.org/2.1.6/docs/convention-Plug-in.html

- Struts 2 tags (link to `<s:url>` and all the rest):
  http://struts.apache.org/2.x/docs/tag-reference.html

- User Stories:
  http://en.wikipedia.org/wiki/User_story

- Java Web Application Basics:
  http://www.onjava.com/lpt/a/671 (oldie but a goodie)
  http://java.sun.com/javaee/technologies/webapps/
  (all the best from Sun)

3
Actions and ActionSupport

In the previous chapter, we had a crash course on how to configure our Struts 2 application and got a (very) small taste of Struts 2 actions—the place where our application does its work. Even if the bulk of our application's functionality resides in service objects, actions are where the service objects are instantiated and used.

In this chapter, we'll examine Struts 2 actions further. While the mantra of "actions are POJOs" echoes in our heads, extending the `ActionSupport` class provides us with quite a bit of functionality, including internationalization (I18N), validation, and so on.

Much of this functionality is provided by a combination of interface implementations and interceptors. We'll cover `ActionSupport`, a utility class implementing most of the commonly used interfaces, as well as a few other handy interfaces. We'll see how we can get a lot out of the framework, without covering how some of the functionality is actually implemented.

We'll implement a prototype of our first user story, entering a recipe. We'll also take a quick detour into some ways of exploring code, including the usefulness of Unix-like command line utilities, and how the ability to create ad hoc tools can really be handy.

ActionSupport and its interfaces

`ActionSupport` is an XWork class that provides default implementations of validation and I18N interfaces. Since many actions require both, it makes a convenient "default" action base class. It's not required for our actions to subclass `ActionSupport`, but it's handy.

`ActionSupport` implements the following six interfaces:

- `Action`
- `Validateable`
- `ValidationAware`
- `TextProvider`
- `LocaleProvider`
- `Serializable`

We'll take a brief look at each of these except `Serializable` (it's boring, and is already familiar to Java developers).

The Action interface

The `Action` interface defines a single method:

```
public String execute();
```

One benefit of implementing `Action` is that reflection isn't required to check for the `execute()` method. We can just cast to `Action` and call `execute()`.

Action's convenience strings

`ActionSupport`, via the `Action` interface, exposes several typical result name strings. For example, we've already seen actions returning "success" and "error". `ActionSupport` defines these as `SUCCESS` and `ERROR` respectively. It also defines `INPUT`, `LOGIN`, and `NONE`. Each of these has the value we'd expect.

`NONE` is a bit different from the rest. It is used when no view is shown by the framework, as when we write directly to the response.

The TextProvider interface

I18N support is provided by the `TextProvider` implementation along with the `LocaleProvider` (discussed later in this chapter). The `TextProvider` interface provides access to standard Java `ResourceBundles` and the messages defined in them. Ultimately, `TextProvider` provides two methods:

- `getText()` which provides an access to a single message
- `getTexts()` which returns an entire `ResourceBundle`

Both the listed methods have several method signatures. We'll focus on the many variants of `getText()`.

The `getText()` method comes in several flavors. The simplest is the `String getText(String key)` method, which retrieves the named message from a resource file. Messages are retrieved in the hierarchical fashion. Messages are retrieved in the following order:

1. `${actionClassName}.properties`.
2. `${baseClass(es)}.properties`.
3. `${interface(es)}.properties`.
4. `ModelDriven`'s model, if action implements `ModelDriven` (discussed later). Steps 1-3 are performed for the model class. However, we'll ignore this feature for now.
5. `package.properties` (and any parent package's `package.properties`).
6. I18N message key hierarchy.
7. Global resource properties.

To demonstrate the process of locating messages, we'll create the following package and file hierarchy:

```
/com/packt/s2wad/ch03/i18n/
/com/packt/s2wad/ch03/i18n/package.properties
/com/packt/s2wad/ch03/i18n/TextExampleAction.java
/com/packt/s2wad/ch03/i18n/TextExampleAction.properties
/com/packt/s2wad/ch03/i18n/TextInterface.java
/com/packt/s2wad/ch03/i18n/TextInterface.properties
/com/packt/s2wad/ch03/i18n/sub/
/com/packt/s2wad/ch03/i18n/sub/package.properties
/com/packt/s2wad/ch03/i18n/sub/TextExampleSubAction.java
/com/packt/s2wad/ch03/i18n/sub/TextExampleSubAction.properties
```

We see a Java package containing `package.properties`, an action class (`TextExamplesAction`), and an interface (`TextInterface`). Each has a corresponding property file. `TextExamplesAction` extends `ActionSupport` and implements `TextInterface`. We have a subpackage with its own `package.properties` file. The subpackage also contains an action class (`TextExamplesSubAction`) extending `TextExamplesAction` with its own property file.

Our first sanity check will be simple. We'll test our `TextExamplesAction` class by looking up a message from the `TextExamplesAction.properties` file. From the list we saw earlier, Struts 2 will look for messages in a property file named after the class.

We'll use the Convention plug-in again, avoiding XML. The action will log the results of a `getText()` call. `TextExampleAction.properties` contains a single entry:

```
from.class.props=Hello from TextExamples.properties!
```

As we're using the Convention plug-in, we need to create a JSP file for our Convention-based action, else Struts 2 will give us an error. For now, we create a dummy JSP file in `/WEB-INF/jsps/i18n/text-example.jsp`. The expurgated version (it's the one without the gannet) of our action looks like this:

```
package com.packt.s2wad.ch03.actions.i18n;
public class TextExamplesAction extends ActionSupport
                                implements TextInterface {
    private static Log log =
        LogFactory.getLog(TextExamplesAction.class);
    public String execute() throws Exception {
        log.debug(getText("from.class.props"));
        return SUCCESS;
    }
}
```

When we access our action at `/i18n/text-examples`, we should see something resembling the following (assuming we're using the `log4j.properties` contained in the chapter's project):

```
DEBUG com.packt.s2wad.ch03.actions.i18n.TextExamplesAction.execute: 15
- Hello from TextExamples.properties!
```

If no message is found for a given key, `getText()` will return `null`.

To avoid going to the console to check our output, let's figure out a way to display our messages on our JSP page. Our first detour serves two purposes:

- It provides a very brief introduction to how Struts 2 exposes values to our JSPs

- It gives us another acronym to add to our growing collection

Detour—action properties, JSPs, and more tags

Traditionally, accessing application data from our JSP page would involve putting a value into either request or session scope. Some frameworks handle it more automatically, for example, Struts 1 would put an `ActionForm` into either request or session scope.

Struts 2 works in a similar fashion. However, Struts 2 simply puts the entire action into scope. (It's actually a bit more complex. The action is actually pushed onto a stack that's in scope, but we'll cover that later.) We then access action properties using Struts 2 custom tags and **OGNL (Object Graph Navigation Language)**, another expression language similar to JSP EL. Another option is to use JSP EL (thanks to Struts 2's custom request wrapper).

 Using the Struts 2 custom tags and OGNL gives us another advantage. We can access action methods, including those that take parameters, directly from our JSP. This is in contrast to JSP EL, which allows access only to properties (although access to functions may appear in JEE 6).

Right now, we just want to display localized messages on our JSP page. As mentioned earlier, we can call action methods from our JSP using Struts 2 tags and OGNL. One of the custom tags is `<s:property>`, which is the most basic way to access action properties (and methods). We specify the action property (or method) with the `value` attribute.

Our stub JSP, which is no longer a stub, will contain the following (the remaining examples in this file will just show the relevant portions):

```
<%@ taglib prefix="s" uri="/struts-tags" %>
    <html>
      <body>
        <dl>
          <dt>From TextExamplesAction.properties via property tag,
              using getText(...):</dt>
          <dd>
            <s:property value="getText('from.class.props')"/>
          </dd>
        </dl>
      </body>
    </html>
```

This JSP will produce output similar to our console output, but in the browser:

This is a little unwieldy. Being lazy programmers, we want to minimize typing as much as possible. As we have access to action properties as well as methods, we could simply put the results of the `getText()` call into an action property.

Action properties are exposed via public getter methods:

```
public String getText1() {
    return getText("from.class.props");
}
```

Now, we can access the text in our JSP via the `text1` action property:

```
<s:property value="text1"/>
```

 Struts 2.1 doesn't actually require a public getter method if we declare the property itself public. OGNL will access public properties without a getter. Whether or not this is a good practice is a debatable issue. The biggest drawback of not following the JavaBean specification is that not all tools or libraries will be as forgiving as OGNL.

Finally, as mentioned, we can access the property via JSP EL. This is achieved using the simplified property access notation introduced in JSP 2.0, reducing the JSP code to a terse:

```
${text1}
```

 Struts 2 wraps requests in a `StrutsRequestWrapper`. This class is responsible for accessing scoped attributes. `StrutsRequestWrapper` will check for properties on the Struts 2 value stack first. If no property is found in the stack, it will defer to the default request wrapper, which searches the normal JEE scopes.

Even with the JSP EL shortcut, this is still a fair amount of work, and it doesn't seem reasonable that we have to write Java code just to look up a message. Struts 2 provides an `<s:text>` tag, meaning more work in our JSP, but less in our Java.

```
<s:text name="from.class.props"/>
```

To protect against missing messages, we can use `<s:text>` tag's body to provide a default message value:

```
<s:text name="an.unlikely.message.name">
  Default message if none found
</s:text>
```

This is similar to the functionality provided by the `getText(String, String)` method.

Which method we use is largely a matter of preference. The `<s:text>` tag is arguably the cleanest, as it's short and it's all in one file.

Continuing with message lookup

Next on the list of places to look for messages are the superclass property files. Our `TextExampleSubAction` class extends `TextExampleAction`. Hence, messages in `TextExampleAction.properties` are available to `TextExampleSubAction`. Messages defined in both files will resolve to the more specific, giving us the ability to override messages for subclasses, just like we can override class functionality.

To demonstrate, we'll add a message under the key `overridden.message` to both `TextExampleAction.properties` and `TextExampleSubAction.properties`. However, the values will be different (you can guess which file contains the following).

```
overridden.message=I am from TextExampleSub.properties
```

We'll add a property and value for the same overridden key to `TextExampleAction.properties`, only in the superclass property file:

```
overridden.message=I am from TextExample.properties
superclass.message=Who's your superclass?
```

We'll add some `<s:text>` tags to a new JSP for the subclass, and to our superclass JSP:

```
<s:text name="overridden.message"/>
<s:text name="superclass.message"/>
```

When we visit `/i18n/sub/text-examples-sub`, we'll see the overridden message from the subclass property file, and also the message defined in the superclass's property file.

Messages may also be placed in interface property files, following class and package hierarchy. Similarly, messages placed in a Java package's `package.properties` file are available to any class contained in that package. What might be slightly less obvious is that Struts 2 will continue searching up the package hierarchy for `package.properties` files until either the message is found or Struts 2 runs out of packages to search.

If we have application-wide message resources, and our actions are not arranged under a single package, we can create and define a global resources bundle. We add an initialization parameter to our `web.xml` file, which defines two more message resource files:

```
<init-param>
  <param-name>struts.custom.i18n.resources</param-name>
  <param-value>
    ch03-global-messages,
    com/packt/s2wad/ch03/misc/misc-messages
  </param-value>
</init-param>
```

These resource files would also be used to resolve message keys. Multiple files, separated by commas, can be defined, and these files may reside anywhere in the class hierarchy.

Parameterized messages

Messages may also be parameterized via the `getText(String, List)` and `getText(String, String[])` methods. As with `getText(String)`, there are also signatures that take a default message (see the API documentation for details).

Parameterized messages take positional parameters. For example, we'll put the following message that takes two parameters into a `package.properties` file in the same package as the `TextExamplesAction` class:

```
params.msg1=You passed {0} and {1}.
```

The {0} and {1} placeholders are filled with the values passed in the parameter list. Calling from Java looks exactly like we'd expect.

```
public String getParams1() {
    return getText("params.msg1", new ArrayList() {{
                    add("Foooo!");
                    add("Baaar!");
                }});
}
```

Funky Java Alert: The code following the `ArrayList` instantiation is normal Java code, although it doesn't look like it. Code like this drives people crazy, and there are situations in which it's wholly inappropriate. However, it is a useful trick to know, and it's not really much of a trick. It's left as an exercise for the reader (including determining when, and why, it might not be appropriate!).

We can also parameterize the text tag in several ways using the `<s:param>` tag. The first way is to just put the parameter values in the tag body:

```
<s:text name="params.msg1">
  <s:param>Fooooo!</s:param>
  <s:param>Baaaar!</s:param>
</s:text>
```

We can also use the `param` tag's `value` attribute and pass in a string. It's very important to note the extra quotes around the value:

```
<s:text name="params.msg1">
  <s:param value="'Foooo!'"/> <!-- See the extra quotes? -->
  <s:param value="'Baaar!'"/> <!-- Don't forget them!    -->
</s:text>
```

The `value` attribute is an object, not an immediate value. In other words, the contents of the `value` attribute are evaluated. If we left the quotes off, we'd see **null** in our output and a warning in our log file (if devMode is turned on).

This gives us a handy way to include action properties in our messages. If we add action properties named `foo` and `bar` to our `TextExamplesAction` class, initialized to "Foooo!" and "Baaar!" respectively, we could write the following:

```
<s:text name="params.msg1">
  <s:param value="foo"/>
  <s:param value="bar"/>
</s:text>
```

Given the previous code fragments and assumptions, visiting `/i18n/text-examples` will produce the same output as the text tags using the immediate values shown earlier.

Our final example of parameterized messages is pretty cool (as cool as parameterized I18N message can be) In addition to providing message parameters using a list (or array) as shown above, we can access action properties directly in our messages.

Instead of using the positional {n} syntax, we can access action properties using the ${...} construct, the same syntax as the `param` tags. For example:

```
params.from.action=From action: ${foo}, ${bar}... wow!
```

The text tag to access this message is as we'd expect:

```
<s:text name="params.from.action"/>
```

Our action's `foo` and `bar` properties will be inserted into the message with no additional work on our part, saving us some JSP code. The expressions allowed in the property file are the same as those allowed in the JSP. This means that we could call action methods, including those that take arguments. This ability may not be useful all the time, but it can often save some irritating Java and/or JSP code on occasion.

The LocaleProvider interface

`LocaleProvider` allows `TextProvider` to get locale information and look up resources based on Java property file names. `LocaleProvider` provides one method, `getLocale()`. The default locale value comes from the browser via the I18N interceptor. By overriding this method we could, for example, return a user's preferred locale from a database.

The Validateable and ValidationAware interfaces

Discussing the complete functionality of `Validateable` and `ValidationAware` at this point is problematic. Much of the functionality depends on several Struts 2 custom tags. We'll defer those details to Chapter 6. Here we'll learn only the minimum necessary.

`Validateable` contains a single method, `void validate()`. `ActionSupport` contains a default implementation that allows for both XML-based and/or annotation-based configurations.

We can implement our own `validate` method in our actions and manually perform validation . We can include default framework validation by calling `super.validate()`. Combining XML- or annotation-driven validation with manual validation (including "business-logic level" validation), along with the ability to define our own custom validators (covered later), covers all of our validation needs.

`ValidationAware` provides a group of methods used to collect error messages related to specific form fields or the action in general. It is also used to collect general informational messages and determine if any errors or messages are present.

These two interfaces work together with the default Struts 2 interceptor stack (specifically the "validation" and "workflow" interceptors) to validate forms and direct application flow based on validation results (specifically the presence of error messages). In a nutshell, if the validation succeeds, the appropriate action method is executed normally. If the validation fails, we're returned to the "input" result.

Implementing our first user story

We actually know enough at this point to prototype one of our user stories. We'll implement this story by hand as a useful exercise, and to help build appreciation for the framework (and reduce your appreciation for your author—however, I can take it!)

One of our user stories, as you can recall, was the following:

- Users can enter recipes to share

The followers of more "traditional" requirement methodologies will be nothing less than horrified by this minimal description of a functional requirement. A traditional version of this story could run across a dozen pages, capturing (or attempting to capture) every nuance of the concept of "recipe entry" including the user interface design, complex validation rules, every possible form field, the underlying data model, and so on.

Once this (portion of the) specification is printed, and the toner has cooled, it will invariably be wrong. Something will have been forgotten. An edge case will have been overlooked. Half a dozen questions about the user interface will surface, all without having written any code or having used even the most minimal of recipe entry systems.

By minimizing functionality, we can very quickly create a low-fidelity prototype, allowing us to vet the basics of our system. While it's not a finished product, it's a way of determining what the finished product will be. Using our prototype can help determine user interface design decisions, spot overly-complex application flow, highlight missing form fields, and so on.

And really, that single sentence does capture the essence of what we need to do, if not all the specifics.

Refining our story

Since we're still learning Struts 2 and prototyping our application, we can afford to make some low-fidelity (lo-fi) assumptions. We'll assume that a "recipe" has an "id", a "name", a "description", a list of "ingredients", and some "directions".

For now, each of these will be a string (except for an `Integer` id). Low-fidelity prototypes, especially early in the development cycle, don't need to reflect the final product with regards to looks, functionality, data models, and so on. Our `Recipe` class is simply a POJO with appropriately named properties. The only note of interest is that the `Recipe` class should have a `toString()` method, giving us a human-readable version of the object.

```
public String toString() {
    return String.format("Recipe (%s) [id=%d, name=%s]",
                          super.toString(), id, name);
}
```

 Including the default `toString()` in our `toString()` methods lets us tell at a glance if two string representations are the same object. This isn't always appropriate, particularly if we'd rather use `toString()` output on a webpage. `String.format()` was a long overdue addition!

The last story refinement is that we require the name and the ingredients, but not the description and the directions. The form will have text inputs for the name and description, and text areas for the ingredients and description (remember — this is a lo-fi prototype).

Creating the recipe form

We'll now flesh out our "new recipe" JSP stub with some input tags. We'll be implementing this form by hand. If you're already familiar with the Struts 2 form tags, bear with me. Starting off on our own makes us much more appreciative of the framework.

Our recipe action will have a `recipe` property, which is the `Recipe` POJO described in the previous section. We'll put our form headers and input elements into a table. Here's a representative element, the recipe name (or at least what we have so far):

```
<tr>
  <td>Name</td>
  <td><input name="recipe.name" type="text" size="20"/></td>
</tr>
```

The most interesting thing (so far) is the `name` attribute. Struts 2 will do the right thing (in general) when encountering request parameters. It will attempt to convert them to the correct type and set the corresponding action property.

In this case, we have a nested object. The `recipe` property is of the type `Recipe`. The `name` property of the recipe is just a string. When we see a form element name, such as the `recipe.name`, what happens (more or less) is roughly equivalent to the following:

```
getCurrentAction().getRecipe().setName(value from form);
```

On top of that, Struts 2 will take care of instantiating a `Recipe` object if one doesn't exist. We can verify this functionality by creating a stub action to process form submissions. We'll call it `NewRecipe` (extending `ActionSupport`). However, for now, we'll just print the recipe to our standard output (hopefully), containing values from the form. Our stub action looks like this (getters and setters elided):

```
package com.packt.s2wad.ch03.actions.recipes;
public class NewRecipe extends ActionSupport {
    private Recipe recipe;
    public String execute() throws Exception {
        System.out.println(recipe);
        return SUCCESS;
    }
}
```

This is just a sanity check to show that the recipe is, indeed, being instantiated and populated. However, at this time there's no real functionality, no results, and so on.

> This is another principle of agile development. Do one thing at a time, verify that it works, and then continue. Here, we're doing something similar to **TDD (Test Driven Development)**. However, *we're* the testers. We'll cover TDD later.

The final piece of our current puzzle is the form tag in the JSP itself. We'll use a plain HTML form tag. As we're staying in our recipe package, and we're using Convention, we can use a relative action path. The form tag will look like this:

```
<form action="new-recipe" method="post">
```

Visiting the page at `/recipes/new-recipe-input` (following the naming conventions of the Convention plug-in) should show us the form. We fill the form using "Java Soup" for the recipe name (along with other details). Now, when we submit the form and look at the console, we should see something like this:

```
Recipe (com.packt.s2wad.ch03.models.Recipe@921fc7) [id=null, name=Java
Soup, etc...])
```

As unassuming as this is, it's actually pretty cool. Struts 2 instantiated a `Recipe` object and filled it with values from our form without any intervention on our part. We don't need to grab values from the request parameters, or use `ActionForm`. It was just a model and an action.

Adding some validation

Now that we know we have a recipe object that can be validated, we'll do that. As our action extends `ActionSupport` (which implements `Validateable`), we can override the `validate()` method, which unsurprisingly performs validation. Inside the `validate()` method, we use `ActionSupport`'s implementation of `ValidationAware`, which includes methods for adding form field errors, keyed by the input element's name.

Our action's `validate()` method implements our refined user story—name and ingredients are required, but not the description and the directions. We'll use Apache Commons Lang's `StringUtils.isBlank()` method. There's no point in creating yet another implementation of a null or whitespace check. (Some folks disagree, and their concerns that it's another dependency and adds a large API for just one method are understandable.)

Each blank field gets an error message, keyed to the name of the input element, and added to a collection of field errors using the `ValidationAware`'s `addFieldError(String fieldName, String message)` method.

Our action's validation method is simple:

```
public void validate() {
    if (StringUtils.isBlank(recipe.getName())) {
        addFieldError("recipe.name",
                        getText("recipe.name.required"));
    }
    if (StringUtils.isBlank(recipe.getIngredients())) {
        addFieldError("recipe.ingredients",
                        getText("recipe.ingredients.required"));
    }
}
```

The validation process depends on interceptors. For now, it's enough to know that if there are any field errors, we'll be returned to our "input" result. We'll add results to our action, an "input" result for when the validation fails, and a "success" result for when it succeeds. Our "input" result will be the same JSP reached through the `/recipes/new-recipe-input` request, whereas our "success" result is a simple thank you page. We'll put the thank you page in `/WEB-INF/content/recipes/new-recipe-success.jsp`.

If we navigate back to our form and try to submit an empty form, we'll find ourselves back on the input form. However, our URL will change from `/recipes/new-recipe-input` to `/recipes/new-recipe`, which is what we'd expect. Adding the required fields and resubmitting shows us our thank-you page. The validation portion of the story is working, but we don't see our validation errors displayed.

Displaying our error messages

`ActionSupport` provides an implementation of `ValidationAware`'s `getFieldErrors()`, which returns a map of field errors keyed by field names. Each map entry is an array. We'll take a sneak peek at another Struts 2 tag, `<s:if>` and use it to determine whether an error message for a specific field exists or not.

We'll add a test to each field to see if an error message exists for that field. If the message exists, we'll display it in a span. For the `name` property, we end up with this:

```
<s:if test="getFieldErrors().get('recipe.name') != null">
  <div class="error">
    <s:property
      value="getFieldErrors().get('recipe.name')[0]"/>
  </div>
</s:if>
<input name="recipe.name" type="text" size="20"
       value="<s:property value="recipe.name"/>" />
```

For now, we can assume there's only one error message for each field, as that's all our `validate()` method does. For multiple errors, we'd have to iterate over all messages. Also, we're using the `<s:property>` tag to reload the field's value. Hence, our form contents are restored when the validation fails.

A simple user story turned into a lot of work! You'll either be delighted, or irritated, to learn that we didn't have to do a large portion of what we just did, thanks to Struts 2's form tags. In fact, most of our JSPs will disappear. We'll cover these tags later.

More action interfaces

We've seen the interfaces supported by the `ActionSupport` class. Combining interfaces (implemented by an action) with interceptors (either the framework's or your own) is how Struts 2 implements the bulk of its functionality.

We can implement additional interfaces to get additional capabilities. We'll cover quite a few useful interfaces here, from both XWork and Struts 2, after a brief detour to explore... ways to explore.

Detour—creating the list of interfaces to explore

As a side note, reinforcing the idea of exploration and ad hoc tool creation, let's think for a moment about how to find information about the environment we're working in. I knew I wanted a list of interfaces from both XWork and Struts 2. However, if we look at the Javadocs for Struts 2 (which, by the way includes the XWork Javadocs), there's no quick way to get a list of all the interfaces.

Standard Javadocs indicate interfaces with italics in the classes frame (lower left by default). That's not a particularly efficient system discovery method, although it works. We could define our own stylesheet that highlights the interfaces, but that's a fair amount of work. We'll see a few ways (out of many available) to extract this kind of information.

Leveraging the IDE

If we're developing in an IDE, there's most likely some form of source or library browser available. For example, Eclipse has a Java Code Browser perspective. Selecting a package shows us a list of the defined types, an icon indicating the interface, class, and so on. We can also filter our view to show only interfaces.

We're currently interested in the interfaces provided by XWork. Browsing the Action interface shows us something similar to the following:

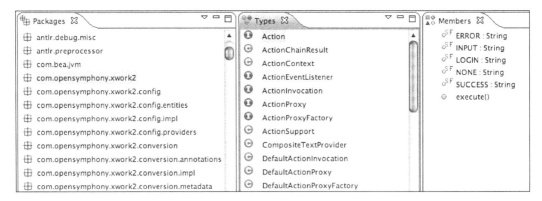

This is helpful. However, if we're trying to get an overview of the system, identify relationships, create printed documentation, and so on, it's not as helpful as it could be.

Using the command line

One quick-and-dirty way to get information like this from a source tree (if we have access to the source code, we can also examine the contents of a JAR file) is by using the grep command, available on all Unix-like systems (and Windows via Cygwin).

If we're running Windows and not using Cygwin, we're selling ourselves short. Cygwin provides much of a Unix-like environment, including the Bash shell and all of the incredibly useful file and text processing tools such as find, grep, sort, sed, and so on. The importance of these tools cannot be over-emphasized, but I'll try. They're really, really important! Really! Honestly, they should be in the arsenal of every developer.

By chaining a few of these simple utilities together, we can create a list of interfaces defined in the source code. With some minor formatting, the output is a list of interfaces we can then explore via Javadocs or the source. The following is one way to get a list of all files in a source tree that declare an interface. Continuing our look at XWork, running the following command line will produce the terse, but useful output here:

```
$ find . -name "*.java" | xargs grep -l "public interface"
./com/opensymphony/xwork2/Action.java
./com/opensymphony/xwork2/ActionEventListener.java
./com/opensymphony/xwork2/ActionInvocation.java
./com/opensymphony/xwork2/ActionProxy.java
./com/opensymphony/xwork2/ActionProxyFactory.java
./com/opensymphony/xwork2/config/Configuration.java
./com/opensymphony/xwork2/config/ConfigurationProvider.java
... etc.
```

Not the prettiest output, but it quickly provides a high-level view of the interfaces defined in the XWork source code without any actual effort. The argument to the grep command is a regular expression. Never underestimate the power of regular expressions. A mastery of regular expressions is an awesome timesaver in so many circumstances, from finding a file to doing incredibly complicated search-and-replace operations.

Repeating the same command in the Struts 2 source tree would generate a list of Struts 2 interfaces. Never underestimate the usefulness of the `find/grep` combination as a "first line of attack" tool set, particularly when we know regular expressions well.

Examining class files

The last method involves looking at Java class files, in this case, extracted from the XWork and Struts 2 core library files. From there, the ASM bytecode manipulation library is used to extract information about each interface that is defined in the class files.

 Bytecode manipulation sounds scary, but it's easier (and more useful!) than you might think. There's a good chance that you're already using some libraries (such as Hibernate or Spring) that use it for some of their functionalities.

The following image was created with a Java byte code exploration tool with a Graphviz back end. The ability to query our code and libraries can be a valuable aid for understanding by suggesting areas of a framework or library to explore, and more.

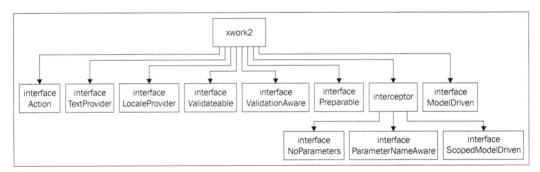

We see a few interfaces we've already touched upon (`Action`, `ValidationAware`, `Validateable`, `TextProvider`, `LocaleProvider`), and several we haven't (but will).

Using the tools we already have, or the tools that we create on an as needed basis, we can facilitate development and learning efforts.

Additional action interfaces

We'll take a brief look at a few more useful interfaces provided by XWork and Struts. We can use our own exploring methods (or just scan the Javadocs) to discover more. Just like it's difficult to over-emphasize how important command line mastery is, it's tough to oversell the value of exploration, writing example and test code, and so on.

Preparable interface

The `Preparable` interface works in concert with the `prepare` interceptor. It defines a single method, `prepare()`, which is executed before any action method. For example, this can be used to set up a data structure used in a JSP page, perform database access, and so on. `Preparable` is most useful when an action has multiple methods, each needing identical initialization. Rather than calling a preparation method each time, we implement `Preparable`, and the framework calls it for us.

Actions with only a single method might not benefit from `Preparable`. The benefit of `Preparable` is that it can remove initialization and setup code from the mainline code. The disadvantage is that it requires the developer to know that the preparable methods are being called by the framework during the request handling process.

Actions containing multiple methods can implement method-specific `Preparable` methods. For example, if we have an action method `doSomething()`, we'd create `prepareDoSomething()`. The `prepare` interceptor would call this method after the `prepare()` method, if it exists.

Accessing scoped attributes (and request parameters)

As we've seen, the request parameters will be set as action properties by the framework. Some web applications will also need access to application-scoped, session-scoped, or request-scoped attributes. A trio of interfaces cover this requirement, another adds accessing request parameters in case we need to access them directly.

These four interfaces, each containing a single method, work in concert with the `servletConfig` interceptor. They allow actions to access scoped data, without tying our actions to the servlet specification. This has a compelling consequence. We can use these actions out of our application server environment, including in standalone applications, or unit and functional tests. (We'll explore testing topics later in the book.)

```
void setApplication(Map application);  // ApplicationAware
void setSession(Map session);          // SessionAware
void setRequest(Map request);          // RequestAware
void setParameters(Map parameters);    // ParameterAware
```

Note that we can access the same objects via `ActionContext` methods. For example, we can access the session attributes with:

```
Map session = ActionContext.getContext().getSession();
```

This is, however, less testable. Therefore, implementing `SessionAware` is preferable.

Accessing servlet objects

While it's not recommended, there are (hopefully rare) times when we absolutely need access to Servlet specification objects, rather than just their attribute or parameter maps. Implementing these interfaces will provide these objects, but tie our action to the Servlet specification.

```
// ServletContextAware
void setServletContext(ServletContext context);
// ServletRequestAware
void setServletRequest(HttpServletRequest request);
// ServletResonseAware
void setServletResponse(HttpServletResponse response);
```

Similar to the attribute and parameter maps, we can also access these objects using a utility class. For example, we could access the HTTP request with:

```
HttpServletRequest req = ServletActionContext.getRequest();
```

As indicated before, this is not the preferred method, as it's more flexible to implement the interface.

Along the same line as the other `*Aware` interfaces is the `CookiesAware` interface, which works with the `cookie` interceptor to provide our action with a map of `Cookies`. This also ties our action to the Servlet specification, although perhaps with less consequence.

```
void setCookiesMap(Map cookies);     // CookiesAware
```

Request parameter/action property filtering

The NoParameters interface (interestingly defined by both XWork and Struts 2, although the Struts 2 version does not appear to add any additional functionality) effectively turns off the normal request parameter framework processing. In other words, implementing NoParameters means that our action won't have its properties set from request parameters. This is only a marker interface and defines no methods.

The ParameterNameAware interface allows an action to declare whether or not it will accept a parameter of a given name via the acceptableParameterName() method. The method should return true if the action will accept a parameter. Otherwise it should return false.

```
boolean acceptableParameterName(String parameterName);
```

This interface also works in conjunction with the params method. There are various ways to use this method. We could create a white list of parameters to accept, or a blacklist to ignore. We'll discover another way to get the same functionality using a parameter filter interceptor, thereby avoiding Java code. However, it's nice to know that the functionality is there.

Summary

This chapter delves into ActionSupport. It explains how ActionSupport, along with a few interfaces and a few Struts 2 tags, allows us to implement a fair amount of functionality. The chapter covers a bit about the I18N and validation support provided by ActionSupport.

The chapter also takes a quick took at a few other interfaces that provide access to scoped attributes (and if needed, direct access to request parameters). We can also access Servlet specification objects, such as the request and response, if we really need to.

All of these interfaces work in concert with interceptors, which we'll discuss in detail later. Even without in-depth knowledge of interceptors, we are already using them. And we could see that they're something worth paying attention to — much of Struts 2's functionality depends on them.

Next on our plate is more about Struts 2 results, including a look at the framework's default result types. We'll also look further at result configuration, type conversion, and how to create our own custom result types.

We'll also add a bit more functionality to our recipe application, sneak a peak at some additional Struts 2 tags (that will make you wonder why I made you type all that JSP in this chapter!), and get our first look at how to fake some data—smoke and mirrors, but handy!

References

A reader can refer to the following:

- Struts 2 and XWork Javadocs (reflects the latest version—may be ahead of releases!):

  `http://struts.apache.org/2.x/struts2-core/apidocs/index.html`

- Cygwin (for those of us unlucky enough not to use a Unix-like system):

  `http://www.cygwin.com/`

- Linux command line reference (not all applicable, but still useful):

  `http://www.pixelbeat.org/cmdline.html`

- Regular Expressions:

  `http://en.wikipedia.org/wiki/Regular_expression`

- ASM bytecode manipulation and analysis framework:

  `http://asm.objectweb.org/`

- Graphviz:

  `http://www.graphviz.org/`

4
Results and Result Types

In the previous chapter, we looked at Struts 2 actions and some of the functionality provided by the `ActionSupport` class. In this chapter, we will look at the other end of action processing—results. Results determine the type of response sent back to the browser after a request. The result configuration is what maps an action's return value (a simple string) to a JSP page, a redirect, another action, and so on.

We've already seen `dispatcher`, the default result type used to dispatch to JSP pages. We'll examine it along with some of the more common result types such as the redirect and FreeMarker results. We'll also create our own custom result type and see how we can integrate it into our application.

The dispatcher result type

The `dispatcher` result type is the default type, and is used if no other result type is specified. It's used to forward to a servlet, JSP, HTML page, and so on, on the server. It uses the `RequestDispatcher.forward()` method.

We saw the "shorthand" version in our earlier examples, where we provided a JSP path as the body of the result tag.

```
<result name="success" type="dispatcher">
  /WEB-INF/jsps/recipe/thanks.jsp
</result>
```

We can also specify the JSP file using a `<param name="location">` tag within the `<result...>` element, in case we don't feel we've typed enough.

```
<result name="success" type="dispatcher">
  <param name="location">
    /WEB-INF/jsps/recipe/thanks.jsp
  </param>
</result>
```

We can also supply a `parse` parameter, which is `true` by default. The `parse` parameter determines whether or not the `location` parameter will be parsed for OGNL expressions. We'll discuss this functionality later in the chapter. However, if you immediately suspect that it could be very useful, you are right.

Configuring results using annotations in Struts 2.1.6 is significantly different from that in Struts 2.0. In Struts 2.0, there was an `@Result` annotation in the Struts 2 configuration package. In Struts 2.1.6, we'd use the `@Result` annotation of the Convention Plug-in.

Convention-based action results only need to be configured manually if we're not using the default, "conventional" result. As an example, consider the following (least-exciting-ever nominee) action:

```
package com.packt.s2wad.ch04.actions.examples;
import com.opensymphony.xwork2.ActionSupport;
public class DispatchResultExampleAction
            extends ActionSupport {
}
```

Assuming the default location for the Convention result pages (JSP in our case), we'd have a JSP located in `/WEB-INF/content/examples/dispatch-result-example.jsp`. To configure a different result location, we can annotate either the entire class or an individual action method.

```
@Results({
    @Result(name = "success",
            location = "/WEB-INF/content/examples/dre.jsp")
})
public class DispatchResultExampleAction
        extends ActionSupport {
}
```

When we visit /examples/dispatch-result-example, we'll get the contents in the dre.jsp file. Note that the name annotation parameter is required even for the default success value. Also note that as with XML, we could supply the type of the result—in this case "dispatcher", with the "type" annotation parameter. This is an additional change from Struts 2.0, where the type parameter was a Class.

The Convention Plug-in does not have a similar parse parameter.

The redirect result type

The redirect result type does exactly what we'd expect. It calls the standard response.sendRedirect() method, causing the browser to create a new request to the given location. As it's a redirect, request parameters will be lost. Struts 2 provides some mechanisms for handling this, which we'll see later.

As with the dispatcher result type, we can provide the location either in the body of the <result...> element or as a <param name="location"> element. Redirect also supports the parse parameter. Here's an example configured using XML:

```
<action name="redirect-result-example">
  <result type="redirect">
    /sanity.action
  </result>
</action>

@Result(name = "success", type = "redirect",
        location = "/examples/dispatch-result-example")
public class RedirectResultExample extends ActionSupport {
}
```

The redirectAction result type

We'll often want to redirect to another action. While we could do that using a redirect result type, we'd need to append the .action (by default) suffix, preceded by a namespace if necessary. A redirectAction result type is quite common, and allows the use of only the action's name without the extension.

```
<result type="redirectAction">home</result>
```

We can provide the action name as the result tag's contents, as shown in the previous section, or by using a `<param name="actionName">` element. Providing a namespace value is only possible using a `<param name="namespace">` element.

```
<result type="redirectAction">
  <param name="namespace">/</param>
  <param name="actionName">home</param>
</result>
```

Using Convention's `@Result` annotation to do the same task looks like the following code snippet.

```
@Result(name = "success", type = "redirectAction",
        location = "dispatch-result-example")
public class RedirectActionResultExample
        extends ActionSupport {
}
```

Supporting a redirect to an action in a different namespace involves using the `params` annotation parameter. The `params` parameter accepts an array of parameter name and value pairs. Some sort of map might be more useful, but Java annotations impose some limitations.

As a further example of the Convention Plug-in, we'll use its `@Action` annotation to create an additional mapping inside the action class.

```
@Results({
    @Result(name = "success", type = "redirectAction",
            location = "dispatch-result-example"),
    @Result(name = "ns", type = "redirectAction",
            location = "home",
            params = {"namespace", "/"})
})
public class RedirectActionResultExample
        extends ActionSupport {
    @Action("nsresult")
    public String useNamespacedResult() {
        return "ns";
    }
}
```

This action class creates the standard Convention-based mapping for
`ActionSupport.execute()` and creates an additional mapping for an `nsresult`
action in the same namespace. The `nsresult` action method returns `ns`, which names
an additional result definition. Note the use of the `params` parameter, where we set
the `namespace` parameter to a `home` action.

The `@Action` annotation is a way to map a URL to a specific action method, similar
to using the `method` attribute inside an XML-based `<action>` configuration element.

The chain result type (action chaining)

The **chain** result type allows us to execute another action as a result of the current
action. This means that the output shown to the browser is ultimately controlled by
the action being chained to.

It's similar to a forward, but includes the chained action's interceptor stack, results,
and so on. In addition, the request parameters will be copied from the original
request. The action being chained from is left on the value stack for access by the
chained action.

The use of action chaining is controversial at best, and is actively discouraged. There
are few valid use cases for it. It can lead to confusing application flow, surprise us
with unexpected interactions with various interceptors (validation, for one, can
become irritating), and so on. When we find ourselves thinking that action chaining
would be a good idea, it's better to take a step back, and examine both our code and
our assumptions. We should also see if a functionality can be moved from an action
into a service layer, a `prepare()` method, or some other option.

So no example! And if we decide to use it, we get what we deserve. Note that there
are examples provided on the Struts 2 documentation wiki. However, there is almost
always a better way to provide whatever functionality we think we need from
chaining actions.

The parse parameter and a usecase detour

Earlier, it was hinted that the `parse` parameter controlled parsing of OGNL
expressions in the `location` parameter. In our JSP pages, we access action
properties using OGNL. It turns out that we have the same capability in our result
configuration (including annotations). This is a big win when used appropriately.

As a simple example, we'll use this functionality to implement a somewhat contrived use case (think administrative functionality).

- A user can enter a recipe ID and view the recipe with that ID.

To keep the JSP size down, we'll use some tags, which we haven't yet introduced—they were hinted at in the previous chapter. Struts 2 has several custom form tags that make the creation of low-fidelity (but functional and reasonable-looking) forms, quick and easy. We'll also start to look at some coding practices. These will ultimately lead us to practices we can put to use to keep our applications agile, changeable, and easier to maintain.

Displaying the form

Our form for entering a recipe ID will contain a single text field, the recipe ID, and a submit button. We'll use some I18N functionality already introduced for the page title and the text field label. Setting the `key` attribute of the form field tags automagically looks up the form element label, sets the form element name, and retrieves the appropriate value from the action when necessary. We'll learn a lot more about form tags in an upcoming chapter. However, sometimes a little teaser can be entertaining.

We'll use the Convention plug-in again. Our action will have only a few responsibilities, including displaying the form, validating the form, and directing us to the action that will actually display the recipe. We don't have to write anything beyond the action definition to display the form:

```
package com.packt.s2wad.ch04.actions.recipes;
import com.opensymphony.xwork2.ActionSupport;
public class ViewByIdAction extends ActionSupport { }
```

We'll create a `package.properties` file containing a title and form element label entry. The important bits of our JSPs are reduced to the following:

```
<s:form action="view-by-id-process">
  <s:textfield key="recipe.id"/>
  <s:submit/>
</s:form>
```

Don't worry! It will all be explained later on. However, much of it is obvious. Also, as you've probably read some of the Struts 2 tag documentation, you've already run across these.

Again, following convention, this will be located in `/WEB-INF/content/recipes/view-by-id.jsp`.

If we view the generated source, we'll see output nearly identical to the table-based HTML that we created in the previous chapter. The logic for displaying form validation error messages is included as well. Hooray, custom tags. Notice that our `<s:form>` tag's `action` attribute points to an action we haven't defined yet.

 We haven't shown the `<s:head>` tag here, but it's actually important. The tag loads the default Struts 2 style sheet, and colors error messages red (not exciting, but we'll run into it again later).

Coding our action

We'll submit our form to another Convention-based action, as seen previously. We'll define this action using Convention's `@Action` annotation that we saw earlier, and create another method in our existing `ViewByIdAction`:

```
@Action(value = "view-by-id-process",
        results = {
            @Result(name = INPUT,
            location =
                "/WEB-INF/content/recipes/view-by-id.jsp")
        })
public String process() {
    return SUCCESS;
}
```

Notice our `@Result` annotation. We've configured an "input" result manually, and determined that it will use the conventionally located JSP page containing our form. We'll learn more about the validation process in a later chapter. However, we can conclude that if there are any validation errors, Struts 2 will return us to the "input" result, our form in this case.

Validating the form will add the following code to our action:

```
public void validate() {
    if (recipe == null || recipe.getId() == null) {
        addFieldError("recipe.id", "Recipe ID is required.");
    }
}
```

If we submit the form without entering a recipe ID, we should see something similar to the following screenshot. The custom tag checks for and displays error messages on a per-field basis—all for free.

Remember when I said you'd wonder why we went through all the trouble of doing it on our own?

Configuring our success result

The next step is to configure a `success` result, that is, what is to be done when validation passes. To demonstrate dynamic results (using OGNL in our results configuration), we'll create a result that redirects to a `view` action, used to view a recipe, potentially from various other pages (like a list of recipes).

We'll add another `@Result` annotation to our `@Action` annotation's `results` parameter:

```
@Result(name = SUCCESS,
        type = "redirectAction",
        location = "show",
        params = {"recipe.id", "%{recipe.id}"})
```

This @Result uses the redirectAction result, sending us to an action named show. The annotation also includes a parameter. Here, we're sending a parameter named recipe.id, and its value is ${recipe.id}.

The %{recipe.id} parameter value is an OGNL expression—the same as we'd use in a Struts 2 custom tag—wrapped in %{} characters. We can also wrap OGNL expressions in %{} when we use Struts 2 custom tags. This is compulsory in some cases.

We can use the same OGNL expressions in our Struts 2 XML configuration files as well, also wrapped in %{} characters. It's important to note that in much of the existing documentation, we'll see OGNL expressions in both XML and annotations using the ${} notation. This is still supported, but changed to include the use of %{} to better match how we use OGNL in our JSP pages.

The bottom line is that we're sending a parameter named recipe.id to the show action (which we haven't written yet), and giving it a value of our recipe's ID, which is entered using our form.

The complete action method, along with its annotations, will look like this:

```
@Action(value = "view-by-id-process",
        results = {
            @Result(name = SUCCESS,
                    type = "redirectAction",
                    location = "show",
                    params = {"recipe.id", "%{recipe.id}"}),
            @Result(name = INPUT,
                    location =
                    "/WEB-INF/content/recipes/view-by-id.jsp")
        })
    public String process() {
        log.debug(String.format("Enter: recipe.id=%d.",
                                recipe.getId()));
        return SUCCESS;
    }
```

Note that we've put a logging statement in our process() method (logging will be discussed in more detail in a later chapter). The reason for this is about to become apparent.

Type conversion sneak attack

If we run the code at this point and submit the form with a reasonable integer value in the form field, we'll notice something rather interesting. When we submit the form, we'll see a log statement that displays the ID we entered.

No big deal, right? The Recipe class's id property is defined as a java.lang. Integer. As we all know, forms can submit only strings. However, it's working.

> In case you didn't know, forms submit strings. This is a source of much confusion. For example, if you looked at the network traffic for a form submission, you'd see only strings. There won't be any type information, no strange binary formats, just strings (file uploads are a bit special). Every form field is submitted as a string, no matter what.

XWork has type conversions built right in for many common types. This means that simple conversions, such as the string-to-Integer seen above, are generally handled transparently by the framework. This saves a fair amount of time and headache during coding. You might not have even noticed. It just seems so natural, and it is. Converting form values to Java objects on our own was tedious, error-prone, and it cluttered up the code that did the real work. We'll cover more about type conversion in Chapter 6.

Something else is happening as well. Even though we have no code that creates a Recipe object, we're logging (to the console) a bit of the recipe property. The framework is creating a Recipe instance as well. Remember instantiating everything on our own? Remember pulling request parameters out on our own, converting them, and copying them into our model object? In many cases, particularly the most common ones, we don't have to do that anymore. This is very helpful in many ways. It saves code, cognitive overhead, and duplication of effort.

Coding the show action

Our view action receives the recipe.id parameter, again into a Recipe object, instantiated and filled by the framework without any intervention from us. Now that's quite handy. For now, as we're not using a database, we're going to look up some fake, hard-coded data—but from where?

One very important principle of agile software development is to decouple our application as much as possible. This means that our individual code chunks should strive to do only one thing, and do it well.

In the past, we would load up our servlets (or framework classes) with all the code to do everything. In Struts 2 terms, we would code a database lookup into our action, handle database exceptions in our action code, marshal (say) a JDBC result set into a business model, and who knows what else.

This is a horrible idea.

However, as we progress through the book, we'll see many reasons why (and how) doing it differently is a really good idea. One of the easiest reasons to highlight is that it makes our code much longer. This increases the cognitive overhead necessary to understand how a particular section of code works, what its purpose is, and so on.

One of the easiest chunks to move out of the mainline code is database access and data marshaling. We'll return to this topic in force in later chapters, especially when we cover testability, Spring, and the mysterious-sounding **Inversion of Control (IoC)** (also known as **Dependency Injection**).

Until then, we'll write a class that pretends it's retrieving recipes from a database — but it's really just a map of hard-coded recipes. We will, however, create a parallel interface that our recipe service will implement. This allows us to write other recipe services that implement the same interface. The code in the action shouldn't have to change once we're retrieving recipes from the database.

For now, it's enough to know that there is an interface, `RecipeService`, which we can use to retrieve a single recipe by ID.

 Notice that it's not called `IRecipeService`. Interfaces can be thought of as classes with multiple implementations. Each implementation is a `RecipeService` for all intents and purposes. Prefixing an interface name with an "I" isn't necessary. The distinction should come on the implementation side, not the interface definition.

For now, the interface defines only what we need — the ability to find a recipe by its ID.

```
package com.packt.s2wad.ch04.services;
public interface RecipeService {
    Recipe findById(Integer id);
}
```

Our implementation is called (somewhat accusingly) `FakeRecipeService`, and is really simple. Some of the code is elided here to make the snippet shorter. The key point to remember is that there's a map of recipes, and we can retrieve them through the `findById()` method.

```
public class FakeRecipeService implements RecipeService {
    private static Map<Integer, Recipe> recipes =
        new LinkedHashMap<Integer, Recipe>() {{
            put(1, new Recipe(1, "Spicy Lentil Pot", ...));
            put(2, new Recipe(2, "Bread and Water", ...));
            ...
        }};
    public Recipe findById(Integer id) {
        return recipes.get(id);
    }
}
```

For simplicity, our low-fidelity prototype recipe service returns a `null` if no recipe is found (whether or not to return a null value is a long-running discussion). Personally, I think it causes problems later on—I'd return a statically-defined `notfound` recipe with a known ID and check for a valid recipe, rather than a null. Null values cause code to blow up, whereas a non-null, but possibly invalid value, may lead to puzzling behavior. However, nothing actually explodes.

Finally, we code our view action, which for now, simply instantiates an instance of the `FakeRecipeService` and uses it to look up our ID (getters and setters not shown). We'll see better ways to handle getting our recipe service later in the book.

```
public class ShowAction extends ActionSupport {
    private Recipe recipe;
    private RecipeService recipeService =
        new FakeRecipeService();
    public String execute() throws Exception {
        recipe = recipeService.findById(recipe.getId());
        return recipe != null ? SUCCESS : "notfound";
    }
}
```

Note that we're returning `notfound` when we don't find a recipe. The Convention plug-in will look for `/WEB-INF/content/recipes/show-notfound.jsp`, and will build the JSP file name using the action name and the action's return value.

Our recipe `show-success.jsp` page just displays the recipe's title, description, and so on. Here's a fragment:

```
<h1><s:text name="recipe.show-recipe.header"/></h1>
<h2><s:text name="ingredients"/></h2>
<p>${recipe.ingredients}</p>
<p>${recipe.description}</p>
...
```

Note that we're using the I18N features in several more places. During our prototyping / low-fidelity phase, we probably don't care if we do that or not. However, it gives us a chance to again see how we can use action properties in our messages. The `recipe.show-recipe.header` message is defined in `package.properties` as follows:

```
recipe.show-recipe.header=Recipe: ${recipe.name}
```

This gives us a localized "Recipe" header along with our recipe's name. Of course, this works only if we don't have localized recipe names… but think low-fidelity!

The FreeMarker and Velocity result types

JSP may be the most common JEE view technology in use. However, it has its detractors due to its verbosity and inability to render outside a server container (in general). Two other popular view technologies are FreeMarker and Velocity — both Java templating engines with simplified markup (compared to JSP).

FreeMarker is used within Struts 2 to create its custom tags (as opposed to using standard Java- or JSP-based tags), so I'll focus on the FreeMarker results (a Velocity discussion would look very similar). FreeMarker will also be covered a bit more when we look at custom themes and templates. FreeMarker does have a few advantages over Velocity. It includes the ability to use custom tags (only Java-based at the time of writing this book, JSP 2.0 tag files aren't yet supported), capture template output into a variable, use built-in conversion and formatting capabilities, and so on. It is a capable replacement for JSP in the view layer.

FreeMarker result configuration

The FreeMarker support in Struts 2 is built-in. Hence, configuring a FreeMarker result looks like the other results types we've seen. Only the FreeMarker library (already a dependency of Struts 2) is required—no additional libraries or plug-ins are necessary. In addition to the `location` and `parse` parameters, FreeMarker results may also specify the `contentType` parameter (which defaults to "text/html") to allow writing other content types. (This is surprisingly handy, for example, when producing XML, CSV, and so on.) The `writeIfCompleted` (false by default) may also be specified, which will write the output to the stream only if there were no errors while processing the template.

As a simple example of using a FreeMarker result, we'll create another show recipe method in our existing action. However, we will use FreeMarker instead of JSP to view the results. Our new method just returns the value of our existing `execute()` method. However, as we're using Convention's `@Action` annotation, it will search for files named after our action name. This means Convention will look for `fmshow-success.ftl` and `fmshow-notfound.ftl`. (It will actually look for the same files, but with a JSP extension. If it doesn't find those, it will look for FreeMarker files next).

```
@Action(value = "fmshow")
    public String fmshow() throws Exception {
        return execute();
    }
```

Remember, this is a low-fidelity prototype at this point. We only have guesses for what the final functionality and data structures will look like. However, we can make semi-intelligent guesses along the way. The more we can show a potential client without coding ourselves into a corner, the better off we are. Our guesses will usually be close, and will help to better identify what the client really wants.

Our FreeMarker template looks much like you'd expect it to (assuming you expected FreeMarker and not JSP). The portion that displays the recipe header and title looks very similar to that of our JSP file:

```
<h1><@s.text name="recipe.show-recipe.header"/></h1>
<h2>
  <@s.text name="recipe.show-recipe.description.header"/>
</h2>
<div id="description">
  ${recipe.description}
</div>
```

The Struts 2 custom tags are used, but with the `<@s.tagname...>` syntax. We can also use FreeMarker's EL notation inside the `${}` characters, just like in JSP, to access the value stack.

The FreeMarker result type may also be used to create various text-based result types very easily because of its `contentType` parameter. For example, by using one of the comma-separated value content types, such as "text/csv", you could create a page that could then be imported into a spreadsheet application. The default dispatcher result type for JSP pages does not have a similar `contentType` parameter, meaning that we must define the content type in the JSP page itself.

With its ability to use Struts 2 custom tags and its concise syntax, FreeMarker can be a compelling replacement for JSP views. There are a few potential gotchas when using FreeMarker results. They are discussed in the Struts 2 documentation wiki in the Tag Developers Guide.

Perhaps the most glaring gotcha is FreeMarker's requirement that tags be declared as "inline" or "block" tags with an inability to switch between the two. For the sake of convenience, some Struts 2 tags are defined as "inline" tags, that is, tags that accept no inner content. For example, the `<s:action>` tag is defined as an inline tag.

As we'll see in the next chapter, the `<s:action>` tag may be used with nested `<s:param>` tags. This use case is currently not possible using FreeMarker.

The XSLT result type

The XSLT result type allows us to transform an action using a specified XSLT file. We don't have to output XML, which is then styled. We simply access our action's properties in our XSLT file, as if we were transforming XML. If we're already invested heavily in XSLT, this result type can be very helpful.

During development, it's handy to turn off Struts 2's built-in stylesheet caching using a "constant" element in our Struts 2 configuration file, or in our `web.xml`. We'll add an initialization parameter to our `web.xml` entry for our Struts 2 filter dispatcher.

```
<init-param>
  <param-name>struts.xslt.nocache</param-name>
  <param-value>true</param-value>
</init-param>
```

To test the XSLT result, we'll create a simple test action, configured using XML. Why aren't we using the Convention plug-in for this example? It turns out that we must play some games with how the Convention plug-in is configured — the default implementations support only a few result types. It's neither impossible nor difficult to extend Convention to handle XSLT results.

```
public class XsltExample extends ActionSupport {
    private String headerText;
    private String testString =
        "really awesome property inserted";
    private List<String> listProperty =
        new ArrayList<String>() {{
            add("Item number one");
            add("The second item");
            add("Yet another item: the third");
    }};

    @Override
    public String execute() throws Exception {
        headerText = getText("header.key");
        return SUCCESS;
    }
}
```

One significant difference with XSLT results is that we do not have access to the Struts 2 tags in our result. Any value we need in our XSLT page must be an exposed action property. This means that our action code must include getters for localized text messages and so on.

The XSLT result assumes our Struts 2 action is exposed with a root element `result`. This is mandatory. The transformation just displays the header text and iterates over the exposed list.

```
<?xml version="1.0" encoding="ISO-8859-1"?>
<xsl:stylesheet version="1.0"
    xmlns:xsl="http://www.w3.org/1999/XSL/Transform">
  <xsl:output method="html" version="4.0"
              encoding="iso-8859-1" indent="yes"/>
  <xsl:template match="result">
    <html>
      <head>
        <title>
          <xsl:value-of select="headerText"/>
        </title>
      </head>
      <body>
```

```
        <h1><xsl:value-of select="headerText"/></h1>
        <table>
          <tr><th>String from list</th></tr>
          <xsl:for-each select="listProperty/*">
            <tr>
              <td><xsl:value-of select="."/></td>
            </tr>
          </xsl:for-each>
        </table>
      </body>
    </html>
  </xsl:template>
</xsl:stylesheet>
```

The XSLT result type takes two optional parameters for including
(matchingPattern) and excluding (excludingPattern) action properties.

The plaintext result

The plain text result type escapes the text sent to the browser, allowing you to see a
raw view of a JSP, for example. The plain text is sent back without any interpretation:
JSP pages won't execute any custom tags, FreeMarker pages won't execute their
directives, and so on. No example is necessary, it's just plain text.

The stream result

The stream result type allows straightforward file downloading from an
InputStream. We can set various parameters such as contentType and
contentDisposition, which do what we would expect them to.

The only requirement for this result type is that our action must either implement
InputStream getInputStream() or a getter for the property specified in the
inputName parameter. However, I suspect the default of inputStream is perfectly
adequate. This getter will be called the source of the stream sent to the browser.

> The showcase example shows the results of a resourceAsStream(...)
> call being returned directly in the getInputStream() method. In
> general, we'll probably attempt resource stream creation in an action's
> execute() method (or whichever method we're executing) to allow for
> the possibility of throwing an exception for a missing file and acting on it,
> and so on.

As this example consists of opening a `FileInputStream` (just like the showcase example, we can open a file as a resource stream, as long as it is on the application classpath), we won't examine it further — let it be an exercise to the reader...

The httpheader result

The HTTP header result type allows the status, error code and message, as well as arbitrary headers, to be set. It also accepts the `parse` parameter, allowing the use of action properties in the results. This could allow, for example, the error message to come from an S2 property file. We'll skip an example of this as well since that's all we can do with it, and it should be self-explanatory.

The Tiles and JasperReports results

These result types are beyond the scope of this book, as each requires knowledge of its respective technology.

Tiles allows the definition of page fragments, which are then composited into complete pages. Tiles results allow tile definitions to be used as the end result of an action execution. Those familiar with Tiles from Struts 1 will recognize the Tiles 2 configuration and tags, although they have changed somewhat.

JasperReports is a reporting engine that can produce reports in several output formats including PDF. The Jasper result tag allows an easy mechanism for rendering the results of an action as a report of any supported output format.

Creating custom result types

Even though Struts 2 ships with most of the results we'll need (and a few we probably won't), there are times when only creating our own results will do. We'll look at a contrived example where having a custom result type saves us some development time upfront.

Let's assume for a moment that our client already has a large number of recipes stored on their file system in a custom format that is neither JSP nor FreeMarker. These recipes, over a thousand of them, are kept in Markdown format. To avoid the overhead of converting the recipes to the site's database format, it's decided that they will be served directly by the application.

Markdown is a lightweight markup used to create HTML. Several blogging engines use it as their default markup because it's very simple and reads well as plain text. It is of limited use in a web application as it has no concept of variables (at least for now). However, it makes for a short, convenient, and contrived example.

The Markdown recipe files are very simple (as is our sample recipe).

- The # characters indicate a header level
- Items prefaced with a * character are put into an unordered list
- Items prefaced with a 1. are put into a numbered list

```
# Macaroni and Cheese
A simple baked macaroni and cheese.
## Ingredients
* Macaroni
* Cheese
* Whole milk
## Directions
1. Cook the macaroni.
1. Mix it with the cheese and milk.
1. Bake at 325F for 35 minutes or until bubbly.
```

By creating a MarkdownResult result type, we can serve these files directly using an action. It will act like a normal dispatcher result that can serve a JSP page, but it serves a converted Markdown file instead.

Again, keeping things simple, we'll ignore things like caching and efficiency, and focus only on the small amount of code necessary to create our own custom result. This task is made easier by subclassing Struts 2's StrutsResultSupport, a class implementing Result that provides some typical functionality, such as the parse and location parameters, which we've seen in other result types.

We'll be using the "markdownj" library, available on SourceForge.

Configuring our custom result type

We'll work a bit backwards, starting with our result configuration. This is a sort of built-in test-driven development step. Our application will fail unless we finish writing our custom result type. We add the following to the top of our `struts.xml` file in our default package element:

```
<package name="default" namespace="/"
        extends="struts-default">
  <result-types>
    <result-type name="markdown"
        class="com.packt.s2wad.ch04.examples.MarkdownResult"/>
  </result-types>
  ...
```

This tells Struts 2 that we can now use a result type `markdown`, and that it is implemented by the `MarkdownResult` class.

Writing the action

Our action is simple, because we're making assumptions in the interests of brevity (as usual).

```
package com.packt.s2wad.ch04.examples;
import com.opensymphony.xwork2.ActionSupport;
public class MarkdownAction extends ActionSupport {
    private String mdid;
    public String getMdid() { return mdid; }
    public void setMdid(String mdid) { mdid = mdid; }
}
```

The XML action configuration is similarly simple:

```
<action name="viewmd"
        class="com.packt.s2wad.ch04.examples.MarkdownAction">
  <result type="markdown">
    /WEB-INF/mdrecipes/${mdid}.md
  </result>
</action>
```

The biggest assumptions are:

1. All of our Markdown-based recipe files live in `/WEB-INF/mdrecipes`.

2. The filenames are all valid URL parameters.

In our case, they're just named `1.md`, `2.md`, and so on. This is not, of course, production-ready code.

We see again how useful accessing action properties in our result configuration can be. Struts 2 handles what essentially is a miniature templating mechanism, saving us the trouble of building up strings ourselves.

Implementing our markdown result type

We need only three simple steps to implement our custom result type:

1. Read the Markdown file.
2. Process the Markdown file.
3. Write the Markdown file.

In real life, we'd pay more attention to error handling.

Our Markdown result looks like this (imports, getters, and setters not shown):

```
package com.packt.s2wad.ch04.examples;

public class MarkdownResult extends StrutsResultSupport {
    private String defaultEncoding = "ISO-8859-1";

    public void doExecute(final String finalLocation,
                          final ActionInvocation invocation)
            throws Exception {
        String markdownInput =
            readFromContextPath(invocation, finalLocation);
        if ((markdownInput == null)
            || (markdownInput.length() == 0)) {
            // FIXME Like our error handling?
        }

        MarkdownProcessor p = new MarkdownProcessor();
        String markdown = p.markdown(markdownInput);

        ActionContext actionContext =
            invocation.getInvocationContext();
        HttpServletResponse response =
            (HttpServletResponse)
              actionContext.get(StrutsStatics.HTTP_RESPONSE);
        byte[] markdownBytes =
            markdown.getBytes(defaultEncoding);
        response.setContentLength(markdownBytes.length);
        response.setContentType("text/html;charset="
                                + this.defaultEncoding);
```

```
        PrintWriter out = response.getWriter();
        out.print(markdown);
    }

    private String
        readFromContextPath(ActionInvocation invocation,
                            String finalLocation) {
        ServletContext servletContext =
            ServletActionContext.getServletContext();
        File inFile =
          new File(servletContext.getRealPath(finalLocation));
        if (!inFile.exists()) {
            // FIXME More awesome error handling.
            return "";
        }
        try {
            return FileUtils.readFileToString(inFile,
                        defaultEncoding);
        } catch (IOException e) {
            e.printStackTrace();
        }
        return "";
    }
}
```

The entry point into StrutsResultSupport classes is the doExecute() method. It receives the current action invocation and the location of the result, which is parsed for OGNL expressions if necessary. In our case, we're passing the Markdown recipe ID from the action into the location using OGNL. Therefore, the finalLocation parameter would be 1.md if we passed an mdid value of 1.

We read the Markdown file in the readFromContextPath() method. Reading a file into a String is boring, so we've used Apache Commons IO's FileUtils class. (Commons IO is required for the default Struts 2 file uploading process; so we shouldn't feel too bad about adding another dependency.) What is (slightly) less boring is how we access things like the ServletContext from within our custom result. This highlights a simple way to get access to the servlet context on the rare occasions we need to tie ourselves to the servlet API (we also saw this in the chapter covering Struts 2 actions).

```
ServletActionContext.getServletContext()
```

I won't talk about it much because using this method ties us to the servlet specification, and we try to avoid that whenever possible. In this case, it was unavoidable as I've packaged the Markdown-based recipe files into our web application for easy deployment, but not on the classpath. Typically, they would live outside the application.

Other than that, it's just a matter of using the MarkdownJ package to transform the Markdown markup into HTML and returning it to the browser with the appropriate headers set. The rest of the `doExecute()` method uses a `MarkdownJ` processor to convert the Markdown file contents and write it directly to the response.

When we make a request to `/viewmd.action?mdid=1`, our result gets the location, `/WEB-INF/mdrecipes/1.md`, thanks to our result configuration. The file contents are run through the Markdown conversion process and get transformed into HTML which, without any styling, will present us with something resembling this:

Summary

The chapter covers most of the standard result types, leaving a few of the more complicated, and a few of the most simple for self-study. The chapter also takes a quick look at the process for creating new result types, should our application need custom functionality.

The chapter also tells how action properties can be interpolated in our result configuration, which can be a very useful technique.

The use case scenario gives us a teasing look at some of the Struts 2 form tags, which help eliminate the bulk of the JSP we wrote on our own in the previous chapter. It would also help us start on the path to agile action coding, which will eventually lead to keeping our code more easily testable (coming up a bit later).

Next on our list are Struts 2's non-form-oriented custom tags, some of which we've already seen (such as `<s:property>`, `<s:if>`). We'll also dive into OGNL, everybody's favorite expression language, and the value stack, from which OGNL gets its data.

References

A reader can refer to the following:

- The `struts-default.xml` defines standard result types (and much more of interest!):

  `http://struts.apache.org/2.x/docs/struts-defaultxml.html`

- The standard result types:

  `http://struts.apache.org/2.x/docs/result-types.html`

- Struts 2 Type Conversion:

  `http://struts.apache.org/2.x/docs/type-conversion.html`

- FreeMarker:

  `http://freemarker.sourceforge.net/`

- XSLT:

  `http://www.w3.org/TR/xslt.html`

- Tiles:

  `http://tiles.apache.org/`

- SiteMesh:

  http://www.opensymphony.com/sitemesh/

- JasperReports:

  http://jasperforge.org/plugins/project/project_home.php?group_id=102

- Markdown:

  http://daringfireball.net/projects/markdown/

- MarkdownJ:

  http://sourceforge.net/projects/markdownj/

5
OGNL, the Value Stack, and Custom Tags

The previous chapter detailed the standard Struts 2 result types, and how to create our own result types. We also saw how to use OGNL expressions in our result configurations to pass along action properties.

Struts 2 uses OGNL as the expression language (EL) for its extensive collection of custom tags, both general tags and those related to user-interface. In this chapter, we'll look at OGNL and the general tags, leaving the UI (form) tags for the next chapter along with form handling.

OGNL

A complete discussion of OGNL's capabilities and syntax is beyond the scope of this book. However, as we go along, we'll cover the most important points necessary to get things done.

 Efforts are underway to allow the use of other expression languages such as JSP EL and MVEL, rather than OGNL (or at least provide the option for doing so).

For now, one of the most important aspects about Struts 2 and OGNL that needs to be understood is the concept of the "value stack". We've already seen that when an action is executed, it's pushed onto the stack, giving us access to its properties from our JSP.

It's more than just a simple stack. It also contains named values, similar to the request and session attributes we're already familiar with. We'll refer to these as stack context values to differentiate them from the objects pushed on to the stack itself. I think of it as both a stack and a scope. We'll also see how we can set our own values in the stack context.

OGNL allows access to both value properties and methods. Value properties are available with a simple named reference, identical to JSP EL. Value methods are called by providing the full method name followed by parenthesis, just like a standard Java call. We're also able to call methods with parameters, as we've already seen.

Contents of the value stack and the <s:property> tag

We've already seen that an action's properties are available on a JSP result page. This is because after an action is executed, it is pushed on to the value stack before moving to the result. So, under most circumstances, the action will be the topmost object on the stack when we get to our result.

We access action properties using the `<s:property>` tag, as already seen—it's a window into the value stack context. It's interesting to note that action properties do not need a public getter method to be accessible—a public property with no getter is also accessible. In fact, a public property with a private getter will also be found (it would be a bit weird, of course). Whether or not this is a good thing is debatable. In general, I recommend sticking to JavaBean conventions, keeping properties private (or protected) and providing public getters and setters.

Escaping values

By default, the `<s:property>` tag will escape HTML-like characters inside it. If a String property's value is "This string's HTML-ish", it will display exactly that, complete with HTML tags. If we want the markup to be recognized by the browser, we must set the `escape` attribute to `false`.

```
<s:property value="propWithHtml" escape="false"/>
```

Any time we render an unescaped property, we must ensure that the property being displayed is properly sanitized and/or escaped before being displayed in order to avoid any of the various **Cross-site scripting (XSS)** attacks. As a simple example, consider a property that had a `<script>` element in it. If we don't escape the property, the JavaScript will be executed when the page is displayed.

Default values

The `<s:property>` tag also allows us to set a default value, which will be displayed when the property itself is null:

```
<s:property value="nullExample" default="A default value."/>
```

Escaping values for JavaScript

We can also specify that property values be escaped for use in JavaScript expressions using the `escapeJavaScript` attribute. Setting `escapeJavaScript="true"` will escape both single (') and double (") quotes for use in JavaScript strings by inserting a backslash (\) before them.

For example, assume our action has the following property:

```
private String javascriptExample =
                    "I haven't got enough \"quotes\".";
```

Also, assume that our JSP page contains the following JavaScript block:

```
<script type="text/javascript">
  var jsFromTag1 = '<s:property value="javascriptExample"
                              escapeJavaScript="true"/>';
  document.writeln(jsFromTag1);
</script>
```

If we view our document source, we'll see the following:

```
var jsFromTag1 = 'I haven\'t got enough &quot;quotes&quot;.';
```

When both the `escapeJavaScript` and `escape` attributes are used, the correct behavior occurs. If the previous example had set `escape="false"`, the `&quot;` characters would not have been replaced by the HTML entities. However, the `escapeJavaScript="true"` seting would cause a leading backslash (\) to be included as with the single-quote examples shown.

If we hadn't used `escapeJavaScript="true"`, we'd have gotten a JavaScript error on the page. The first single-quote in our string would signal the end of the JavaScript string, and the rest of the string is obviously not valid JavaScript.

Other value stack objects and the debug tag

There are several other important properties on the value stack that can be accessed by name. These properties are in the stack *context*, and must be referred to using the # character As of this writing, is appears as though this is no longer necessary in many circumstances due to changes in the way stack context values are looked up.

We can get a view of everything on the stack by using the `<s:debug>` tag, which creates an HTML view on our page of the stack and stack context. During development, it's often handy to include this as the last content on the page. It renders a link, which when clicked, exposes the stack and stack context in all its glory. A portion of its expanded output is shown in the following screenshot:

[Debug]

Struts ValueStack Debug

Value Stack Contents

Object	Property Name	Property Value
	locale	en_US
	nullExample	null
	errorMessages	[]
	errors	{}
	nonNullExample	I can haz value?
com.packt.s2wad.ch05.actions.examples.PropertyTagAction	javascriptExample	I haven't got enough "quotes".
	actionErrors	[]
	texts	null
	fieldErrors	{}
	escapeExample	I have embedded HTML.
	actionMessages	[]
com.opensymphony.xwork2.DefaultTextProvider	texts	null

Stack Context

These items are available using the #key notation

Key	Value
last.bean.accessed	null
struts.actionMapping	org.apache.struts2.dispatcher.mapper.ActionMapping@e522a6
com.opensymphony.xwork2.ActionContext.locale	en_US
session	{}
current.property.path	null

Most importantly, the application, session, and request scopes of our application are all exposed directly (unsurprisingly) using the `#application`, `#session`, and `#request` names. Request parameters are available using the `#parameters` name. The code snippet shown here directly accesses an attribute in each of the scopes:

```
<s:property value="#application.anAppAttribute"/>
<s:property value="#session.aSessionAttribute"/>
<s:property value="#request.aRequestAttribute"/>
<s:property value="#parameters.aRequestParameter"/>
```

Note specifically that there is no #page name, and in order to access page-scoped attributes, we must use the #attr name. Using the #attr name will cause all scopes to be searched in a typical JSP EL order—application, session, request, and page. The following snippet will return the same results as the previous snippet (assuming there are no "shadowing" attributes, that is, attributes of the same name in different scopes). This is the lengthy equivalent to using the JSP EL shorthand.

```
<s:property value="#attr.anAppAttribute"/>
<s:property value="#attr.aSessionAttribute"/>
<s:property value="#attr.aRequestAttribute"/>
<s:property value="#attr.aPageAttribute"/>
```

Of course, accessing scoped attributes can also be done using the normal JSP 2.0 EL ${} or with JSTL's <c:out> constructs.

There are some other debugging options available by using the debug request parameter. For example, if we append debug=xml to a request, we'll get back an XML representation of the value stack. However, that's *all* we'll get back, meaning that in some browsers we'd have to view the page's source to get a readable view.

We can also use debug=console and get a pop-up box allowing us to query the value stack using OGNL expressions directly, drilling down into objects contained on the stack interactively.

These options require that the debug interceptor is active (which it is in the default interceptor stack).

The <s:debug> tag is handy as we can just add it to the bottom of our page and get a collapsible view of the stack with essentially zero effort. Note that in Struts 2.0, the <s:debug> tag does not escape property values, which can lead to unexpected consequences, particularly if we have <script> tags in the displayed value. This is resolved in Struts 2.1.

A dirty EL trick

Referring to a simple property, such as anActionProperty, with an <s:property> tag feels like a throwback to the beloved <c:out> days. Struts 2 provides a custom request wrapper allowing the use of JSP 2.0 EL to access properties without the syntactic noise of <s:property>, allowing us to use the shorter JSP 2.0 EL notation to refer to objects on the value stack.

```
${anActionProperty}
```

Struts 2 does this by first checking the value stack of the named property. If it isn't found on the value stack, it's passed off to the normal JSP lookup, which will check the various JEE scopes. This is very convenient, but can throw people off if they're not aware of the trick being played. Note that this dirty EL trick, as it uses the normal Struts 2 stack lookup mechanism first, follows the same property/getter access rules described earlier.

 Some people don't like mixing paradigms like this. This decision is a stylistic one, rather than a technical decision. While I try to avoid mixing Struts 2 and JSTL tags in the same JSP, using the ${ . . . } notation saves time (and typing).

The <s:set> tag

The set tag assigns the results of an OGNL expression to a variable, optionally setting a scope (defaults to `action` scope, rather than the four typical servlet scopes). This tag is useful when we have a complicated or deeply nested expression, we need to access it over and over again, and don't want to type much. Such deeply nested expressions can also be very computationally expensive. Using an `<s:set>` tag can save typing as well as execution time.

```
<s:set name="shorter" value="deeply.nested.value.getter"/>
...
<s:property value="#shorter"/>
```

The "#" character is now optional—current documentation doesn't reflect this. We can also reference stack context values without the leading "#".

Calling static methods from OGNL

OGNL allows us to call static methods by using the `@full.package@methodName()` notation. In order to use this functionality, we must enable static method access in any of our configuration methods (`struts.properties`—not recommended, a `struts.xml` constant, or a `web.xml` Struts 2 filter initialization parameter). Setting `struts.ognl.allowStaticMethodAccess=true` enables static method access.

As a simple example, consider a utility class that repeats a string a given number of times. We can call it from a JSP page such as:

```
<s:property
    value="@com.packt.s2wad.utils.UtilClass@repeat(20, '*')"/>
```

This will return the asterisk repeated twenty times.

Conditionals

Struts 2 provides three tags for dealing with conditionals: `<s:if>`, `<s:elseif>`, and `<s:else>`. Unlike JSTL's `if` construct, we can have a complete `if-elseif-else` decision tree without a surrounding `<c:choose>` tag, making the Struts 2 version slightly cleaner. Both `<s:if>` and `<s:elseif>` take a single attribute `test`, which does what we'd expect.

```
<s:if test="aBooleanExpression">
  Printed when test is true.
</s:if>
<s:elseif test="aDifferentBooleanExpression">
  Printed if previous test was false and this one is true.
</s:elseif>
<s:else>
  Printed if neither were true.
</s:else>
```

The `test` attribute accepts any valid OGNL expression, including expressions that call action methods, static methods (assuming static method access is enabled), and so on.

One OGNL expression gotcha is often encountered when testing string. In OGNL, a single character inside single quotes is a character, not a string. If we assume an action property `testMe`, a string containing a single letter A, the following test will not work:

```
<s:if test="testMe == 'A'">
  This won't print; 'A' is a character, not a string.
</s:if>
```

We can force OGNL to compare strings using double quotes around A:

```
<s:if test='testMe == "A"'>
  Ah, much better--this prints.
</s:if>
```

Collections and iteration

There are several tags provided for dealing with collections, from the typical iteration to some fairly sophisticated tags for manipulating lists and defining custom iteration. OGNL, too, provides some sneaky tricks that we'll cover briefly.

The <s:iterator> tag

In its simplest form, `<s:iterator>` is a compact way to iterate over a list. First, we'll iterate over a list of strings, displaying the current item by using `<s:property/>` with no attributes. This works because the iterator tag pushes each item on to the top of the stack, and a property tag with no `value` attribute will display the object on the top of the stack. This is convenient. However, as we'll see later, it can lead to an interesting gotcha! when the object in the collection has a property with the same name as an action property.

```
<ul>
  <s:iterator value="listOfStrings">
    <li><s:property/></li>
  </s:iterator>
</ul>
```

The object of the current iteration can also be named using the `var` attribute (`id` in Struts 2.0). The following is equivalent to the previous snippet, the only difference being that we now name the current object of the iteration. However, the named object is still on the top of the stack. We can access it either using the name as shown here, or using a bare property tag as shown above.

```
<ul>
  <s:iterator value="listOfStrings" var="anItem">
    <li><s:property value="anItem"/></li>
  </s:iterator>
</ul>
```

Iterating over a `java.util.Map.Entry` is similar. When iterating over a map, each item is a `Map.Entry`. We can access the map key and map value by using the `key` and `value`, again using the convenience of having each item in the collection being pushed on to the stack.

```
<ul>
  <s:iterator value="mapStringString">
    <li>
      <s:property value="key"/> : <s:property value="value"/>
    </li>
  </s:iterator>
</ul>
```

Again, we can still use the `var` attribute to name each entry value:

```
<ul>
  <s:iterator value="mapStringString" var="entry">
    <li>
      <s:property value="#entry.key"/> ==
      <s:property value="#entry.value"/>
    </li>
  </s:iterator>
</ul>
```

Tracking iteration status

Tracking iteration status—which iteration we're on, whether it's an even or odd iteration, and so on—are pretty common needs. The iterator tag's `status` attribute defines an `IteratorStatus` instance, accessible using the # prefix (because it's a variable we're creating, not pushing onto the stack) that defines several useful properties that can be used for a host of functionality.

```
<table>
  <s:iterator value="list1" status="stat">
    <tr>
      <td><s:property value="#stat.index"/></td>
      <td><s:property value="#stat.count"/></td>
      <td><s:property value="#stat.even"/></td>
      <td><s:property value="#stat.odd"/></td>
      <td><s:property value="#stat.first"/></td>
      <td><s:property value="#stat.last"/></td>
      <td><s:property value="#stat.modulus(2)"/></td>
      <td><s:property value="#stat.modulus(4)"/></td>
      <td><s:property value="#stat.count % 4"/></td>
    </tr>
  </s:iterator>
</table>
```

The `index` and `count` properties are similar. However, `index` is zero based and `count` is one based. The `even`, `odd`, `first`, and `last` properties are exactly what we'd expect, booleans that are true if their respective conditions are true. The `modulus` method is a convenience method that can be used instead of an equivalent OGNL expression, which is also shown above.

> The `even` and `odd` properties, as well as the `modulus` method, are based on the `count` attribute and not on the `index` attribute. The iterator status provides a `modulus` method. Using it creates code that's just as long as using the "%" operator. It's not clear to me that the `modulus` method is particularly convenient, since it's just as many characters, and arguably less clear, than using "%".

CSS detour: Alternating table row background color

One common use of these properties is for alternating row coloring in a table. This can be done in several ways. One of the ways could be to name our style classes evenTrue and evenFalse, and then using the even property (of course, the same applies for the odd property). The other option is to create row0 and row1 classes (or however many class names we need for our chosen modulus), and using either the modulus attribute or an expression using the modulus operator "%".

It's also possible, and probably more readable to create variables using <s:set> and using them in our CSS class names, especially if we're using only even/odd classes. The following example shows several of these possibilities. I wouldn't recommend using all of them at once. However, by picking and choosing among techniques, it's possible to come up with some relatively cleaner ways of styling simple HTML tables. (CSS tricks and tips are discussed in more detail in a later chapter, but this is an easy one.)

Note again that the dirty EL trick can be used here too, rather than embedding large quantities of <s:property> tags. It makes a substantially cleaner, easier-to-read JSP page.

Using the combination of appropriate class names, the status iterator variable, and the dirty EL trick, we've created a simple, but effective table layout. We'll assume that we have a requirement that the first and last rows have their own styles. We alternate between two styles for each row, except that the last column alternates between four styles. (Contrived scenarios are beautiful for highlighting functionalities, aren't they?) Here is the example:

```
<%@ taglib prefix="s" uri="/struts-tags" %>
...
<style>
  table { border-collapse: collapse; }
  td { padding: 0.24em; }
  .firsttrue { border-top: 2px solid black; }
  .lasttrue { border-bottom: 2px solid black; }
  .firstfalse { }
  .lastfalse { }
  .row0 { background: #fff; }
  .row1 { background: #aaa; }
  .row2 { background: #555; color: white; }
  .row3 { background: #000; color: white; }
</style>
...
<table>
  <s:iterator value="list1" status="stat">
    <tr class="row${stat.count % 2}
               first${stat.first} last${stat.last}">
```

```
            <td>${stat.count}</td>
            <td><s:property/></td>
            <td class="row${stat.count % 4}">${stat.count % 4}</td>
        </tr>
    </s:iterator>
</table>
```

Rather than explicitly check for the first and last rows, we give each row several class names—one created from the current iteration count modulus two (giving us our alternating rows), and two created by appending the `first` and `last` status attributes of the iterator's status. Note that when we access the `stat` variable using JSP EL's `${}` notation, we do not use a # character. Using it may result in an error in many recent JSP containers.

In our CSS, we create classes that reflect a "true" status for the first and last rows, and apply it to our table row elements. Hence, each row will always define either a `firsttrue` or `firstfalse` class. However, only `firsttrue` is defined as a class (the same thing for `last`). This will produce output similar to the following:

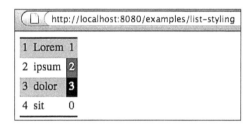

We could, of course, use a combination of `<s:if>` and `<s:set>` tags, similar to the following, to achieve the same effects. However, it's nearly not so contrived. Kidding aside, code similar to the previous code snippet is a double-edged sword. It's concise and interesting, but not always easy to maintain. This is where documentation comes in handy. A simple JSP comment can clear things up. The "maintainable" way looks like this:

```
<s:if test="#stat.first">
    <s:set var="trFl" value="'firsttrue'"/>
</s:if>
<s:elseif test="#stat.last">
    <s:set var="trFl" value="'lasttrue'"/>
</s:elseif>
<s:else>
    <s:set var="trFl" value="''"/>
</s:else>
```

Notice that we're using immediate string values as the `value` attribute arguments in the `<s:set>` tags. We'd then use `${trFl}` (for `tr first/last` — naming variables is hard!) as a class for our table row elements.

```
<tr class="row${stat.count % 2} ${trFl}">
```

Is the trade-off worth it? The HTML sent to the browser will be shorter, but we've added nine lines to the JSP code that produces it. Decisions like this are what make programming so entertaining.

Personally, I like playing little tricks and reducing code size, as long as it remains maintainable. This has led co-workers to claim that I won't be happy until the entire application is a single line. I'm okay with that accusation, as it meshes nicely with my Lisp background! To be clear, I don't advocate using tricks just for the sake of using them. Also, obfuscating code just to appear "clever" is not a good idea. But code can be expressed clearly and succinctly, as I believe it should be, even when using advanced techniques.

The <s:generator> tag

We may never need to use the generator tag. However, we'll discuss it briefly. It's used to generate a list, which is pushed on to the value stack (and popped on the closing tag). We give it a string `val` attribute (that is, surrounded by quotes) with each element separated by the character specified in the `separator` attribute. (You may wonder why it is "val" and not "value". That's the beauty of open source volunteer projects) The resulting list can be iterated using the iterator tag.

```
<s:generator val="'1, 2, 3, 4'" separator=",">
  <ul>
    <s:iterator>
      <li><s:property/></li>
    </s:iterator>
  </ul>
</s:generator>
```

We can also supply a `var` attribute (`id` in Struts 2.0), which names the generated collection, allowing an iterator tag to reference it by name. This allows us to use the generator without nesting our iterator inside the generator tag.

```
<s:generator val="'1, 2, 3, 4'" separator="," var="to4list"/>
...
<ul>
  <s:iterator value="to4list">
    <li><s:property/></li>
  </s:iterator>
</ul>
```

There are two potential gotchas though.

It's not a list, it's an iterator!

A list created by the generator tag isn't really a list—it's an iterator. Once the iterator has been iterated over, we can't iterate over it again. We must re-generate the iterator with another generator tag.

```
<s:generator val="'1, 2, 3, 4'" separator="," var="to4list"/>
<s:iterator value="to4list"><s:property/></s:iterator>
<s:iterator value="to4list"><s:property/></s:iterator>
```

Only the first `<s:iterator>` tag will do what we want. The second will produce no output because the `to4list` iterator has nothing left to iterate.

Silent death

Here's a subtle and completely silent gotcha! Take a look at the following code:

```
<s:generator val="'1, 2, 3, 4" separator=",">
  <ul>
    <s:iterator>
      <li><s:property/></li>
    </s:iterator>
  </ul>
</s:generator>
```

It might be fairly obvious in isolation. However, in the thick of a JSP, it might slip by unnoticed, breaking your render. If you didn't see it, check in the `val` attribute and look for a missing single quote. This will fail silently. You've been warned.

Another potential stumper (Struts 2.0 only)

As mentioned, the `id` attribute is deprecated (use the `var` attribute in Struts 2.1). However, in Struts 2.0, accessing the named generator is a bit counter intuitive. We cannot simply use the `#theId` notation. You must use the `#attr.theId` notation, as shown here:

```
<s:generator val="%{'1, 2, 3, 4'}" separator="," id="myList">
  <ul>
    <s:iterator value="#attr.myList">
      <li><s:property/></li>
    </s:iterator>
  </ul>
</s:generator>
```

In Struts 2.1.1+, we can simply refer to it as **#myList** (my lasting contribution to the Struts 2 project is in a tag that most people will never use... the generator's value was placed into page scope in Struts 2.0) .

What is <s:generator> for?

At first, it's not clear why we'd want to use a generator tag, as we can do the previous task by creating an immediate list to use in an iterator tag as we do next:

```
<ul>
  <s:iterator value="{1, 2, 3, 4}">
    <li><s:property/></li>
  </s:iterator>
</ul>
```

Note the subtle difference between how the list is being created—the value in the iterator tag is a list, an immediate OGNL list. The generator tag creates a list by parsing a string. Therefore, if we received a comma-separated string from an action, we could easily process each item by using the generator tag. This is a big benefit when we don't have the ability to modify the action code ourselves, as the list parsing functionality arguably belongs in the action itself.

The generator tag has two other attributes—count and converter. These attributes further control the iterator created by the tag. The count attribute puts an upper bound on the number of elements included in the iterator. For example, if a list could contain 100 items, setting the count to 10 would mean only the first 10 items in the list would be included in the iterator.

The converter attribute expects an implementation of IteratorGenerator. Converter, which defines a single method, Object convert(String). This method defines how to convert each element of the generated iterator.

As an example, we'll consider a use case where we need a list of sequential dates, seven days starting today. Our action defines a getter, returning a Converter implementation, that just adds the integer value of each item in the generator to the current date (imports elided):

```
package com.packt.s2wad.ch05.actions.examples;
public class GeneratorConverterAction {
    public IteratorGenerator.Converter getCalConverter()
            extends ActionSupport {
        return new IteratorGenerator.Converter() {
            private Calendar cal = Calendar.getInstance();
            private Date now = new Date();
            public Object convert(String sOffset) {
```

```
            int offset = Integer.parseInt(sOffset);
            cal.setTime(now);
            cal.add(Calendar.DAY_OF_MONTH, offset);
            return cal.getTime();
        }
    };
  }
}
```

The JSP uses the generator tag and specifies a converter. We output the converted generator value with an `<s:date>` tag. We'll cover this in a moment. For now, just assume it does precisely what it looks like it does.

```
<s:generator val="%{'0,1,2'}"
             var="dates" separator=","
             converter="calConverter"/>
<s:iterator var="aData" value="#dates">
  <s:date name="#aData" format="yyyy-MM-dd"/> 
</s:iterator>
```

It outputs something similar to the following (depending on the date, of course):

```
2009-02-18  2009-02-19  2009-02-20
```

Our action creates a `Calendar` instance, and uses it in the `Converter` implementation as the "base date" to add our offset to (mandatory error handling removed for clarity). Only the `Converter` implementation is interesting.

The <s:append> tag

The append tag takes a number of collections using `<s:param>` tags and creates one big collection. We must supply a `var` attribute (id in Struts 2.0) with the append tag. (Oddly, in Struts 2.0, we do not need to use the `#attr.theId` as described in the generator tag. We can simply use `#theId` as shown here.)

The `param` tags provide unnamed parameters, with each value being a list. The resulting iterator does exactly what we'd expect. It iterates over each collection in order. Here, we'll provide immediate lists in the `param` tags. We can also use collection properties from an action, values from a generator tag, and so on.

```
<s:append var="append1">
  <s:param value="{1, 2, 3}"/>
  <s:param value="{'a', 'b', 'c'}"/>
</s:append>
```

```
<s:iterator value="append1">
  <s:property/> 
</s:iterator>
```

This will produce the following:

```
1 2 3 a b c
```

The <s:merge> tag

The merge tag is similar to the append tag. However, it will "weave" the given collections together, returning the first item of each collection first, followed by the second item in each collection, and so on. If the lists are of different lengths, the woven collection will weave up to the shorter list's length and continue by completing the iterations using only the longer-length lists. It won't stop after the shortest list has been exhausted.

```
<s:merge var="merge1">
  <s:param value="{0, 1, 2}"/>
  <s:param value="{'a', 'b', 'c', 'd', 'e', 'f'}"/>
</s:merge>
<s:iterator value="merge1">
  <s:property/> 
</s:iterator>
```

This snippet will produce the following:

```
1 a 2 b 3 c d e f
```

Notice that all items in both lists are iterated over, and that the values of the two lists are woven together until the short list runs out of elements, at which point the iteration continues with items from the longer list. The same logic applies regardless of how many lists there are.

The <s:subset> tag

The subset tag is used to filter a collection, resulting in an iterator we can use in an iterator tag. In its simplest form, you can filter based on the start index of the collection and/or limit the number of items from the collection that will be iterated over.

As with the other collection tags, we can define the name of the iterator for later use using the `var` attribute (`id` in Struts 2.0). The collection being filtered is specified using the `source` attribute (neither `val` nor `value`... I know...)

The following code shows examples of the `start` and `count` attributes on immediate lists, with the produced output shown immediately below the JSP that produces it.

```
<s:subset source="{1, 2, 3, 4, 5, 6, 7, 8}" start="3">
  <s:iterator> <s:property/> </s:iterator>
</s:subset>
```

This will produce the following:

```
4 5 6 7 8
```

```
<s:subset source="{1, 2, 3, 4, 5, 6, 7, 8}" count="3">
  <s:iterator> <s:property/> </s:iterator>
</s:subset>
```

This will produce the following:

```
1 2 3
```

```
<s:subset source="{1, 2, 3, 4, 5, 6, 7, 8}"
          start="3" count="3">
  <s:iterator> <s:property/> </s:iterator>
</s:subset>
```

This will produce the following:

```
4 5 6
```

As with the earlier collections tags, it will also accept a collection on the top of the stack. We could write the last example using a generator tag.

```
<s:generator separator="," val="%{'1, 2, 3, 4, 5, 6, 7, 8'}">
  <s:subset start="3" count="3">
    <s:iterator>
      <s:property/>
    </s:iterator>
  </s:subset>
</s:generator>
```

This will produce the following:

```
4 5 6
```

Can you spot the difference? Just in case the difference isn't obvious, do something like displaying the class name of each item of the iteration. I'd leave how to do that as an exercise for the reader, but it's so handy I won't make you work for it: `<s:property value="class.name"/>`. But you already knew that!

Arbitrary filtering with the <s:subset> tag

For arbitrary filtering, we supply a `decider` attribute, which specifies an implementation of the `SubsetIteratorFilter.Decider` interface. `Decider` defines a single method, `boolean decide(Object)`, which determines if an object in the collection should be included in the subset. For example, to filter a small list of letters for vowels, we can create a `Decider` implementation that will allow only vowels to be included in our subset. Again, we create a getter in our action that returns the anonymous implementation, named in tribute to our great once-leader (imports elided... there's another political joke here):

```
package com.packt.s2wad.ch05.actions.examples;
public class SubsetFilterAction extends ActionSupport {
    public SubsetIteratorFilter.Decider getTheDeciderer() {
        return new SubsetIteratorFilter.Decider() {
            public boolean decide(Object o) throws Exception {
                String s = (String) o;
                return s.matches("[aeiou]");
            }
        };
    }
}
```

On the JSP side, we generate a list of several letters and supply the subset tag with our `Decider` implementation:

```
<s:generator separator="," val="%{'a, b, c, d, e, f'}">
  <s:subset decider="theDeciderer">
    <s:iterator> <s:property/> </s:iterator>
  </s:subset>
</s:generator>
```

This will produce the following:

```
a e
```

The `Decider` implementation, of course, can be arbitrarily complex and operate on any type of object, giving us the ability to easily filter lists in our view layer. Should we? Well, that's a debate for another book. Some folks might argue that this type of work should be done at a higher level, say in our action or service object.

Dirty OGNL secrets

We can play some really interesting games with OGNL. Again, whether these games should be played in our JSP pages is debatable, but it's all very fun. What we just did by creating a new class and using one of the lonelier Struts 2 tags, can be done in a single OGNL construct using only the iterator tag. OGNL has some functionality that will be familiar to users of Lisp and Smalltalk — the ability to collect items from a list that match a specified criterion.

Yes, that is what we did in the previous example. However, we can do it entirely in OGNL, in a single line (even if it causes our friends to stop speaking to us):

```
<s:generator separator="," val="%{'a, b, c, d, e, f'}"
             var="letters"/>
<s:iterator value='%{#letters.{?#this.matches("[aeiou]")}}'>
  <s:property/>
</s:iterator>
```

I am going to let this example stand on its own, mentioning only that `#this` refers to each element contained in the list. This functionality is covered in the OGNL documentation.

We can also project across collections, that is, gather only specified properties from each object in the collection. For example:

```
<s:iterator value="{1,'a',4.5}.{class.name}">
    <s:property/> 
  </s:iterator>
```

This produces:

```
java.lang.Integer  java.lang.Character  java.lang.Double
```

There are a lot of dirty OGNL secrets. Use them at your own risk. However, remember that your peers will be forced to give you cool points—right after beating you about the head and shoulders...

 Remember: Work is in progress on the road to Struts 2.1 to make the EL pluggable. So, you may or may not be able to make use of the OGNL functionality that will be presented here. However, it will probably always remain as one of the EL options if your project chooses to use it.

The <s:sort> tag

The last collection tag we'll cover is the sort tag, which takes a `source` attribute for the collection (like the subset tag). It also takes a `comparator` attribute, which specifies a `java.util.Comparator` implementation exposed by the action. The sorted collection may be exposed (a sordid collection?!) with the `var` attribute (`id` in Struts 2.0) if we'd rather refer to it later.

We'll cheat a little bit by using `java.lang.String`'s `CASE_INSENSITIVE_ORDER` static `Comparator` because writing our own is uninteresting. (You knew about that, right? Running through the API documentation is always a good idea!) We'll use OGNL's ability to reference static members and use it directly.

```
<s:generator separator="," val="%{'f, d, C, a, E, B'}">
  <s:sort
      comparator="@java.lang.String@CASE_INSENSITIVE_ORDER">
    <s:iterator>
      <s:property/>
    </s:iterator>
  </s:sort>
</s:generator>
```

This will produce the following:

```
a B C d E f
```

Are the collection tags useful?

Iterator is unquestionably useful, especially for those of us who prefer not to mix-and-match JSTL and Struts 2 tags whenever possible. The other tags are debatable, it's largely a matter of preference. They're certainly handy in small doses. They can be used to speed up page development, occasionally reduce the amount of Java code, and in cases where a decider or comparator could be returned based on action logic.

Referencing other pages and actions

Struts 2 includes a three-page URL-related function used to include the output of a servlet, JSP, or action, or create a URL for later use.

The <s:include> tag

The Struts 2 `<s:include>` tag is equivalent to JSTL's `<jsp:include>` tag. It takes a `value` attribute to specify the JSP (or servlet; it's just a `RequestDispatcher.include` under the covers) and an `id` attribute, which doesn't appear to do anything.

We can specify an arbitrary number of request parameters by nesting the `<s:param>` tags. Of course, when we dispatch to a JSP or servlet, we can't access those parameters with Struts 2 tags because no value stack will be created (this only happens for action-based URLs). However, we can access the parameters using the `HttpServletRequest` object—for example, by using JSP EL and the `params` object.

The <s:action> tag

The `<s:action>` tag allows the inclusion of action execution. It's like using a `<jsp:include>`, but with an action instead of a servlet.

The most important attributes are `name`— naming the action to include, and `namespace`—the namespace of the action, which defaults to the current namespace.

```
<s:action name="includedAction"/>
```

If we try using this tag as shown above, we hit a snag as nothing shows up in our browser where the action's output should be. To get the rendered output of the action referenced by the `<s:action>` tag, we must set the `executeResult` attribute to `true`. We then see the normal output of the action rendered in the page containing the `<s:action>` tag.

```
<s:action name="includedAction" executeResult="true"/>
```

That naturally leads us to wonder why we'd want to use the `<s:action>` tag without the `executeResult` attribute. The answer to that lies in the `var` attribute (`id` in Struts 2.0). The `var` attribute will put a named instance of the action class itself in the stack context (for this use we *must* use the "#" character or it won't work!) allowing us to access the action's properties.

```
<s:action name="someOtherAction" var="includedAction"/>
<s:property value="#includedAction.propertyOfAction"/>
```

Some people use this technique as a way to initialize data and use it in a page. In some ways, it's the same as action chaining with finer-grained control. We only need to execute the actions to initialize their properties needed on a specific page. While a valid technique, such initialization probably belongs in a service object used by any action that needs that data. (As we'll see later, we can get that type of functionality very easily by using Spring.)

Another interesting `<s:action>` attribute is `ignoreContextParams`, which determines whether or not the context parameters (such as action properties, and so on) from the current request are included in the request to the action referenced by the `<s:action>` tag.

There is a somewhat ugly gotcha regarding the `ignoreContextParams` attribute. Under some circumstances, it may look as though it's being completely ignored. This has to do with the interceptor configuration. By default, it includes the "chain" interceptor, which copies the current action's context (including properties) to the included action, even if `ignoreContextParams` is set to true. This is only an issue if the included action has properties with the same name as the action you're using the `<s:action>` tag from, and we don't want the properties copied. There are a few ways around this, which we'll discuss in Chapter 8. For now, just be aware that our interceptor configuration can produce subtle, difficult-to-diagnose behavior under certain circumstances.

As with the `<s:include>` tag, we can use the `<s:param>` tag to supply an arbitrary number of parameters to the included action. Unlike `<s:include>`, we can make better use of those parameters without resorting to scriptlets. We can pass in typed parameters as well. For example, if the action being included has a `List<String>` property named `list1`, the code snippet shown next will pass a `List` to the action. The `List` can be used by the action itself or in its view.

```
<s:action name="includedAction" executeResult="true">
  <s:param name="foo">I'm a simple String.</s:param>
  <s:param name="list1" value="{'11','22','33','44'}"/>
</s:action>
```

You might notice that I didn't use a simple `value="{1,2,3,4}"` in the previous code snippet: that would actually create a list of integers. I also didn't use `value="{'1', '2', '3', '4'}"`, as that would create an array of characters. Putting multiple characters in single quotes forces OGNL to create a `String` instead of a `Character`. The right way to define this immediate `List<String>` is to use `value='{"1", "2", "3", "4"}'`. OGNL can sneak up on us sometimes.

Finally, `<s:action>`'s `flush` attribute works similar to `<jsp:include>`'s `flush`.

Note that the action tag can introduce subtle issues under certain circumstances. Details have been discussed on the Struts user mailing list.

The <s:url> tag

The `<s:url>` tag is used to create (wait for it...) URLs that can be used by standard HTML anchor tags or, as we'll see when we discuss Struts 2's Ajax capabilities, the Struts 2 Ajax tags.

There are two ways to create a URL with the `url` tag—using the `value` attribute for non-action URLs, and the `action` and `namespace` attributes when referring to an action.

We use the `value` attribute when we refer to nonaction resources inside our webapp. This can be used if the application isn't based entirely on Struts 2. For example, if we have servlets or raw JSP pages as well as configured actions, used for image tags, CSS files, and so on.

It can also be used to create external references. Doing so requires a scheme included in the `value` attribute, although it doesn't need to be a valid scheme. Any value, as long as there's a ":" after the first character, will create a non-context-relative URL.

As with other tags we've seen, we can store the generated URL in the stack context by using the `var` attribute (`id` in Struts 2.0), and refer to it later with an `<s:property>` tag using the # OGNL stack context reference character.

```
<a href="<s:url value='localJsp.jsp'/>">Local Resource</a>
<s:url value="http://struts.apache.org" var="strutsUrl"/>
<a href="<s:property value="#strutsUrl"/>">Struts Home</a>
<!-- Using JSP EL in a JSP 2.0 container -->
<a href="${strutsUrl}">Struts Home</a>
```

Creating a URL to a configured action uses the `action` attribute, using the name (alias) of the action as the value of the attribute. Note that using an invalid action name will not result in an error on the page. However, if the `struts.devMode` constant is set to `true`, we'll see an error in the log file.

```
<s:url action="anAction" var="localAction"/>
<a href="${localAction}">Action in current namespace</a>
```

Use the `namespace` attribute to refer to an action in a different namespace.

```
<s:url action="anAction" namespace="differetNamespace"
       id="nsAction"/>
<a href="${nsAction}">differentNamespace</a>
```

The `method` attribute allows us to specify a specific method in the action class to be run. By default, the `execute()` method of an action is run. As we've already seen, configuring an action and including a `method` attribute in a Struts 2 configuration file is another way to specify which action method is run by default.

```
<s:url action="anAction" method="anActionMethod"/>
<!-- Produces .../anAction!anActionMethod.action -->
```

Recall that the exclamation point is associated with dynamic method invocation, which lets us specify an action's method in the URL. This feature is enabled by default, but might be considered a security risk. We can disable dynamic method invocation by setting the `struts.enable.DynamicMethodInvocation` constant in our Struts 2 configuration file or in our `web.xml`.

I occasionally find using dynamic method invocation to be helpful. Others either perceive it as a security risk or think of it as tying the JSP too closely to the Java implementation. It depends on the application and how its security is configured. This is another one of those features that may not work for every project or organization. Turning it off is quick and easy. The same functionality (specifying a particular method to run on an action class) can be achieved by configuring another action in the Struts 2 configuration file without any risk, or by using an `@Action` annotation in a Convention-based action.

The configuration and JSP snippets shown next will execute the action method specified, irrespective of whether or not the dynamic method invocation has been enabled.

```
<!-- struts.xml snippet -->
<action name="actionRunningMethod" class="anActionClass"
        method="anActionMethod">
...
<!-- JSP snippet -->
<s:url action="actionRunningMethod"/>
```

Of course, we could create a link to an action using the `value` attribute by simply putting in the URL (along with the action suffix—by default ".action") or by using JSTL's `<c:url>` tag. While a minor point, doing so makes it more difficult to change action extensions, and is indicative of the fact that we can't use a few of `<s:url>`'s other attributes.

Adding an `anchor` attribute will allow us to specify a named location on the destination page.

```
<s:url action="anAction" anchor="top">
<!-- Appends "#top" to the URL created by the tag. -->
```

As with the `<s:action>` tag, we can use the `<s:param>` tag to add request parameters to the generated URL. The `encode` attribute of `<s:url>` controls whether or not the parameter values are URL-encoded. The `escapeAmp` attribute of `<s:url>` controls whether or not any ampersands between parameters are encoded, which is required for XHTML.

The `includeParams` attribute controls whether or not request parameters from the current request will be included in the generated URL. It currently defaults to `get`. Our next example assumes we've visited a page with the URL `/recipe/show.action?id=5` (we're assuming we're already in the `/recipe` namespace). A value of `all` will include all parameters (like a form POST) and is rarely what we'll want.

```
<s:url action="edit" includeParams="get"/>
<!-- Produces /recipe/edit.action?id=5 -->
<s:url action="edit" includeParams="none"/>
<!-- Produces /recipe/edit.action -->
```

We can define an application-wide setting for `includeParams` in our Struts 2 configuration file. The default is `get`, which is probably not what we want. In general, it's easiest to set the default to `none`, and on occasions, we need included parameters to set the option in the `<s:url>` tag, usually set to `get`.

```
<struts>
  <constant name="struts.url.includeParams" value="none"/>
  . . .
```

The last three attributes are `forceAddSchemeHostAndPort`, `scheme`, and `includeContext`, each of which controls what we'd expect. Setting a value in the `scheme` attribute will cause the generated URL to use whatever scheme is specified. Normally, we won't need to set this.

The `forceAddSchemeHostAndPort`, when set to `true`, will create a complete URL including the scheme, host, and port. Again, it's rare we'd use this.

Lastly, `includeContext` (set either to `true` or `false`) determines if the web application context will be included in the generated URL. This defaults to `true`, which is what we want.

Summary

In this chapter, we cover Struts 2's generic (read: non-user-interface) tags, including the most useful ones, such as `iterator`, `if-elseif-else`, and `url`. The chapter also covers several tags which we're not likely to use, such as generator and merge. (But it's nice to know they're there and you never know, they might be the exact answers we need some day!)

The chapter explores the power of OGNL—an unusually expressive language (when in the right hands) for those brave enough to use all of its capabilities. We also cover the value stack—both a stack and a context, which can throw people off.

In the next chapter, we'll take a look at the Struts 2 form tags. We'll also take a quick look at file uploading and how to prevent double-submits (assuming our business model doesn't depend on charging people twice for every purchase).

References

A reader can refer to the following:

- Struts 2 Generic (non-UI) Tags:

  `http://struts.apache.org/2.x/docs/generic-tag-reference.html`

- Struts 2 OGNL and OGNL Basics:

  `http://struts.apache.org/2.x/docs/ognl.html`

  `http://struts.apache.org/2.x/docs/ognl-basics.html`

- Opensymphony OGNL URL:

  `http://www.opensymphony.com/ognl/`

6
Form Tags

The previous chapter explored the Struts 2 generic tags and ventured a bit further into the wild lands of OGNL. In this chapter, we'll take a look at the Struts 2 form tags that handle the usual HTML form input elements. We will also take a look at some combination tags that group two or more form controls together, creating more complex controls.

As we look at the form tags, we'll get our first introduction to Struts 2 themes and templates, which control the HTML emitted by the UI tags. We'll also take a look at how to upload files, and one way to help prevent double submits using Struts 2.

Form tag basics

We saw earlier that we could do all our form tags and error reporting manually using JSP, some conditionals, and some OGNL. A chapter later, we saw that there was an easier way to do it, and we cursed the author.

We'll explore the topics of themes and templates later in the book. For now, all we really need to know is that entire applications, single forms, or individual form elements have a theme. Themes determine how the Struts 2 form tags are rendered on our page.

Struts 2 form tags are rendered by FreeMarker templates (Struts 2.1.6 also saw the addition of a few pure Java tags). The templates handle the basic form element HTML. Most of them also include some layout, field error checks, and so on.

Different themes use different templates. The nutshell version of theme functionality is that the **simple** theme does nothing for us other than render HTML input elements. The "**xhtml**" theme uses a table layout and includes field error messages (as do the rest), whereas the **css_xhtml** puts everything inside `<div>` tags and relies on CSS for layout. Finally, the **ajax** theme embeds Ajax functionality, but otherwise it is the "xhtml" theme.

A theme can be set at the application level for use in every form element by setting a configuration constant—`struts.ui.theme`. Here, we'll set the default theme to `"xhtml"` (already the default) in a Struts 2 configuration file (as usual, we can also use a filter initialization parameter, or the `struts.properties` file):

```
<struts>
  <constant name="struts.ui.theme" value="xhtml"/>
```

We can set the theme in several other ways, each overriding a less-specific setting. The theme of a tag is determined by:

1. Checking the `theme` attribute of the Struts 2 form input element itself.
2. Checking the `theme` attribute of the Struts 2 form tag that surrounds it.
3. Checking a scoped `theme` attribute (as usual, following the page-request-session-application hierarchy).
4. Finally, checking the configuration file value.

The rest of this chapter assumes the "xhtml" theme (handy for prototyping), but will occasionally set the theme to `simple` when we don't want any of the table markup.

The "xhtml" theme in a nutshell

The "xhtml" theme, as mentioned, uses a table layout. The `<s:form>` tag emits an HTML `<form>` tag and a `<table>` tag inside it. Each "xhtml" theme form element tag renders a two-column table row—the first column holding the label and the second column holding the input element.

If a form is validated and has field errors, the input element templates will also render individual field errors above the input element and change the CSS class of the label to indicate the error.

This is handy most of the time, but a bit irritating occasionally (we'll learn how to fix the irritation in Chapter 12). However, during these irritating times, however, we can always look back at the amount of work we did in Chapter 3 to duplicate a small portion of the "xhtml" theme. We can also recognize that for simple use cases, it's an overall win. And when it isn't a win, we can either revert to doing it by hand, using a different theme, modifying an existing theme, or creating our own.

The <s:head> tag

The `<s:head>` tag is a bit different in that it's not actually a form tag. However, it does include both Struts 2 JavaScript utilities, and a theme-specific style sheet. The `<s:head>` tag should be in the `<head>` section of our pages. It loads the default CSS styles and the Struts 2 javascript from the Struts 2 static directory.

Any stylesheet we load after the `<s:head>` tag will take precedence. Hence, we can still use our own styles for form elements, labels, errors messages, and so on.

The <s:form> tag

The `<s:form>` tag, of course, renders an HTML `<form>` element. In the "xhtml" theme, it also renders a `<table>` tag in preparation for the form element tags to come:

```
<s:form action="anAction">
</s:form>
<!-- Renders as: -->
<form id="anAction" name="anAction"
      action="path/to/action" method="post">
  <table class="wwFormTable">
  </table>
</form>
```

We'll look at styling in Chapter 12, but it's convenient to see which classes are used in certain circumstances. The "xhtml" theme renders the form table with the wwFormTable class.

The `<s:form>` tag takes a slew of parameters, all of which are detailed in the official Struts 2 documentation. We need only a few to get basic functionality.

The action attribute defines which Struts 2 action the form will be submitted to. We don't put the .action extension (or whatever the action extension is) on the attribute value. Leaving out an action attribute indicates that we're submitting the action that rendered the `<s:form>` tag to the current action (postback).

If the action is in a different namespace, we use the namespace attribute, as with the `<s:url>` tag.

The method attribute does the same as in an HTML `<form>` element—setting the form submission type as either GET or POST. It defaults to POST. This attribute does *not* define the action method to be run, it is the form submission type.

The validate attribute determines if some client-side validation will be performed. However, it defaults to false indicating that only server-side validation will be run (when applicable). We'll discuss client-side validation further when we cover the various validation configuration options.

The form's id attribute will default to the value of the action attribute. We can define our own with the id attribute. We can also set our own CSS styles and classes with the cssStyle and cssClass attributes.

Common input element tag attributes

Each input element tag has a slew of possible attributes, but we need only a few for the most basic functionality. The big three are `name`, `value`, and `label`, which can all be set with the `key` attribute. However, we'll go over what they all mean.

Values, labels, and names (and keys)

The `name` attribute determines the name of the submitted value, just like the `name` attribute of an HTML form input element. As we've already seen, if the action we're submitting to contains a property of the same name, the form value will be set on that property (with the help of XWork's type conversion).

```
<!-- Value will be initialized to action's "foo" property
 value (null values will be blank, *not* "null") -->
<s:textfield name="foo" />
```

The `value` attribute, if specified, sets the initial value of the input element. If no `value` is specified, the value will be initialized from the action property in the `name` attribute. The `value` attribute can be an OGNL expression.

```
<!-- Sets text element's value to "hello" -->
<s:textfield name="foo" value="%{'hello'}" />
<!-- Sets text element's value to "10" -->
<s:textfield name="foo" value="%{5 + 5}" />
```

The `%{}` syntax forces Struts 2 to evaluate the expression. The Struts 2 tag documentation lists which attributes are evaluated (in theory), but that may mean by default. The `value` attribute is listed as not being evaluated. However, when wrapped in the OGNL escape sequence `%{}`, the attribute will be evaluated. Some people prefer to use the `%{}` characters around all OGNL expressions to resolve any ambiguity. Suppose that we use the following:

```
value="hello"
```

This would actually put the word `hello` into the text input, without calling `getHello()` in our action. In this particular case, we must use the `%{}` characters to force evaluation:

```
value="%{hello}"
```

In this case, our action's `getHello()` method is called.

The `label` attribute sets the label of the input element. We can set this to a simple string and use our action's `getText()` methods, if we extended `ActionSupport` (remember Chapter 3?). We might set an input element's label as we see here:

```
<s:textfield name="text1" label="%{getText('text1')}" />
```

This uses the same resource lookup logic we've seen previously.

The `key` attribute replaces all three attributes, cleaning up our JSP pages quite a bit. It does the label text lookup and sets the name attribute. For the `key` attribute to work properly, our action must extend `ActionSupport`, as we're relying on its `getText()` methods. The `key` attribute reduces the most common use case to:

```
<s:textfield key="text1" />
```

One possible disadvantage of the `key` attribute is that our label messages must have the exact same name as our field names. Sometimes, we'll see labels named by the field name, and a prefix or suffix, such as `text1.label`.

If our application is not internationalized with messages stored in resource files, this might seem like an extra, unnecessary step. In some cases, particularly in smaller applications, it can be frustrating and is arguably not worth the extra hassle. However, separating text like this can make both development and documentation easier. It may also provide long-term benefits not originally anticipated.

All the rest

Most of the standard HTML input element attributes are supported. As with `<s:form>`, CSS styles and classes are handled with the `cssStyle` and `cssClass` attributes. All the event handler attributes are supported. A complete attribute list for each tag is available on the Struts 2 documentation wiki.

Basic rendering

The next question is: how does the label and input element get rendered in relationship to the table element that was rendered by the `<s:form>` tag. To answer this briefly, the label goes in the first table cell and the input element in the second. Given the Struts 2 form defined like this:

```
<s:form action="anAction">
  <s:textfield key="text1" />
</s:form>
```

We'll get (once it's formatted nicely) something like the following:

```
<form id="anAction" name="anAction" ...>
  <table>
    <tr>
      <td class="tdLabel">
        <label for="anAction_text1" class="label">
          Text1 label from resource file
        </label>
```

```
        </td>
        <td class="tdLabel">
          <input type="text" name="text1" id="anAction_text1"/>
        </td>
      </tr>
    </table>
  </form>
```

We'll see later that the tags also render error messages if there are any errors present.

But I don't want tables

The default table layout may not work for a particular application. In that case, we can use the simple theme (which may actually be too simple, as error messages are not rendered) or the css_xhtml theme. If neither of these work, we must either create a custom theme (which can be as simple as taking an existing theme and tweaking it slightly, or as complicated as completely redoing every template) or avoid the Struts 2 form tags altogether, which may make sense in some circumstances.

Basic form input elements

We'll cover the basic form input elements briefly, leaving a more detailed exploration for the official Struts 2 documentation. However, it's helpful to get a quick flavor of what's available. Most of it is obvious. However, when it's not, we'll go a bit more in depth.

The <s:textfield>, <s:password>, and <s:hidden> tags

We've already seen `<s:textfield>` in the previous examples. It renders a text input element and accepts the `maxlength` and `size` attributes as a normal HTML text input element. It is used to enter strings, numbers, and so on. The `<s:password>` and `<s:hidden>` tags render password and hidden fields, respectively. The `<s:hidden>` tag does not render a label.

```
<s:textfield key="firstname" />
<s:password key="password" />
<s:hidden key="hiddenField" />
```

The <s:textarea> tag

The `<s:textarea>` tag renders an HTML `<textarea>` tag, taking similar attributes like `cols`, `rows`, and so on.

```
<s:textarea key="directions" />
```

The <s:label> tag

The <s:label> tag isn't an input element per se, but can still be useful. It renders a table row, as the other input elements do, and emits two HTML <label> tags. The first label is like the other input elements — the label is either defined explicitly using the label attribute or by lookup using the key attribute.

The second label is the value of the named element. Instead of rendering an input element, the <s:label> tag renders the value in an HTML <label> tag, providing a read-only view of the value. For example, assume that our action property firstname is set to Albert (and we have a message named firstname):

```
<s:label key="firstname" />
```

It will be rendered as:

```
<tr>
  <td>
    <label for="firstname" class="label">
      First Name:
    </label>
  </td>
  <td><label id="firstname">Albert</label></td>
</tr>
```

Styling the label containing the data can be done using the normal cssClass and/or the cssStyle attributes. Note that this only styles the label containing the data (column two) and not the label for the label (column one). We can use CSS tricks and style label elements, but it is just not as flexible as it could be.

The <s:radio> tag

The <s:radio> tag renders a collection of radio buttons. As such, the tag requires a List or Map to be used for the radio button values. There are various ways to control what gets rendered as the radio button value and label. The simplest method is to supply a List of any type. Its toString() representation will be used as both the value and the label. In our action:

```
public List<String> getGenderOptions() {
    return new ArrayList<String>() {{
        add("Male"); add("Female"); add("Other");
    }};
}
```

We then use the radio tag, providing a `list` attribute value. Here, we use the `key` attribute to retrieve both the form element label and define the action property that will be set.

```
<s:radio key="gender" list="genderOptions" />
```

We can also use an immediate list:

```
<s:radio key="gender" list="{'male', 'female', 'other'"/>
```

This renders a row of radio buttons like this:

Gender: ○ male ○ female ○ other

Relying on the `toString()` representation is fine for simple types, such as strings or integers. However, complex values usually require the specification of `listKey` and `listValue` attributes. These attributes specify which bean properties will be used for the radio button value and label. Perhaps confusingly, the `listKey` property is used as the radio button value, while the `listValue` property will be used as the label.

For example, our action property `coolBeans` is a collection of beans, each with `id` and `text` fields. We could specify our `<s:radio>` tag like this:

```
<s:radio key="stringFromRadio" list="coolBeans"
        listKey="id" listValue="text"/>
```

Radio button collections can also be created from maps. The map keys will be used as the radio button values, the map entry's `toString()` being used as the label. We cannot use the `listKey` and `listValue` with maps. If we use them, we'll get a FreeMarker exception.

This is a bit of a hassle, as that means we can only use a map containing simple objects, or we must provide a `toString()` method suitable for use on our view side. In other words, we can't have a more complete `toString()`, which could be used for logging, and so on.

Maps, of course, are generally unordered. If we need the radio buttons to appear in a specific order, we'd need to use a `TreeMap` or another ordered map.

The <s:checkbox> tag

The `<s:checkbox>` tag renders a single `checkbox`. At the time of this writing it only works well with `Boolean` (or boolean) properties. Attempting to preselect a checkbox with, for example, a string value only works if the string is `true` or `false`.

```
<s:checkbox key="checkbox1" />
```

We can set the value that will be sent back to the browser with the `fieldValue` attribute:

```
<s:checkbox key="checkbox1" value="Y" fieldValue="Y"/>
```

Browsers do not send a value for unchecked checkboxes to the server on a form submit. This causes some confusion, particularly among those who choose not to learn how browsers work. In the "xhtml" theme, the `<s:checkbox>` tag also renders a hidden element containing the current value of the checkbox property.

```
<tr>
  <td valign="top" align="right"></td>
  <td valign="top" align="left">
    <input type="checkbox" name="checkbox1" value="true"
           id="forms1_checkbox1"/>
    <input type="hidden" id="__checkbox_forms1_checkbox1"
           name="__checkbox_checkbox1" value="true" />
    <label for="forms1_checkbox1" class="checkboxLabel">
      Checkbox 1
    </label>
  </td>
</tr>
```

Notice the funky name for the hidden input element. The hidden form value is used by the `checkbox` interceptor. The `checkbox` interceptor looks for request parameters with a leading __checkbox_. If anything is found with no corresponding checkbox value, it indicates that the checkbox wasn't checked and the hidden value is set on the checkbox's action property. It's a nice way to work around how browsers handled unchecked checkboxes, neatly encapsulated in a custom tag and an interceptor. Our mainline code doesn't have to worry about any of this anymore (Yes, no more `ActionForm.reset()`)

The <s:checkboxlist> tag

The `<s:checkboxlist>` tag, of course, renders a list of checkboxes. It operates similar to the `<s:radio>` tag, except that the action property being set should be a collection (or array) rather than a single value. Similar to the `<s:radio>` tag, using a map will result in the map keys being the checkbox value and the map entry's `toString()` as the label. You may also use the `listKey` and `listValue` attributes, as with the radio tag.

```
<s:checkboxlist key="cblist" list="listOfCbs"/>
```

At the time of writing this chapter, the hidden fields rendered by the `<s:checkbox>` tag are not rendered by `<s:checkboxlist>`. For example, if we needed to do something with the collection of options that were unselected, we'd need to do that on our own.

Moreover, as of this writing, `<s:checkboxlist>` ignores the `cssClass` and `cssStyle` attributes, making styling it a bit more problematic than the other UI tags.

Using the <s:checkboxlist> tag to implement a user story

Let's return to our recipe application for a moment, create a user story, and prototype an implementation. This user story, like all user stories, is short and sweet:

- Users can check off any number of recipe types (like "appetizer", "dessert", and so on).

First, we'll create a `RecipeType` class, which seems to consist only of an integer ID and a string name. Mercifully, we won't list the code here (it's as we'd expect).

We'll also create a `RecipeTypeService` interface and a fake implementation, as we did with the recipes. We give the interface a `getAll()` method, returning a list of `RecipeType`s. The fake implementation just returns a hard-coded list.

For now, our recipe class will get a `List<String>` `recipeTypes` to hold its collection of recipe type names, and our `FakeRecipeService` is modified to add some recipe types to each of our test recipes.

We'll also take this opportunity to modify our new recipe form to use Struts 2 tags, significantly cleaning it up and again making us crabby as we didn't do it that way in the first place. As a brutal reminder, here's what the JSP looked like for just the recipe name:

```
<tr>
  <th>Name</th>
  <td>
    <s:if test="getFieldErrors().get('recipe.name') != null">
      <div class="error">
        <s:property
            value="getFieldErrors().get('recipe.name')[0]" />
      </div>
    </s:if>
    <input name="recipe.name" type="text" size="20"
          value="<s:property value="recipe.name"/>" />
  </td>
</tr>
```

Converting the form to use Struts 2 form tags, putting our labels in a resource file, and adding the new recipe type field, reduces our form JSP to this:

```
<s:form action="newRecipe">
  <s:textfield key="recipe.name" />
  <s:textfield key="recipe.description" />
  <s:checkboxlist key="recipe.recipeTypes"
                  list="recipeTypeOptions"
                  listKey="name" listValue="name" />
  <s:textarea key="recipe.ingredients" rows="5" cols="40" />
  <s:textarea key="recipe.directions" rows="5" cols="40" />
  <s:submit />
</s:form>
```

It's marginally cleaner (just like I have a marginal penchant for understatement).

In the above JSP fragment, we see that we're providing the list of recipe type options using an action property named `recipeTypeOptions`. Here's the rub: to get to our form we're requesting `/recipes/new-recipe`, and relying on Convention Plug-in to create the backing action for us. We need a way to get the recipe types into our action for use on the JSP.

There are several ways to accomplish this. We could just put the recipe types into application scope, so they can be used across the application with no database calls. However, this is not contrived enough for a book example. Therefore, we'll look at two additional options.

One solution would be to create a recipe action subclass — `NewRecipeAction`. It would implement the `Preparable` interface and contain a `recipeTypeOptions` property. We'd put code in its `prepare()` method to load up the recipe types.

We'll go a second route. We'll create a single class, NewRecipeAction, which implements Preparable, and uses the @Action annotation to create another URL handler. Both the initial form display (handled by ActionSupport's default execute() method) and the form submit (defined using the @Action annotation) are handled in the same class. The action, minus saving new recipes, and without imports, getters, and setters is shown next:

```
package com.packt.s2wad.ch06.actions.recipes;
public class NewRecipeAction extends ActionSupport
    implements Preparable {

    private Recipe recipe;
    private Collection<RecipeType> recipeTypeOptions;
    private static RecipeTypeService recipeTypeService =
        new FakeRecipeTypeService();

    public void prepare() throws Exception {
        recipeTypeOptions = recipeTypeService.getAll();
    }

    @Action(value = "new-recipe-process")
    public String process() {
        // Handle saved recipe.
        return "thanks";
    }
}
```

We'd also need to make sure that validation errors return us to /recipes/new-recipe. There are several ways we could do this with the Convention Plug-in, including using the @Result annotation to define an "input" result.

The <s:select> tag

The <s:select> tag renders a select box, with the options filled from its list attribute, similar to the radio and checkbox list tags.

As with the other collection-oriented tags, if our collection is contained in a map, the map key will be used as the value, and the map's toString() value will be used as the option text. When using a map, the listKey and listValue attributes are ignored. However, the select tag doesn't give us a FreeMarker exception. The attributes are just ignored, and we get a select box with empty values and text.

The optional headerKey and headerValue attributes specify an <option> rendered first, at the top of the list of options. This can be used to specify instructional text—for example, "-- Select State --" or similar. The headerKey attribute specifies the header option value, while the headerValue specifies the header option's text.

The `emptyOption` attribute specifies whether or not a blank `<option>` will be generated at the top of the `<option>`s, although, if one is specified after the header option. In general, it's likely that only one of the `emptyOption` and `headerKey`/`headerValue` attributes is used—it's not a requirement though (it's fine to use both, at least from a technical standpoint).

The `<s:select>` tag also accepts a `multiple` attribute, which does what we expect. Additionally, if the value passed to the tag (through either the `key` or the `value` attributes) is a collection, the multiple preselects will be rendered appropriately.

The <s:optgroup> tag

The `<s:optgroup>` tag provides an HTML `<optgroup>` element within a `<s:select>` tag. It takes a `label` attribute to specify the label of the option group. It can either be an immediate value or a `getText()` call as we've seen previously.

The `<s:optgroup>` tag is a bit quirky when using a list as an argument to the `list` attribute. If we use a map as the `list` argument, everything is fine (although once again, providing `listKey` and `listValue` attributes produce a FreeMarker exception). When we use a `List`, we must provide both the `listKey` and `listValue` attributes, or we'll receive a FreeMarker template exception.

One potential gotcha with `<s:optgroup>` is that if all our options are contained in optgroups, we must still provide a list to the surrounding select tag because the `list` attribute is required. We can use OGNL's immediate list syntax to provide this:

```
<s:select name="optg1" list="{}">
```

Not a huge deal, but it is something to keep in mind.

The <s:submit> tag

The `<s:submit>` tag renders a "submit" input element. Either the `key` or the `value` attributes may be used to specify the text of the submit button. As usual, the `key` attribute will perform a property lookup, while the `value` attribute will use its value as the button text.

The submit button accepts a `type` attribute, which may be `input`, `button`, or `image`. The `input` type renders a normal submit input element, while the `button` and `image` types render what we'd expect. IE (of course) has certain issues with `button` input elements. However, if we are targeting other browsers, `button` inputs are nice because we can use different values for the button text and value.

The `<s:submit>` tag also accepts the `action` and `method` parameters. These require a bit of hackery on the server side to let us specify the action we'll submit to, and/or the action method to execute, when we click to submit.

If we specify an `action` attribute and examine the emitted HTML (always a good idea), we'll notice that the input element's `name` attribute has changed to `action:` plus whatever we specified as the `action` attribute's value. Similarly, specifying a `method` attribute sets the `name` to `method:` plus the value of the method attribute.

If we specify both, the input element's `name` attribute is set to `action:` plus the `action` and `method` attributes joined by "!" (an exclamation mark). The action-plus-method attributes require that dynamic method invocation is enabled, and may not always leave the expected URL in the browser's address bar, if such things matter to us.

The `<s:reset>` tag

This tag renders a "reset" input element. It accepts the same attributes as the `<s:submit>` tag. However, if neither the `action` nor the `method` attributes are specified as a normal HTML reset, it will just clear the form and will not perform a submit.

Combination form tags

Struts 2 provides a set of "combination" form tags that combine several HTML input elements together and provides some enhanced functionality (think of them as simple HTML/JavaScript widgets).

Getting these tags to do what we want can sometimes be more trouble than it's worth. While these tags do provide some value for simple use cases, we'll often find that using their functionality within an existing design can be problematic. It may be a better idea to either create our own components or graduate to a real client-side framework.

`<s:combobox>` tag

The `<s:combobox>` tag renders both a text input element and a select box.

```
<s:combobox key="combo1" list="hellos" />
```

The text element can be filled directly, or by changing the select box's value. The text value is updated only when the select box value changes, meaning, we'll almost always want to include either the `emptyOption` or the `headerKey/headerValue` attributes.

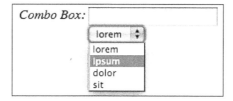

As the text box won't be filled (or cleared) if the select box value is empty, the default behavior of the `<s:combobox>` tag may not always be what we want. Also, selecting an empty option will not clear the text box — the JavaScript checks for nonempty values.

Using a map for the `list` attribute will again act in a way that is a bit counter intuitive. The `listKey` and the `listValue` attributes are ignored completely, although no exception is thrown. However, if the map uses something like an integer as its key, the text box will be filled with an integer rather than text, opposite of what we probably want.

The `<s:updownselect>` tag

The `<s:updownselect>` tag renders a select box along with an optional set of buttons for moving the currently selected list item (or items) up or down in the list, or to select all items in the list. Note that all the items in the list are submitted. This is a control for ordering a list, not for selecting individual list items.

```
<s:updownselect key="updown1" list="goodbyes"/>
```

The creation of the buttons is controlled by three attributes — `allowMoveUp`, `allowMoveDown`, and `allowSelectAll` — each of which controls the button we would expect. The label for each may be specified with the `moveUpLabel`, `moveDownLabel`, and `selectAllLabel` attributes. The defaults are "^", "v", and "*".

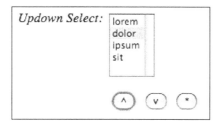

Again, the `listKey` and `listValue` attributes are ignored if the `list` attribute evaluates to a map, but no exception is thrown.

The <s:optiontransferselect> tag

The `<s:optiontransferselect>` tag renders two select boxes along with a set of buttons for moving selected options between the two selects, moving all elements from one to the other, and ordering selections within each. Button rendering and button labels are controlled by a long list of attributes.

The only required attributes are:

- `list`: Specifies the options for the lefthand select box (the "select from" list)
- `doubleList`: For the righthand select box (the "select to" list, allowing for initially selected items)
- `doubleName`: Provides a name for the entire component — the action property that will be set on form submission

The simplest use looks like this, and renders as follows:

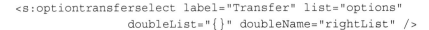

```
<s:optiontransferselect label="Transfer" list="options"
                doubleList="{}" doubleName="rightList" />
```

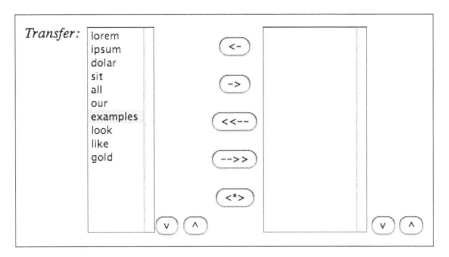

The usual suspects for list-oriented attributes are available for both the rendered select boxes — prefix the attribute name with `double` to apply to the second (righthand) select box. The same applies for event handler attributes. For example, the `onclick` attribute is for the lefthand list, whereas the `doubleOnclick` attribute is for the righthand list.

All entries of the righthand select box are submitted.

Leaving the doubleName element blank, might, at the minimum, cause the tag to be nonfunctional, and might actually lock up some browsers and spike the CPU.

Note that the previous image also used some minimal CSS to get the empty righthand box. If there are no preselected list items, it will collapse on itself, would be narrow, and would look odd.

All of the control buttons are optional and are controlled using tag attributes. For example, the buttons labeled **<<--** and **-->>** (which move the original list of items into the lefthand or righthand boxes) can be removed by setting the allowAddAllToLeft and/or allowAddAllToRight attributes to false.

Perhaps surprisingly, removing the "add all" buttons won't change the height of the combination control. Setting the size attribute doesn't quite work either. We actually need to set both size and doubleSize to reduce the height of the entire control.

There are also attributes for specifying JavaScript to run on the click of any of the buttons, and so on (see the Struts 2 documentation wiki for an exhaustive list).

The <s:doubleselect> tag

Finally, the <s:doubleselect> tag renders two select boxes where selecting an item in the first select box (the lefthand select) determines which values are visible in the second select box (the righthand select). The collection for the second select box is chosen using an OGNL expression. The example provided on the Struts 2 documentation wiki looks something like the following, but has only two elements in the lefthand list. Here, we're using a three-element list, making the doubleList attribute's OGNL a bit awkward.

```
<s:doubleselect
    doubleName="dsel2"
    list="{'one', 'two', 'three'}"
    doubleList="top == 'one' ? {'1a', '1b'}
                        : top == 'two' ? {'2a', '2b'}
                                    : {'3a', '3b'}"/>
```

At the time of writing this book, the JavaScript generated for this tag fails under Convention-based actions because of the hyphen in the action names (this will be addressed later). Note also that we must use CSS if we want equally sized select boxes.

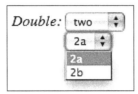

For longer lists (in either select box), the immediate lists aren't really an option. However, we recall that OGNL can call arbitrary methods with parameters. Using this and the idea that the currently-selected item in the first select box is called "top", leads us to the following solution. It's more realistic because in many (most?) applications, both sets of lists will come from the server.

```
<s:doubleselect doubleName="dsel4"
                list="doublelist1"
                doubleList="getDoublemap1(top)"/>
```

Here, we've created a method `getDoublemap1(String s)` in our action that returns the appropriate collection type for our application. We just use the currently selected value of the first list to determine the contents of the second list.

Uploading files

The `<s:file>` tag renders a standard file form element. The file upload itself is handled using the `upload` interceptor, included in the default interceptor stack (we'll cover that part later). For now, it's enough to know that the file upload interceptor puts uploaded files in a temporary directory and (as we'll discover), deletes them after the action executes.

Handling a single file is straightforward. The temporary uploaded file is available to us as a `java.io.File` in the action, as are the original filename and content type. Let's say we want to upload a single file to an action property named (unimaginatively) `file1`:

```
<s:form action="file1" enctype="multipart/form-data">
  <s:file key="file1"/>
  <s:submit/>
</s:form>
```

Our action has a `File` property, as well as string properties, for both the file name and content type (getters and setters not shown).

```
private File file1;
private String file1ContentType;
private String file1Name;
```

The `upload` interceptor sets those action properties for us. The `File`'s filename will be system-generated and will consist of the default temporary directory and a temporary file name. The file name property will be the name of the file on the client's computer and will vary depending on what browser the client is using. Some browsers return the full pathname of the file, while others return only the file name.

We can change the temporary upload directory (it defaults to the container's `javax.servlet.context.tempdir` property) by setting a parameter on the `upload` interceptor (which we'll see in Chapter 8).

Note that we must download the **Commons File Upload** and the **IO libraries** (unless we want to use and configure a different multipart parser) and include them on our web app's classpath. The standard download doesn't (as of this writing) include these dependencies. Even if we're not uploading files, we must have those libraries on the classpath, or our application will fail on startup.

If we're paying attention (and have our logging set up to show INFO-level messages from the Struts 2 hierarchy) after our action processes the file upload form submission, we'll see a message from the `upload` interceptor saying that it has deleted the temporary file.

This means that, by default, we must copy uploaded files to a permanent location if we need them after the action executes. This is made trivial with the Commons IO library `FileUtils.copyFile(File, File)`, or a similar method. Expecting the file to be saved in the temporary upload directory is a common file upload gotcha. If we want to keep uploaded files after action execution, we must copy them to their final destination(s).

Preventing double submits with the <s:token> tag

We all hate being charged twice for a single purchase and double submits are really irritating (and occasionally expensive). Struts 2 provides the `<s:token>` tag (along with two interceptors, `token` and `tokenSession`) to help eliminate double submits. We'll sneak a peek at the `token` interceptor's configuration to see how to use the `<s:token>` tag.

The default interceptor stack doesn't include the `token` interceptor. We must add it to the actions that need it (or our default interceptor stack) in our Struts 2 configuration file, or using the `@InterceptorRefs` and the `@InterceptorRef` annotations of our Convention Plug-in.

```
<action name="dsub"
        class="com.packt.s2wad.ch06.examples.DoubleSub">
  <interceptor-ref name="token"/>
  <interceptor-ref name="defaultStack"/>
  <result name="input">/WEB-INF/content/examples/doublesub.jsp
    </result>
  <result name="invalid.token">
    /WEB-INF/content/examples/doublesub.jsp</result>
  <result type="redirectAction">thanks</result>
</action>
```

We then put the `<s:token/>` tag in our form:

```
<s:form action="dsub">
  <s:token/>
  <s:textfield key="text1"/>
  <s:submit/>
</s:form>
```

The `<s:token/>` tag puts a unique identifier in the form that's checked by the `token` interceptor. The first time we submit the form, we're redirected to the "thanks" page. If we hit the **back** button in our browser (taking us back to the form) and submit again (or if we double-click the submit button), we're taken to the same page—courtesy the result named `invalid.token`, returned by the token interceptor (not our action).

The session token interceptor handles a double submit with a bit more sophistication (we'll cover it briefly in Chapter 8).

Another common technique to avoid double-submits is to disable the submit button or link using JavaScript, eliminating the need for techniques such as the `<s:token/>` and the interceptor combination.

Summary

This chapter covers the Struts 2 user interface tags and how they can be used to significantly reduce the amount of clutter on our JSP pages. The chapter also takes a quick look at file uploading and double submission prevention. We also get a hint of the power and the utility of the themes and templates used by Struts 2 to generate tag HTML.

In the next chapter, we'll take a look at form validation using both XML and annotations, avoiding manual validation, thereby cleaning up our action code further. We'll also see how to create our own validators. We'll also look at the closely related topic of type conversion, that is, taking form values (always strings, remember) and converting them into useful Java objects. We've already seen some examples of this. However, we'll now cover more, including collection support and how to create our own type converters.

References

A reader can refer to the following:

- Struts 2 UI Tags Documentation:

    `http://struts.apache.org/2.x/docs/ui-tag-reference.html`

7
Form Validation and Type Conversion

In the previous chapter, we covered the Struts 2 form tags. We started to see how the framework, including its interceptors, themes, and templates, provide a lot of out of the box power. In this chapter, we'll continue our exploration of form topics, looking at form validation and its spooky cousin, type conversion.

Validation helps to ensure that only appropriate data is passed to our actions. Type conversion converts form data (which is always sent from the browser as a string) to various Java types such as Integers, Dates, or our own custom conversions.

In this chapter, we'll take a more detailed look at:

- How to configure form validation in various ways
- The validations supplied by the framework
- The basics of type conversion
- How to customize type conversion and validations for our specific application needs

Form validation

Validation is a topic that could fill up a book in itself. There's client-side validation, server-side validation through either XML or annotations (or both) available on both actions and models, Ajax validation, custom validation, interceptor stack interaction, issues relating to type conversion, manual validation, and so on.

We'll whittle this down somewhat and provide a basic validation overview, highlighting how using even a small amount of configuration or annotations, we can create complex and robust validations.

Manual validation

As we saw during our discussion regarding ActionSupport's Validateable and ValidationAware interfaces, the validate() method will be run during the default workflow, returning to the "input" result if there are any validation errors.

In Chapter 3, we implemented some simple validation on some recipe fields by manually calling Commons Lang StringUtil.isBlank() on our action properties, adding field errors for each blank field.

We can, of course, run any code in the validate() method. This means that validation can run the entire gamut, from the simple presence of a value to arbitrarily complex business-side validation, using services or in the validation method (not recommended in general).

However, for simple form validation it can be quicker and easier to use either XML-based validation or annotation-based validation.

Configuring XML validation

Struts 1 users will be familiar with XML-based validation. Struts 2 provides similar XML-based validation with an added bonus, which is similar to the message resource file lookup. Validation configuration files are located hierarchically, named after an action, its parent classes, or its interfaces.

To get started, we'll rework our simplistic recipe validation to use XML-based validation. Previously, we were validating manually in our new recipe action's validate() method.

```
public void validate() {
    if (StringUtils.isBlank(recipe.getName())) {
        addFieldError("recipe.name",
                    getText("recipe.name.required"));
    }
    if (StringUtils.isBlank(recipe.getIngredients())) {
        addFieldError("recipe.ingredients",
                    getText("recipe.ingredients.required"));
    }
}
```

We'll delete that method. Our XML-based form validation will mirror our original manual validation criteria — the name and the ingredients must not be blank. We'll create an XML validation file in the same package as our action, and name it `NewRecipeAction-validation.xml`. The naming convention is simple; it's our action's class name with an appended `-validation.xml`. There are a few additional naming conventions detailed on the Struts 2 documentation wiki.

```
<!DOCTYPE validators PUBLIC
  "-//OpenSymphony Group//XWork Validator 1.0.2//EN"
  "http://www.opensymphony.com/xwork/xwork-validator-1.0.2.dtd">
<validators>
  <validator type="requiredstring">
    <param name="fieldName">recipe.name</param>
    <message>Recipe name is required.</message>
  </validator>
  <field name="recipe.ingredients">
    <field-validator type="requiredstring">
      <message>Recipe ingredients are required.</message>
    </field-validator>
  </field>
</validators>
```

The first thing we notice from the above code is that there are two different ways to specify validation for a specific field. We can either use a `<validator>` element and provide the field name in a `<param>` element, or use a `<field>` element.

When we have a single validation for a field, it really doesn't matter which convention we use. As validation becomes more complex, the `<field>` convention becomes more readable because it groups validations more logically.

If we submit our form with one of the required fields missing, we are taken back to the form, our field label is red, and the appropriate messages from our validation file for the missing fields are displayed.

Let's add an additional validation. We'll now require that the recipe name must be at least three characters long. We add the following to our validation XML file:

```
<validators>
  ...
  <validator type="stringlength">
    <param name="fieldName">recipe.name</param>
    <param name="minLength">3</param>
    <message>
      Directions must be at least ${minLength} characters long.
    </message>
  </validator>
```

Perhaps we can now see one reason why the `<field>` element makes more sense for field-specific validations. Using `<validator>` elements and supplying the field name parameters gives a disjointed view of what's actually intended, even though it works. It makes more sense to group validations by field, rather than by validation type:

```
<field name="recipe.name">
  <field-validator type="requiredstring">
    <message>Recipe name is required.</message>
  </field-validator>
  <field-validator type="stringlength">
    <param name="minLength">3</param>
    <message>
      Directions must be at least %{minLength} characters long.
    </message>
  </field-validator>
</field>
```

We're able to include the `minLength` parameter in our error message. Validation messages can include OGNL expressions and refer to anything available on the OGNL value stack. (Yes, that includes action properties—another big win.)

Note again that as of Struts 2.1, we can use the same `%{}` OGNL notation in our property and validation files (as we do here) as we use in our JSP pages. Previously, only the `${}` notation was supported, which led to some confusion.

Customizing validation messages

There are several ways to customize and improve our validation messages, which have so far been specified explicitly. The first thing we notice is that our validation messages repeat, more or less, the field names defined in our `package.properties` file.

Because we can use OGNL to access the value stack, even in our validation files, we can use our action's `getText()` method to include the field name defined in the property file. (This may not always be possible due to grammar, capitalization, or other requirements, but we'll get to that.) Here's a fragment showing this technique with the recipe name field.

```
<field name="name">
  <field-validator type="requiredstring">
    <message>%{getText(fieldName)} is required.</message>
  </field-validator>
  <field-validator type="stringlength">
    <param name="minLength">3</param>
```

```
    <message>
      %{getText(fieldName)} must be at least %{minLength}
      characters long.
    </message>
  </field-validator>
</field>
```

The `fieldName` value is set with the `<field>` element's `name` attribute by Struts 2. This allows us to remove a common point of duplication and eliminate field label and validation message field name mismatches.

Our next observation is that the entire message can be localized. We can move our messages into our `package.properties` file (or another file in the file lookup hierarchy), while maintaining our OGNL method calls and parameters. The `<message>` elements now use a `key` attribute to define the messages, for example:

```
<field name="name">
  <field-validator type="requiredstring">
    <message key="requiredstring"/>
  </field-validator>
  <!-- etc. -->
```

Our property file now has an entry containing our original message verbatim.

```
requiredstring=%{getText(fieldName)} is required.
```

Eventually, we might move global validation messages like this into either a global resource file or a root `package.properties` file.

Also note that we've already run into a potential grammar problem due to our "ingredients" validation with our `requiredstring` message. The message "Ingredients is required" sounds awkward to many English speakers. Instead, it is better expressed as "Ingredients are required" — the perils of obsessive-compulsive web application development!

What validations are available?

The default validations are defined in the XWork 2 library and include a basic set of validators. It is likely that most projects will either need to define their own custom validators, or use a combination of pre-built and manual validation. Manual validation is particularly useful when there are complex business-side validations that cannot be expressed in XML, or are too awkward to be expressed. It also allows the re-use of existing business logic.

The requiredstring validator

We've already seen the `requiredstring` validator, but there is a parameter available we didn't cover. The `trim` parameter defines whether or not the string will be trimmed using the `java.lang.String.trim()` method prior to performing the validation. The parameter has `true` as its default value. Hence, if we want the user to be able to enter only spaces, we must set the `trim` parameter to `false` using the `<param>` element.

```
<field-validator type="requiredstring">
  <param name="trim">false</param>
  <message key="requiredstring"/>
</field-validator>
```

In general, this is rarely what we want, which is why it defaults to `true`.

> The `trim` parameter only trims the string for the length check. It does not trim the field value itself—don't expect a trimmed string in the action. We'll see a few ways around this as we move through the book.

Note that the `requiredstring` validator is not the same as the `required` validator, and has a different behavior. The `required` validator (covered shortly) checks for `nullness`. Browsers send an empty string (""), not null, when a text element isn't filled in. This means a text input field element's action property will never be null, it will always be the empty string. Therefore, the `required` validator's check won't work for a text input field.

The stringlength validator

We've also seen the `stringlength` validator, but not its `maxLength` or `trim` parameters. The `trim` parameter works the same way as it does with the `requiredstring` validator.

The `maxLength` parameter does what we'd expect—setting an upper bound on the length of the field value. To demonstrate `maxLength`, we'll change our recipe name validation to require a name between three and eight characters and create a validation message including the upper and lower bounds.

```
<field-validator type="stringlength">
  <param name="minLength">3</param>
  <param name="maxLength">8</param>
  <message key="stringlength"/>
</field-validator>
```

Creating a parameterized `stringlength` message is similarly easy.

```
stringlength=%{getText(fieldName)} must be between %{minLength} and
%{maxLength} characters.
```

However, this isn't a generic string length validation message. Some length requirements apply only to a minimum number of characters, with no limit set for maximum number of characters (or the opposite). Fixing this leads us to a side trip into the world of validation messages.

Detour—playing games with validation messages

There are many games we can play to create robust, human-readable error messages under very complex circumstances. The easiest solution to fix our `stringlength` validation message is to provide separate messages depending on whether or not we've specified the `minLength` and/or `maxLength` parameters.

```
stringminlength=%{getText(fieldName)} must be at least %{minLength}
characters.
stringmaxlength=%{getText(fieldName)} must be under %{maxLength}
characters.
stringminmaxlength=%{getText(fieldName)} must be between %{minLength}
and ${maxLength} characters.
```

We then use the appropriate message key in our field validator configuration, and rely on the developer to use the correct message. We'll come back to this, as developers rarely do the right thing.

Next, we'll create a new requirement, which states that we must echo the data entered back to the user along with the number of characters actually entered, focusing on the recipe name field.

 At the time of writing this book, there appears to be no trivial way to access the actual value being validated from an external message file. Hence, we will be going back to using messages in our validation file.

Once again, we'll rely on OGNL's ability to call arbitrary methods.

```
<field-validator type="stringlength">
  <param name="minLength">3</param>
  <param name="maxLength">8</param>
  <message>
      Name must be between %{minLength} and %{maxLength}
      characters; '%{recipe.name.trim()}' is
      %{recipe.name.trim().length()} characters.
  </message>
</field-validator>
```

Our next requirement change is that we must use the `stringMinLength` or `stringMaxLength` messages (currently defined in our properties file) depending on whether or not the value we entered is too long or too short. This provides a more specific error message. Again, OGNL allows us to do this relatively easily.

```
<message>
  <![CDATA[%{name.trim().length() < minLength ?
                  getText('stringMinLength') :
                  getText('stringMaxLength') }
  ]]>
</message>
```

The CDATA allows us to use the < comparison operator. OGNL's ternary operator allows us to check the length of the trimmed data and retrieve the appropriate message. The last requirement we'll give ourselves is to put our message in a property file (for I18N), but retain the use of our minimum length and maximum length messages. This is harder.

As noted, the current crop of XWork validators don't provide trivial access to the value being validated, but they're still accessible using OGNL and some knowledge of the value stack during validation. During validation, the top-most stack item is the validator itself (meaning it would be trivial to expose the value being validated). The next item down the stack is our action, meaning our action properties are also available.

By using OGNL's map-style access to action properties, we can construct an ugly, but requirement-achieving OGNL statement allowing us to move our message into a property file, giving us a `stringminmaxlength` message that looks like this (formatted nicely):

```
stringminmaxlength=
  %{[1][fieldName].trim().length() < minLength
    ? getText('stringminlength')
    : getText('stringmaxlength') }
```

We already know that `fieldName` refers to the name of the field being validated. The weird bit is the `[1]`, which looks like an array reference without the array. This is OGNL-speak. An `[n]` by itself references the stack minus the first *n* elements. This means that when our expression is evaluated against the value stack, we'll start searching from the nth element and move down. The `[fieldName]` portion uses map-style notation to access the action property named inside the brackets (here, whatever value `fieldName` contains).

With clever use of OGNL, we can put all sorts of functionality in our validation messages (and any other message, for that matter), including I18N-ed pluralization rules. Sometimes it looks a little scary, but we laugh in the face of danger to meet our client's many and perverse requirements.

I have been a bit deceptive (here, by "a bit", I mean "a lot") because the above capability just discussed is very cool and handy. Now, let's talk about our big but... Our current recipe action is using a `Recipe` class instance in the form. Our OGNL treachery will work only if the field name isn't nested.

In other words, we're validating `recipe.name`. This means we're trying to use the OGNL expression `${[1]['recipe.name']}`, which we'll discover doesn't work. This breaks some of the convenience of the message tricks we have just discussed.

As we'd expect, there's a workaround, though bulkier. Recall that `ActionSupport`'s `getText()` method comes in many flavors, including one that takes a list of message parameters. This sounds promising, and it turns out that it fixes all our problems (at least those surrounding this particular validation message requirement).

In our validation file, where we have easy access to our `recipe.name` property, we can define our message as follows:

```
<message>
  <![CDATA[
    ${recipe.name.trim().length() < minLength
      ? getText('stringminlength', {recipe.name,
                                    recipe.name.length()})
      : getText('stringmaxlength', {recipe.name,
                                    recipe.name.length()}) }
  ]]>
</message>
```

We also update our `stringminlength` and `stringmaxlength` messages and use the standard Java positional parameter notation (not OGNL, there's no "$" or "%") to access the parameters passed in with the `getText()` call (we'll only show `stringminlength`).

```
stringminlength=${getText(fieldName)} must be at least
    ${minLength} characters; ''{0}'' has a measly {1}.
```

Of course, we went a bit crazy in this example, choosing the minimum or maximum message when we could have used a single message. This was more to show off some of the capabilities provided to us by OGNL at several levels of the validation message process.

The required and int validators

The `required` validator checks for the nullness of a form field. This is a little bit misleading. However, as even empty form fields are sent to the server, they won't be null, the HTTP parameters are empty strings. The notable exceptions are unchecked checkboxes. Even that is not entirely true with the use of the Struts 2 `<s:checkbox>` tag (recall its use of hidden fields), so even checkbox properties won't be null.

To explain a bit further, we'll show a first attempt at validating two numbers (example form just has text fields for both):

```
<s:form action="reqint">
  <s:textfield key="reqint"/>
  <s:textfield key="reqInteger"/>
  <s:submit/>
</s:form>
```

Our action has `reqint` and `reqInteger` properties—the first a primitive, the second an object. The reason for having one of each will become clear shortly (getters and setters elided):

```
public int reqint;
public Integer reqInteger;
```

Our first attempt at a validation file defines an `int` validator for each field, expected to be in the range of `10` to `20` (both inclusive).

```
<field name="reqint">
  <field-validator type="int">
    <param name="min">10</param>
    <param name="max">20</param>
    <message>
      'int' must be between ${min} and ${max} (inclusive).
    </message>
  </field-validator>
</field>
<field name="reqInteger">
  <field-validator type="int">
    <param name="min">10</param>
    <param name="max">20</param>
    <message>
      'Integer' must be between ${min} and ${max} (inclusive).
    </message>
  </field-validator>
</field>
```

When we visit the form URL, we notice that the input element for the `int` field `reqint` is already filled in with a "0", whereas the `Integer` field `reqInteger` is empty. This is because the default value of a primitive `int` is 0, while the default value of an `Integer` is `null` (this alone may determine whether we use primitives or objects as properties).

If we submit the form as is, we'll get the message saying that `reqint` must be between 10 and 20. However, there is no message for the `reqInteger` field even though it's empty, and clearly not between 10 and 20.

Why? The `int` validator (more precisely, its parent class) does not do the range comparison if the value is `null`. This is where the `required` validator makes an appearance. It must be used for non-primitive properties that should have a value.

We just add the `required` validator to the `reqInteger` `<field>`:

```
<field-validator type="required">
  <message>Missing the 'Integer' value.</message>
</field-validator>
```

When we submit a fresh form, we'll now get an appropriate error message when the `reqInteger` field is empty.

But wait, there's more

Everything looks good until we enter a non-numeric value. If we enter "adf" in both fields, we get back two different messages for each field. The `int` field gives us the `int` error, the `Integer` field gives us the required error, and both claim that there's an "Invalid field value". Something has happened behind the scenes, producing a message we didn't define.

This error message appears due to a type conversion error ("adf" is not a valid numeric value, at least in base 10) and is added to our field-specific by the `conversionError` interceptor. We can disable this by removing the interceptor from our action's interceptor stack if it meets our application's needs.

We can override the type conversion error message in our property file. We can either override the global I18N key `xwork.default.invalid.fieldvalue` or create individual error messages for each field by creating messages named `invalid.fieldvalue.xxx`, where xxx is the name of the field.

The double validator

The `double` validator works like an `int` validator, but validates doubles. However, the `double` validator has parameters for both inclusive and exclusive range comparisons (the `int` validator is always inclusive). Because floating point numbers are inherently inaccurate, we might occasionally need both inclusive and exclusive comparisons.

The parameters are named `minInclusive`, `maxInclusive`, `minExclusive`, and `maxExclusive`, each being what we'd expect. Any parameter that is set will be checked, and any combination is legal. For example, we would specify both inclusive parameters and only one exclusive parameter, and so on.

Using a `Double` property requires the use of the `required` parameter, as with the `int` validator. Primitive `double` parameters will be filled beforehand in the form with their default value "0.0" (unless of course our action initializes it in some way).

The email validator

The `email` validator ensures that a field is a valid email address. Technically, it only validates most email addresses, but covers the majority of common addresses. The regular expression for validating an RFC-compliant email address is about one page long, and is not to be trifled with. (To paraphrase an old joke: I had a problem validating email addresses. I decided to use regular expressions, and then I had two problems.)

The `email` validator is a subclass of the `regex` validator discussed next. One potential gotcha is that if we're using a string property for the address, we must use the `requiredstring` validator to make sure there's an email address to validate.

The url validator

The `url` validator, unlike the `email` validator, is not a `regex` validator subclass. It uses an XWork utility class to check for valid URLs using the default `java.net.URL` constructor (with a trivial hack so HTTPS URLs are properly validated).

As with the `email` validator, if we use a string property for the URL, we'd need to use the `requiredstring` validator if a URL is required.

The date validator

As the name suggests, the `date` validator validates dates, with optional `min` and/or `max` parameters for validating date ranges. Our action property is usually a `java.util.Date`.

Recall again that the server receives a string parameter from the form—everything comes from the browser as a string. We'll cover how this type conversion works in a bit. For now, the short explanation is that XWork has a default set of type converters, one of which knows how to convert strings into dates. By default, XWork will use the Date.SHORT format for the appropriate locale. Failing to do this, it will use the default system locale.

The regex validator

The regex validator accepts arbitrary regular expressions (Java syntax) and validates the input field against that expression. If the field being validated with the regex validator is required, we need to use the requiredstring validator, as we've already seen.

The regex validator also accepts the trim parameter and an additional caseSensitive parameter if the regular expression is case sensitive. The default value is true.

A complete discussion of regular expressions is outside the scope of this book. However, they're very useful as a general tool. Having a reasonable grasp of regular expressions is among the most valuable tools in our toolbox.

The expression and fieldexpression validators

Both the expression and fieldexpression validators take arbitrary OGNL expressions in their expression parameters, which are evaluated and used to determine a validation's success or failure. Almost any validation can be performed using one of these two validators, although the supplied convenience validators should be used when possible.

In general, anything more complex than the convenience validators should probably be encapsulated in business logic and used in a validate() method rather than encoded in our validation configuration. However, in some instances, these validators are handy. This is particularly true for simple expressions, such as comparing email and email confirmation fields.

That being said, as OGNL lets us call arbitrary methods (static or not), almost any validation can be captured using these validators. If we have exposed business logic, it may be easier to use those services using OGNL. Different people prefer different techniques.

As a quick example, we'll validate an email address against a confirmation email address. We will stipulate that it must not start with the string "dave" (as people named Dave are generally a little shifty). We'll use the `fieldexpression` validator (to keep out those nasty Daves), and will use the `expression` validator for the confirmation address validation.

Our validation for our two email addresses looks like this:

```
<field name="email">
  <field-validator type="email">
    <message key="email.required"/>
  </field-validator>

  <field-validator type="requiredstring">
    <message key="required"/>
  </field-validator>

  <field-validator type="fieldexpression">
    <param name="expression">!email.startsWith('dave')</param>
    <message key="keep.daves.out"/>
  </field-validator>
</field>

<field name="cemail">
  <field-validator type="email">
    <message key="email.required"/>
  </field-validator>

  <field-validator type="requiredstring">
    <message key="required"/>
  </field-validator>
</field>
```

Our `expression` validator is not tied to a specific field, unlike the other validations we've seen so far.

```
<validator type="expression">
  <param name="expression">email.equals(cemail)</param>
  <message key="confirm"/>
</validator>
```

Submitting this form with non-matching emails, along with the condition stated above (name shouldn't start with the string "dave"), doesn't display our confirmation error message. Only field-specific error messages are displayed by the standard Struts 2 form tags. We must use the `<s:actionerror>` tag to display the nonfield errors:

```
<s:actionerror/>
```

This displays a bulleted list of all non-field-specific error messages. There are corresponding `<s:actionmessage>` and `<s:fielderror>` tags, each displaying what we'd expect. The `<s:fielderror>` tag accepts either a `value` attribute or `<s:param>` elements that name the field whose errors will be displayed.

Note that our check for strings not starting with "dave" could also call a utility method (for example, a service object injected into our action). Business-oriented rules such as this one, whenever possible, should exist in re-usable objects, so that can be used throughout the application.

Assuming such an object exists, our `fieldexpression` validation might look like this:

```
<field-validator type="fieldexpression">
  <param name="expression">
    !emailService.excluded(email)
  </param>
  <message key="email.excluded"/>
</field-validator>
```

Combining validation methods

We can also combine manual and XML validation by implementing `validate()` in our action, calling `super.validate()` to run the XML validation. We can then perform any additional validation. For example, we could remove the email exclusion check from our XML validation and put it in our action's `validate()` method, as shown here:

```
public void validate() {
    super.validate();
    if (emailService.excluded(email)) {
        addFieldError("email",
            getText("email.excluded",
                    new String[] { getText("email.label") }));
    }
}
```

Moving the field validation into our action means we need to manually pass the name of the field (retrieved from our property file) to our validation error message. The field name will no longer refer to the `fieldName` value, but would instead be a standard Java resource positional parameter.

The conversion validator

The `conversion` validator checks to see if there was a conversion error on the field in question. This can be used if the `conversion` interceptor is not in our interceptor stack (which we'll discuss later), and we want a specific conversion error message. We've already seen how other validator's error messages are enough to catch conversion errors, rendering the `conversion` validator unnecessary in many circumstances.

The visitor validator

The `visitor` validator is used primarily when we're implementing the `ModelDriven` interface or validating domain objects directly, which we haven't discussed yet. In short, using the `visitor` validator allows us to validate a form field using a model-specific validation file. This can make more sense than action-specific validation, depending on our application.

Configuring validation with annotations

All of the validations we've seen so far can be configured using annotations rather than XML. Validation annotations can be applied at the action method level using the `@Validations` annotation, or the property level by annotating property setters.

Annotation validators require a `message` parameter, even if a `key` element is specified. It's used as a default message if the message specified by the key can't be found in a resource file. It can be a blank string, a message from a `getText()` call, a warning message saying the key is missing, an actual error message, and so on.

OGNL expressions are available to our annotations, just like our XML.

The @Validation annotation

Classes that will be validated using annotations may use the `@Validation` annotation at the type (class or interface) level. It is a marker annotation taking no parameters. It used to be required, but isn't anymore.

On a side note, making the `@Validation` annotation optional may be marginally less work for us, but makes it marginally more difficult for tools to determine if a class has validation annotations. It's not a major issue from a technical standpoint, but is an example of the typical tradeoffs developers often make.

The @Validations annotation

As mentioned, there are two ways annotations can be used for form validation. They can be applied at the property level by annotating setter methods, or at the action method level by grouping them with the @Validations annotation.

The @Validations annotation accepts several parameters that group similar validations together. This allows all required validations to be grouped together, all email validations to be grouped together, and so on. There is a group element for each included validation type (except for double, as we'll discuss soon).

The following groupings are available:

1. requiredFields
2. requiredStrings
3. intRangeFields
4. stringLengthFields
5. regexFields
6. emails
7. urls
8. dateRangeFields
9. expressions
10. fieldExpressions
11. customValidators
12. visitorFields

As a brief example, we'll look at a @Validations example for an email address and some required fields. We might validate the action class as follows:

```
@Validations(
    emails = { @EmailValidator(fieldName="email",
               message = "Invalid email address.",
               key="valEmail") },
    requiredStrings = {
       @RequiredStringValidator(fieldName="email",
        message="Email is required.", key="required") },
    requiredFields = {
       @RequiredFieldValidator(fieldName="aRequiredInteger",
        message="Integer is required.", key="required"),
       @RequiredFieldValidator(fieldName="aRequiredDouble",
         message="Double is required.", key="required")
    }
)
```

When specifying field-level validations with the @Validations annotation, the fieldName element must be provided to tie validations to fields.

There are a couple of issues we must take into consideration while deciding if we'll use the action-method-specific validations using the @Validations annotation, or if we'll annotate each property setter method.

The first is that if we have an action class with multiple methods, which we want to execute and validate separately, we'll have an issue. The @Validations annotation is not method-specific. Regardless of which method is annotated and which one is executed, all validations found within the @Validations annotation will be executed for *all* methods.

Another less serious issue is that specifying a @DoubleRangeFieldValidator using the @Validations annotation is more trouble than it's worth, as the @Validations annotation (for now) does not have a double validations grouping. We can still validate doubles by using a customValidators block. For fun, we'll see what that would look like.

```
customValidators = {
    @CustomValidator(type="double", fieldName="reqDouble",
        message="dblMinMax", key="dblMinMax",
        parameters={@ValidationParameter(name="minInclusive",
                                          value="-10.0"),
                    @ValidationParameter(name="maxInclusive",
                                          value="10.0")})
}
```

That wasn't as much fun as we'd hoped for. It does show how custom validations can be specified through annotations, even if the parameter passing is a bit unwieldy.

The @SkipValidation annotation

@SkipValidation marks methods that should be excluded from validation. Depending on our requirements, we can use this annotation to work around the limitation of the @Validations annotation. It's particularly helpful if we have validations handled using setter validation annotations, but want to skip them for certain action methods.

The @RequiredFieldValidator annotation

This is the annotation analogous to the required validator and there is nothing much interesting to add to the discussion. However, remember that the message element is required, even if you provide a key element with a resource key.

The @IntRangeFieldValidator annotation

The annotation version of the `int` validator accepts the `min` and `max` elements, and operates in the same way as its XML counterpart. If we're validating an `Integer` (a non-primitive integer), we must also specify the `@RequiredFieldValidator`, just as we would with XML-based validation.

Specifying multiple validation annotations on a property setter is a simple matter of listing each appropriate annotation and no grouping is necessary as with action methods. A required `Integer` property can then be annotated as follows.

```
@RequiredFieldValidator(key="required",
    message="!!! MISSING required MESSAGE !!!")
@IntRangeFieldValidator(key="intMinMax", min="-10", max="10",
    message="!!! MISSING intMinMax MESSAGE !!!")
public void setReqInteger(Integer reqInteger) {
    this.reqInteger = reqInteger;
}
```

Again, our `message` element could include an actual error message, complete with arbitrary OGNL expressions. Here, we're warning that the error message wasn't found.

The @DoubleRangeFieldValidator annotation

This is analogous to the `double` validator and accepts all the configuration elements as its XML counterpart. As mentioned, the only caveat regarding the `@DoubleRangeFieldValidator` is that if used at the action method level inside a `@Validations` annotation, we need to pretend it's a custom validator. This works, but it adds a fair amount of syntactic overhead to define its parameters.

The remaining validation annotations

Each of the remaining validation annotations are similar to the annotations already discussed and are analogous to their XML counterparts. Their documentation is available both on the Struts 2 documentation wiki and in the Struts 2/XWork 2 API documentation.

For the sake of completeness, we'll list them here:

1. `@EmailValidator`

2. `@UrlValidator`

3. `@DateRangeFieldValidator`

4. `@StringRegexValidator`

5. @ExpressionValidator

6. @FieldExpressionValidator

7. @ConversionErrorFieldValidator

8. @VisitorFieldValidator

(You didn't really want me to rewrite the existing documentation, did you?)

Client-side validation

In addition to server-side validation available using both XML and annotations, we can also use client-side validation. This is handled using JavaScript injected by the Struts 2 form tags. Client-side validation is turned on by setting the `<s:form>` tag's `validate` attribute to `true`.

The client-side validation mechanism depends on the theme being used. When using the "xhtml" or css_xhtml themes, it's pure JavaScript client-side validation, whereas using the ajax theme uses Ajax-based validation.

 Client-side validation requires the presence of XML or annotation validation. The server-side configuration is used to create the appropriate JavaScript.

When using the `@Validations` annotation on an action method, we must remember to provide the `fieldName` element for our field validations. Failure to provide the `fieldname` element will result in the failure of our client-side validation with a FreeMarker exception. We must use the `fieldName` element anyway, but forgetting it sometimes leads to a difficult-to-diagnose error.

Client-side validation supports a smaller number of validators, which are listed here:

1. required

2. requiredstring

3. stringlength

4. regex

5. email

6. url

7. int

8. double

There are a couple of things to remember when using client-side validation.

The client-side `required` validator works differently than the server-side. The client-side version checks and flags empty strings. The server-side version checks for a null value, which doesn't work for string fields (empty fields are empty strings, not null).

Lastly, the Struts 2 form element tags have a `required` attribute. The `required` attribute is not tied to any validation process. It just controls whether or not there is a `required` indicator (by default, an asterisk "*") rendered in the form field's label.

In other words, if we need a form field to be required, we must still use the `required` or `requiredstring` validators. Adding the `required` attribute to a form input element tag alone is not enough.

Custom validators

The built-in validators are great for simple validations. The `regex` and `expression` family can handle more complicated validations. We will, however, need a custom validator sometimes.

The bulk of string-related validations can be handled by the `regex` validator, or by combining it with one or more expression validators—particularly if we're well versed in regular expressions. (If you haven't already noticed, I think regex fluency is very important.)

When our system has existing business-side validation rules, however, using a custom validator makes sense. In our newest contrived example, we'll say our system has a `classification` field, and we have existing business logic that validates the format of this field.

As there's already code, duplicating the functionality using the `regex` validator is unnecessary. And worse, it introduces another potential failure point in our system. In addition, if the validation ever changes (for example, the number of digits can either be three or four, but four-digit classifications must begin with "1" or "2"), we'd have to change our code in two places and not just one. This is generally a recipe for disaster.

Instead of using the `regex` validator, we can create and register a validator that uses the existing `classification` validation code rather than run the risk inherent in repeating ourselves. The existing validation logic exists in a `ClassificationService` class containing a static validation method with the signature `boolean isValidClassification(String)`.

We're implementing a field validator, so we'll extend Xwork's `FieldValidatorSupport`. We need to implement only the validate method—`void validate(Object)`. Validation errors are signaled by the presence of field errors in our action's field errors collection (which `ActionSupport` provides, or we can implement manually).

The following is the majority of our classification validator (imports elided):

```
package com.packt.s2wad.ch07.examples.classification;
public class ClassificationValidator extends FieldValidatorSupport {
    public void validate(Object o) throws ValidationException {
        String val = (String) getFieldValue(getFieldName(), o);
        if (!ClassificationService.isValidClassification(val)) {
            addFieldError(getFieldName(), o);
        }
    }
}
```

During normal operation, the `validate()` method gets an instance of the action we've submitted to. Here, we're getting the value of the field from the action, and adding field errors to our action.

We must register our validator, so Struts 2 knows what we're referring to in our validation configuration. We create a `validators.xml` and place it in the root of our classpath. (Earlier versions of Struts 2 required us to include the default validators, which is no longer a requirement.)

```
<?xml version="1.0" encoding="UTF-8"?>
<!DOCTYPE validators PUBLIC
  "-//OpenSymphony Group//XWork Validator Config 1.0//EN"
  "http://www.opensymphony.com/xwork/xwork-validator-config-1.0.dtd">
<validators>
    <validator name="classification"
class="com.packt.s2wad.ch07.examples.classification.
ClassificationValidator"/>
</validators>
```

We can now use our `classification` validator in our action using annotations. (We could just as easily use it in our validation XML, but we're bored of that. It's too easy in the XML, we just use the `classification` type.)

In this example, our action has a single `classification` property. We annotate its setter with the `@CustomValidator` annotation. We have no parameters, so we can keep things clean.

```
@CustomValidator(type="classification",
                 message="Invalid classification")
public void setClassification(String classification) {
    this.classification = classification;
}
```

We could even assume a static property in the classification service that defines an invalid classification message:

```
@CustomValidator(type="classification",
message="${@com.packt.s2wad.ch07.examples.classification.
ClassificationService@INVALID_CLASSIFICATION}")
```

Okay, so OGNL's static method is a thing of both beauty and horror.

We could also do this validation in an action's `validate()` method. If our classification service is injected, it might be cleaner. (We'll discuss injection when we cover testing. It's not as scary as it sounds, and no needles are involved.)

Deciding where to put this type of logic might include considering the implementation of the validation logic, how often the "classification" validation is used, organization coding standards, and so on. Having declarative (or annotation-driven) validation can also ease the creation of various documentation (as opposed to Java-only validation).

It's quite easy to use our custom validator in either `@Validations` annotations using the `@CustomValidator` annotation or on a property setter. Unfortunately, at the time of writing this book, the ability to create a custom validation annotation (instead of using `@CustomValidator`) was difficult to integrate into the default XWork annotation validation configuration.

Type conversion

We've already seen some type conversions, often without even being aware of it. Remember our `int` and `Integer` form validations? Our action simply declared values as the `int` and the `Integer`, and we didn't give it any more thought, even when we mysteriously ended up with a new `Recipe` object.

The problem

As has been mentioned already, web browsers only and always send back strings. In times not-so-long past, we could see a lot of code fragments similar to the following (assuming an `anInt` property):

```
String s = request.getParameter("anInt");
int anInt = NumberUtils.toInt(s, 0);
doSomething(anInt);
```

Okay, that's not much extra code because we're making use of Apache Commons Lang and its `NumberUtils` class to hide the potential `NumberFormatException`. We are also making use of Java 1.5's auto-boxing for the `int` to `Integer` conversion.

However, in Struts 2 the code is simply:

```
doSomething(anInt);
```

Busting out our trusty command line tool `wc` (for "<u>w</u>ord <u>c</u>ount" — it's pretty handy for low-resolution size comparisons), we confirm that it's one-third the line count and one-fifth the character count. There's more to this than simply less typing. There is a significant reduction in cognitive overhead, as our code is more focused on what we're actually doing. The conversion code was ancillary to our actual task, doing something to our `Integer`.

The solution

Type conversion! Well, the above old school code was type conversion too, but it happened "in the foreground" and we were doing it manually. Ideally, the type conversion should happen behind-the-scenes, letting us focus on what we're really trying to accomplish. Our goal, after all, isn't converting integers — it's *doing* something with them.

Struts 2 has built-in type conversion that is usually intuitive. We didn't really think about it when we did our integer validation. The validators depend on type conversion to convert the form values into something they can use. It's entirely possible to never need to understand most of how type conversion works (except, perhaps, collections).

Obviously, there's out of the box support for integers, both primitive and objects. Numeric support includes bytes, shorts, longs, doubles, `BigIntegers`, and `BigDecimals`. `Date` and `Calendar` types are also supported. There is also support for `Maps` and `Lists`. We'll take a look at that next, after looking at how to create our own converters.

Nested conversions are also possible. In other words, if we have a domain object, such as a recipe, its properties can be converted. Our recipe had only string properties, so we don't need it yet. We'll look at an example later when we cover collections.

Defining our own converters

We can also create our own type converters to supply functionality not included by default. For example, the included `BigDecimal` type conversion breaks if our input string has extra spaces at the end (an oversight, I'm sure). We'd like to fix that. (Note that we'll learn a better way to implement this in Chapter 8.)

Type conversion usecase—trimmed BigDecimals

The default Java `BigDecimal` parsing doesn't really like extra spaces. (We already know that we should be using the `BigDecimal` class for accurate calculations involving money, among other things, right?)

We could work around this in several ways. We could use a string property, trim it ourselves, and do the `BigDecimal` conversion in our action. However, this completely defeats the purpose of the type conversion process. Let's create a custom type converter (which seems like the best solution, given the section of the book we're in).

Custom type conversions generally implement the `ognl.TypeConverter` interface or, a bit more cleanly, extend the `StrutsTypeConvertor` class. It defines two methods, `convertFromString(Map, String[], Class)` and `convertToString(Map, Object)`, which do as we'd expect (although the parameters look odd at first).

We've left the error handling and logging in place not only to show how simple error handling and logging is (perhaps a bit over-done here), but also to highlight how little application code has to do with the actual problem being solved. There's also a potential subtle exception message issue, just to see if you're paying attention!

Often, there's a lot of boilerplate code dedicated to two goals: making sure our code doesn't break, and if it does, ensuring that it's easy to figure out why it broke, and how to fix it. We'll discuss error handling and logging soon.

Our conversion implementation is reasonably straightforward.

```java
public class BigDecimalConverter extends StrutsTypeConverter {
    public Object convertFromString(Map context,
                                    String[] values,
                                    Class toClass) {
        if (values == null) {
            return null;
        }
        if (values.length != 1) {
            String msg = String.format("Array too big: [%s]",
                         StringUtils.join(values, ", "));
            throw new TypeConversionException(msg);
        }
        return values[0] == null ? null
                : new BigDecimal(values[0].trim());
    }

    public String convertToString(Map context, Object o) {
        if (!(o instanceof BigDecimal)) {
            String msg =
              String.format("No BigDecimal supplied; object was %s",
                         o.getClass().getCanonicalName());
            throw new TypeConversionException(msg);
        }
        BigDecimal val = (BigDecimal) o;
        if (val == null) {
            return null;
        }
        return val.toString();
    }
}
```

The last step is to inform Struts 2 that we'd like to use this type converter for a specific property on our form. If we assume an action `TestBigDecimal` with an exposed `BigDecimal` property `myBigOne`, we can create a file in the same package as `TestBigDecimal` named `TestBigDecimal-conversion.properties`, which will look like this:

```
myBigOne=com.packt.s2wad.ch07.examples.conversion.BigDecimalConverter
```

We name the property that will use our type converter and provide the class of the type converter to use. Pretty straightforward, but very XML-ish! We can also use an annotation and eliminate another external file.

To use our `BigDecimalConverter` with annotations, we annotate our action class with the `@Conversion` marker annotation, so that it's scanned for `@TypeConversion` annotations. The `@TypeConversion` annotation is applied on property setters and is straightforward as shown here:

```
@TypeConversion(converter =
    "com.packt.s2wad.ch07.examples.conversion.BigDecimalConverter")
public void setBig(BigDecimal big) {
    this.big = big;
}
```

Configuring conversion across the entire application

The only issue left is that we have to configure all `BigDecimal` properties using either XML or annotations. This is not a big deal for occasional needs, but hardly convenient if they're scattered across an entire application. To configure type conversions across an entire application, we create a file named `xwork-conversion.properties` on the root of our classpath and fill it with type and converter pairs:

```
java.math.BigDecimal=
    com.packt.s2wad.ch07.examples.conversion.BigDecimalConverter
```

Custom type conversion is handy

Using whatever parsing mechanism necessary, it is similarly straightforward to create arbitrarily complex type converters such as coordinates (for example, convert a string "5, 10" into a `Point` object), URLs (there's a `url` validator, but the result is stored in a string—it could just as easily be a `URL` object, and probably should be), and so on. Ultimately, we're still turning a string (repeat after me: the browser always sends strings!) into a domain object—we're just doing it in an unobtrusive way.

Hiding this functionality and keeping type conversion out of our mainline code is really handy. It reduces the amount of code contained in our actions and the cognitive load needed to understand that code. We still need to remember that type conversion is taking place—it's another place to look if things go wrong.

Collections

Struts 2 also provides automatic type conversion for collections, including maps. By using OGNL's array (or map) syntax in our forms, Struts 2 will not only automatically convert specific data types, but will also put that data into a collection. Our actions receive a collection of domain objects, with no intervention from us.

Usecase—adding a list of ingredients

To demonstrate this capability, we'll return to our client's application. As it stands, the ingredients are a simple text area. One of the requirements is to have a list of individual ingredients, with each ingredient having a quantity and a name.

Recall that we have already created a `ShoppingListItem` class with the `name` and `quantity` properties. We'll modify our `Recipe` class and change its `ingredients` property to use the existing `ShoppingListItem` (getter and setter not shown).

```
private List<ShoppingListItem> ingredients;
```

We will also update our recipe view page and iterate over the ingredients:

```
<s:iterator value="recipe.ingredients">
  <tr>
    <td><s:property value="quantity"/></td>
    <td><s:property value="name"/></td>
  </tr>
</s:iterator>
```

We will also change our `FakeRecipeService` to use the new data type. Notice that the `Recipe` class has been graced with an `addIngredient()` method. This might seem like an unnecessary addition, but we'll consider two things after looking at how we create sample data.

```
Recipe recipe2 = new Recipe(2, "Java");
recipe2.setRecipeTypes(new ArrayList<String>() {{
    add(FakeRecipeTypeService.RECIPE_TYPE2.getName());
    add(FakeRecipeTypeService.RECIPE_TYPE4.getName());
}});
recipe2.addIngredient(new ShoppingListItem("1",
                            "Large lack of abstractions"));
recipe2.addIngredient(new ShoppingListItem("Lots", "typing"));
```

Why add addIngredient()?

The most obvious benefit is also the least interesting—there's a little less typing. We might skip the convenience method, so that adding an ingredient looks more like this:

```
recipe2.getIngredients().
        add(new ShoppingListItem("Lots", "typing"));
```

That's longer, but not ridiculously so. The actual big win is that we're exposing that much less of our `Recipe` class's implementation. Remember how object-oriented programming was supposed to hide implementation details? There's nothing hidden about a `getIngredients()` call. No big deal, we say.

In this case, that's probably true. However, consider the very simple case of changing how we store our collection of ingredients. Let's say we now need to store our ingredients in a map, indexed by the ingredient ID. Suddenly, our decision to expose our list doesn't seem so good, and we must change all of our code that uses the `getIngredients()` method, as it's tied to using a list (well, collection).

By using an `addIngredient()` method, we've provided a layer of isolation from the underlying implementation. Assuming that we don't need to pass in any additional information when adding an ingredient, the only code that has to change is isolated within the `Recipe` class's implementation.

Sometimes, a small amount of effort up front can reduce potential development hassles down the road, even when it seems trivial and unimportant.

Updating our new recipe form

Our new requirement states that a recipe form will have fields for ten ingredients (`ShoppingListItems`). (We'll see how to add rows dynamically when we cover JavaScript, one of the world's most misunderstood languages.) There are several changes to be made in order to meet our new requirements.

First, we need to generate appropriate form tags for each of the ten ingredients. In order to make use of the built-in collection conversions, our form tags need to end up looking like typical array notation, one for each ingredient.

```
<input type="text" name="recipe.ingredients[0].name"/>
<input type="text" name="recipe.ingredients[1].name"/>
<!-- ... and so on ... -->
```

We could do this manually, but that seems like a poor solution. A quick solution is to build the text tags inside an iterator.

```
<s:iterator value="{1, 2, 3, 4, 5, 6, 7, 8, 9, 10}"
            var="idx" status="stat">
  <s:textfield name="recipe.ingredients[%{#stat.index}].quantity"/>
  <s:textfield name="recipe.ingredients[%{#stat.index}].name"/>
</s:iterator>
```

Struts 2.1.7+'s iterator tag includes "begin", "end", and "step" attributes, to support looping similar to JSTL's "forEach" tag.

The `name` attribute includes an OGNL expression inside the field name, and is similar to the OGNL we've already seen. It simply uses the index of the iterator as the array index of the recipe's ingredients list.

 Simply, you say? What's simple about `[%{#stat.index}]`?! The `#stat.index`, which we've already seen, just refers to the iterator tag's status. The `%{}` forces OGNL evaluation, so we get the index value inside the square brackets. The rest is simple array notation. Piece of cake! The coolest part hasn't even happened yet, though.

Note that we don't really need the array index notation here. Struts 2 will notice that there are multiple values for the same form parameter, and will do the right thing. However, if we need to guarantee an order, it's best to leave them in. Recipe ingredients are usually listed in the order of use. Hence, order is significant here.

If we visit our new recipe form at /recipes/new, we see something like this (truncated after a couple of our new ingredient fields):

New Recipe

Name:
Description:
Recipe Types: ☐ Main Dish ☐ Side Dish ☐ Appetizer ☐ De

We're definitely on the right track, but there are a few glaring deficiencies. We need a label for our ingredient fields, and it'd be a lot nicer if the ingredient's quantity and name fields were lined up on the same row.

We can create labels in a resource file, as we've done in the past. Our default label will be Ingredient #n where n will be the list element from our iterator, the numbers 1 through 10. There are actually two ways in which we could do this. As we define a `var` attribute in our `<s:iterator>` tag, we know there's a variable named `idx` available on the value stack, and we remember that the value stack is available in our message resources. We could then create a message resource such as this:

```
recipe.ingredientn=Ingredient #${idx}
```

(Here, the # symbol has nothing to do with OGNL—it just means a number!)

We could add the label to one of the text fields using the `getText()` call as shown here:

```
<s:textfield label="%{getText('recipe.ingredientn')}" size="5"
        name="recipe.ingredients[%{#stat.index}].quantity"/>
```

This is acceptable, but it creates a dependency between our JSP page and our resource file. If a developer changes the name of the iterator (the iterator tag's `var` attribute), the message will be broken. We're lazy, and we're certain to break this later.

Instead, we'll use the same `getText()` trick we've used before, and pass in an argument to the message resource. Our message will look like this:

```
recipe.ingredient=Ingredient #{0}
```

To use this message, our text tag will contain the following `label` attribute:

```
label="%{getText('recipe.ingredient', { #idx })}"
```

Slightly tricky OGNL, but it's still relatively straightforward. Our array of arguments to `getText()` is an OGNL immediate list. It consists of a single element, the named `var` of our iterator, with the # notation as usual. We could also just use the status variable, and pass in `#status.count`.

In Java, this call would look like this:

```
getText("recipe.ingredient", new String[] { idx });
```

The other issue was that our ingredient's quantity and name text fields are putting themselves in separate table rows because we're using the default "xhtml" theme. We'd like them on a single line, and will associate a label with each line.

We're not up to themes and templates yet, but here's a simple trick. We can set the theme for a single element by using the `theme` attribute. The simple theme renders only the input element—no table rows, no table cells, and no labels. Also, there are no error messages. Hence, there's still a hole in our solution, but we have to stop somewhere.

Our solution (for this chapter) will build the table row and table cells, normally built by the Struts 2 tags and the "xhtml" theme, on our own. In the first cell, where Struts 2 puts its labels, we'll put our label, using the Struts 2 property tag. The second cell gets the text inputs. We'll force them to render themselves using the simple theme, which renders no extraneous stuff.

```
<s:iterator value="{1, 2, 3, 4, 5, 6, 7, 8, 9, 10}" status="stat">
  <tr>
    <td>
      <s:property value="getText('recipe.ingredientn',
                     { #stat.count })"/>
    </td>
    <td>
      <s:textfield theme="simple" size="5"
         name="recipe.ingredients[%{#stat.index}].quantity"/>
      <s:textfield theme="simple" size="30"
         name="recipe.ingredients[%{#stat.index}].name" />
    </td>
  </tr>
</s:iterator>
```

Visiting our page now shows a more reasonable form, as shown in the following figure:

We'll skip ingredient validation. However, recall that an action's `validate()` method can easily call `super.validate()`, which will call any XML- or annotation-based validation. It will then add other validation logic such as iterating over recipe ingredients and checking for values, and so on. But we still need to get the recipe ingredients into our `Recipe` instance, right?

Before we cover submission of this form, we'll take a quick look at our `Recipe` class again, looking at its `toString()` method. Here, it's creating a verbose, human-readable dump of the important bits, useful in console output.

```
public String toString() {
    return String.format("%s [id=%d, name=%s, type(s)=[%s],
                         ingredients=[%s]]",
                         super.toString(), id, name,
                         StringUtils.join(recipeTypes, ", "),
                         StringUtils.join(ingredients, ", "));
}
```

It just returns a string that combines all the data we need together (using Apache Commons Lang's `StringUtils.join()` method because we've spent a lot of time poring over the Apache Commons Javadocs, right?). We looked at `Recipe.toString()`, so we'd understand what's in our `NewRecipe` action's `execute()` method.

```
public String execute() throws Exception {
    System.out.println(recipe.toString());
    return SUCCESS;
}
```

Not much, but we know that after we submit the form, we can check our console and, in theory, we should see a nice readable dump of our new recipe, complete with its ingredient list. However, we're worried because we haven't really written any code.

Sure, we wrote a `Recipe` class and a `ShoppingListItem`. We also wrote a JSP that pretended like our form was returning instances of `ShoppingListItem` in our recipe's ingredients list. Our form had already assumed that we could blithely use `recipe.name`, and it would be put into a `Recipe` object.

For the Struts 1 coders out there, remember copying `ActionForm` properties into a domain object with `BeanUtils.copyProperties()`?. Also, make `ActionForm` and `BeanUtils.copyProperties()` Or worse yet, copying the properties over by hand? Wasn't it fun?

New Recipe

Name:	S2 App	
Description:		
Recipe Types:	☑ Main Dish ☐ Side Dish ☐ Appetizer ☑ Desse	
Ingredient #1	1	Mediocre programming language
Ingredient #2	1	Awesome expression language
Ingredient #3	Lots	of great ideas

The above figure shows the form we're submitting. After we hit the **submit** button, the Struts 2 type conversion process takes hold. For example, it knows that when we specify a text field named `recipe.name` on our form, we don't just have a string, but rather a `Recipe` class with a `name` property. Better yet, on seeing `recipe.ingredients[0].quantity`, it assumes that the `Recipe` class has a list of `ShoppingListItem`s, each having a `quantity` property. And we didn't have to tell it anything.

When we check our console, we see the following (formatted for some amount of legibility):

```
com.packt.s2wad.ch07.models.Recipe@7c6dff [
  id=null,
  name=S2 App,
  type(s)=[Main Dish, Dessert],
  ingredients=[
    ShoppingListItem@ed5f47 [quantity=1,
                        item=Mediocre programming language],
    ShoppingListItem@a4662 [quantity=1,
                        item=Awesome expression language],
    ShoppingListItem@92fe37 [quantity=Lots,
                        item=of great ideas], ...
```

Something really helpful has happened. We're not dealing with strings, but with domain objects, without writing any of the code ourselves! This is a thing of beauty. Our mainline code is about as simple as anything can be.

Map-based collections

Maps are handled similarly, using the map key in OGNL's [] syntax instead of an array index. (OGNL's () (parentheses) syntax is used only for indexed collection access, discussed on the Struts 2 documentation wiki.) For our current requirements, we will just use a list. However, putting values into maps is a very common need when dealing with collections of data relating to a specific instance (such as a checkbox list of recipe IDs, and so on).

Summary

This chapter covers the basics of Struts 2 form validation, configurable through both XML and annotations. We also see that it's easy to combine manual and automatic validation by calling `super.validate()` to run the automatic validation, and implementing additional validation manually

The chapter also explains how to create custom validators that can be used as easily as built-in validators when configured using XML, and nearly as easily using annotations.

Struts 2 also provides a basic set of type converters and can automagically marshal form values into our domain objects, saving a tremendous amount of boilerplate code.

In the next chapter, we will finally take the framework functionality that we've put off for the first seven chapters. This is primarily to reinforce the idea that it's possible to accomplish quite a bit without having an in-depth knowledge of one of the fundamental components of Struts 2 — interceptors.

Are you excited yet?

References

A reader can refer to the following:

- Struts 2 validation:

  `http://struts.apache.org/2.x/docs/validation.html`

- Struts 2 Type Conversion (covers more complex use cases than we had room for):

  `http://struts.apache.org/2.x/docs/type-conversion.html`

8
Interceptors

In the previous chapter, we looked at form validation, which is configurable using both XML and annotations. We also saw how to create our own custom validators. We examined type conversion, and realized that it's both more intuitive and less intrusive to let the framework handle mundane housekeeping chores.

Now, we'll cover one of the "holy grails" of Struts 2—interceptors. In many ways, interceptors are the heart of Struts 2. We've already seen that quite a bit of behavior is implemented by interceptors, even without understanding precisely how they work or are configured. Validation, type conversion, file uploads, double submit tokens, action chaining, and the `Preparable` interface are all behaviors tightly coupled to interceptors.

In this chapter, we will cover:

- How to configure interceptors and interceptor stacks (ordered groups of interceptors)
- The interceptors we've already used (and some we haven't)
- Ways to use custom interceptors to implement "cross-cutting" functionality required across the entire application (or parts of the application)

The basics

Interceptors are similar to servlet filters. They're executed in the order in which they're declared. Each has access to the same action invocation, just as each filter has access to the same request. Each can modify program flow. Each wraps request processing, allowing processing before and after the request.

Interceptors are grouped into interceptor stacks, which are named and ordered collections of interceptors. Stacks can be configured both per-package and per-action. The most specific configuration is the one that's used. In other words, if we have configured an action to use a specific stack that would be the only stack used.

Configuring interceptor stacks

Struts 2 ships with several pre-configured interceptor stacks. We've been using the default stack (configured in the `struts-default.xml` file, which configures the `struts-default` package). For many purposes, it's all that's necessary. The `struts-default.xml` file defines the standard interceptors and a number of stacks that contain various combinations of the standard interceptors.

Looking at the `struts-default.xml` file's `struts-default` package definition, we see two major parts to the `<interceptors>` element:

- `<interceptor>` elements: to define interceptor names and classes
- `<interceptor-stack>`: to name and group together both individual interceptors and other named interceptor stacks

If nothing else, knowing how interceptors and stacks are defined allows us to find the class names, and hence the Javadocs of the interceptors we're using. Here's a representative portion of the interceptors in the `struts-default` package:

```
<package name="struts-default" abstract="true">
  ...
  <interceptors>
    <interceptor name="fileUpload"
      class="org.apache.struts2.interceptor.FileUploadInterceptor"/>
    <interceptor name="i18n"
      class="com.opensymphony.xwork2.interceptor.I18nInterceptor"/>
    <interceptor name="token"
      class="org.apache.struts2.interceptor.TokenInterceptor"/>
    <!-- etc. -->
```

Each interceptor element consists of a unique name and a fully-qualified implementation class.

Interceptor stacks are named, ordered collections of interceptors. For example, Struts 2 defines an interceptor stack named `basicStack` as follows:

```
<interceptor-stack name="basicStack">
    <interceptor-ref name="exception"/>
    <interceptor-ref name="servletConfig"/>
    <interceptor-ref name="prepare"/>
    <interceptor-ref name="checkbox"/>
```

```
    <interceptor-ref name="params"/>
    <interceptor-ref name="conversionError"/>
</interceptor-stack>
```

In this case, each of the `<interceptor-ref>` elements refers to a specific interceptor. However, the definition of the `validationWorkflowStack` is slightly different:

```
<interceptor-stack name="validationWorkflowStack">
    <interceptor-ref name="basicStack"/>
    <interceptor-ref name="validation"/>
    <interceptor-ref name="workflow"/>
</interceptor-stack>
```

One reference is to the `basicStack` interceptor stack, while the other two are individual interceptors. Recall that interceptors are executed in order. This includes interceptor stacks. If we're using the `validationWorkflowStack`, each interceptor in the `basicStack` is executed, followed by the `validation` and `workflow` interceptors.

Configuring interceptors

An interceptor's configuration also accepts parameters in `<param>` elements. For example, we've already seen that validation is skipped for an action's `input()` method. This is possible because the `validation` interceptor subclasses the `MethodFilterInterceptor`, which defines an `excludeMethods` parameter. The parameter is interpreted as a comma-separated list of method names for which the interceptor should not be executed.

We'd add a parameter to configure our previous `validationWorkflowStack` from above, in order to exclude a list of methods from validation (as the `defaultStack` does).

```
<interceptor-stack name="validationWorkflowStack">
  ...
  <interceptor-ref name="validation">
    <param name="excludeMethods">
      input,back,cancel,browse
    </param>
  </interceptor-ref>
  ...
```

The default stack for a package is defined using the `<default-interceptor-ref>` element inside a package definition. For example, the `struts-default` package defines the default interceptor like this:

```
<package name="struts-default" abstract="true">
    <!-- ... -->
    <default-interceptor-ref name="defaultStack"/>
</package>
```

We can create our own interceptor stacks within our packages and modify the default behavior using interceptor configuration parameters. This includes creating a default interceptor stack to use for all actions within the package.

As a simple (but realistic) example, we might want to create a default stack that removes interceptors that our application never uses. We'll assume that we don't want to use the `profiling` and `modelDriven` interceptors, along with the `chain` and `alias` interceptors because we never chain our actions. Our package definition would include the following, copied from the `strutsDefault` stack, with several interceptors removed:

```
<interceptors>
  <interceptor-stack name="appDefault">
    <interceptor-ref name="exception"/>
    <interceptor-ref name="servletConfig"/>
    <interceptor-ref name="prepare"/>
    <interceptor-ref name="i18n"/>
    <interceptor-ref name="debugging"/>
    <interceptor-ref name="fileUpload"/>
    <interceptor-ref name="checkbox"/>
    <interceptor-ref name="staticParams"/>
    <interceptor-ref name="actionMappingParams"/>
    <interceptor-ref name="params">
      <param name="excludeParams">dojo\..*,^struts\..*</param>
    </interceptor-ref>
    <interceptor-ref name="conversionError"/>
    <interceptor-ref name="validation">
        <param name="excludeMethods">
          input,back,cancel,browse
        </param>
    </interceptor-ref>
    <interceptor-ref name="workflow">
        <param name="excludeMethods">
          input,back,cancel,browse
        </param>
    </interceptor-ref>
  </interceptor-stack>
</interceptors>
<default-interceptor-ref name="appDefault"/>
```

Again, we see the `excludeMethods` parameter for the `validation` interceptor. If our action method naming convention differed from the Struts 2 assumptions, we could create our own list of excluded method names.

Configuring interceptors for individual actions

We can declare and configure interceptors on a per-action basis in our `<action>` elements. Configuration done this way affects the action being configured.

 It's important to note that if we declare any interceptor for an action, we must declare *all* interceptors for that action.

To demonstrate, let's assume that we have an action method named `doNotValidate()` for which validation should not be run. We could configure the `validation` interceptor to ignore that method (along with the others) like so (note that this is an incorrect example):

```
<!-- Incorrect "validation" interceptor configuration. -->
<action name="brokenConfiguration"
        class="com.packt.s2wad.ch08.BrokenConfigurationAction">
  <interceptor-ref name="validation">
    <param name="excludeMethods">
      input,back,cancel,browse,doNotValidate
    </param>
  </interceptor-ref>
</action>
```

Technically, this will do what we want. It won't validate the `doNotValidate()` method. However, we've actually configured only the `validation` interceptor here. None of the other `defaultStack` interceptors will be run. This is almost never what we want (particularly as the `validation` process relies on the `workflow` interceptor).

As declaring all the interceptors just to change the `excludeMethods` parameter would be silly, another mechanism exists. The easiest way is to use the `defaultStack` stack and configure just the `validation` interceptor. This is shown here:

```
<action name="correctConfiguration"
        class="com.packt.s2wad.ch08.NowWorkingAction">
  <interceptor-ref name="defaultStack">
    <param name="validation.excludeMethods">
```

```
        input,back,cancel,browse,doNotValidate
      </param>
    </interceptor-ref>
  </action>
```

This will configure the action to use a `defaultStack` stack and configure the `excludeMethods` parameter for the `validation` interceptor. The syntax is obvious and simple—`interceptorName.parameterName` will set the named parameter on the named interceptor. This affects the interceptor stack for *only* this particular action. When we define interceptors for an individual action, we're actually creating new instances of those interceptors, specific to the action.

The same configuration method can be used for other interceptors and interceptor stacks, including our own. If we're using a stack that contains multiple stacks, we can also set parameters using a `<param>` element. The syntax would be `stackName.interceptorName.parameterName`.

How interceptors work

Interceptors implement the `Interceptor` interface, which defines three methods: `void destroy()`, `void init()`, and `String intercept(ActionInvocation invocation)`. We'll cover implementation details when we start writing our own interceptors, but we'll look at some basics in order to understand how the included interceptors do their work.

Some interceptors do their work regardless of the action being invoked. Some only execute after checking for marker interfaces implemented by the action. The `ActionInvocation` has an `action` property, which is the actual action instance being invoked. By performing an `instanceof` check on the action being invoked, an interceptor can determine if it should process the request or continue normally.

The `intercept()` method returns a string, the return type of typical action methods. This allows interceptors to return their own result, or allows the action invocation to continue normally by returning the results of the `ActionInvocation`'s `invoke()` method. This method passes the action invocation to the next interceptor or, finally, the action itself.

 As interceptors have access to the action being invoked, they are free to change the state of the action in arbitrary ways. Because of this power, it's important to understand how interceptors work, and to be aware of interceptor and interceptor-action interaction. It's a powerful mechanism, but can lead to very interesting behavior at times. Actions do not exist in a vacuum.

Interceptors in the default stack

We'll introduce ourselves to many of the interceptors defined by Struts 2, focusing first on those in the default stack (defaultStack). The default stack contains around a dozen and a half interceptors, several of which we've already used (even if we didn't know it).

We'll cover the interceptors in the same order they're declared in the default stack because order is important. As we read through the next sections, we'll try to keep in mind that these interceptors are executed in this order, for every action invocation, when using the default stack. After we cover the default stack interceptors, we'll take a quick look at a few additional ones that are handy to know about.

The exception interceptor

The exception interceptor maps exception classes to the named Struts 2 results. In a nutshell, the exception interceptor wraps the entire action invocation, allowing exceptions thrown by the remaining interceptors and our actions (and anything called by our actions) to be caught and handled within the framework. We'll explore exceptions in the next chapter.

The alias interceptor

The alias interceptor allows us to rename an action property between actions and is primarily used with action chaining. For example, one action might have a property named "foo" while another action uses the name "bar". The alias interceptor lets us put the "foo" property into the second action's "bar" property.

If you think this seems like a good way to cause yourself trouble, you're probably right. However, it may be invaluable under certain (pathological?) circumstances. One (reasonably) legitimate use would be to transform parameters from our actions to third-party actions. A stretch, perhaps, but one never knows.

The servletConfig interceptor

The servletConfig interceptor sets various servlet-specification-related variables (for example, the session attribute map) on appropriate actions. We discussed the servletConfig interceptor when we covered the ApplicationAware, SessionAware, RequestAware, ParameterAware, ServletRequestAware, ServletResponseAware, and the ServletContextAware interfaces.

All this interceptor does is check for the implementation of each of the interfaces listed earlier (plus `PrincipalAware`) and set the appropriate action property if the action implements the corresponding interface.

For example, if our action implements `SessionAware`, it must implement the method `void setSession(Map)`. The `servletConfig` interceptor checks for an implementation of `SessionAware`. If found, it casts the action to `SessionAware` and sets the session attribute map using the `setSession()` method, using code similar to the following (it's more or less the same idea for the other interfaces):

```
public String intercept(ActionInvocation invocation)
            throws Exception {
    Object action = invocation.getAction();
    ActionContext context =
        invocation.getInvocationContext();
    if (action instanceof SessionAware) {
        ((SessionAware) action) setSession(context.getSession());
    }
```

Interceptors are not always complicated. The behavior they encapsulate may be simple, as shown in the above example. The beauty of interceptors is that they provide a known place to put cross-cutting functionality without polluting mainline code.

The prepare interceptor

The `prepare` interceptor checks for actions that implement `Preparable`, and when it finds one, it executes the action's `prepare()` method. We also saw that we can define method-specific "preparable" methods.

The interceptor checks for `prepareXxx()` methods using reflection, where `Xxx` is the action method being invoked. If we were executing an action method `list()`, the interceptor checks for `prepareList()` (and `prepareDoList()`) and calls it if found.

The `prepareXxx()` method is called before the `prepare()` method.

The prepare interceptor accepts an alwaysInvokePrepare parameter, controlling whether or not the prepare() method is invoked. It defaults to true. If we have no prepareXxx() methods, setting it to false just means that prepare() won't be called — probably not what we want. Consider a scenario where we have multiple methods for the same action. For one of them we don't want prepare() to be called, but still want its prepareXxx() method to be called. The prepare interceptor can be really handy in such situations.

The last bit of potential confusion is that the prepare interceptor is a subclass of MethodFilterInterceptor. This means we could configure the interceptor to skip calling any of the prepare() methods, based on the action method being invoked by using the excludeMethods or the includeMethods parameters. By default, it is configured to include all action methods.

The use of Preparable requires diligence. It creates non-locality between our action's code and its behavior. As the prepare methods aren't being called explicitly, it can create confusion, particularly to those unfamiliar with the framework. Although it's convenient, knowing the complete request flow, including the interceptors, is important. "Spooky action at a distance", applied to web frameworks.

The i18n interceptor

The i18n interceptor handles setting the locale by examining the request for a parameter named request_locale (by default). Including the parameter sets the locale in the user's session. The interceptor then removes the parameter, so the framework doesn't try to set it on our actions.

This interceptor accepts an optional parameterName parameter, naming the parameter the interceptor will look for. It also accepts an attributeName parameter, defining the session key where the locale will be stored.

The chain interceptor

The chain interceptor works along with action chaining, which we examined earlier. The chain interceptor makes the current action's properties available to the next.

The chain interceptor accepts both the excludes and the includes parameters, defining defining lists of parameters that will be excluded or included between the actions. If an includes parameter is provided, only those parameters will be set on the chained action.

The debugging interceptor

The debugging interceptor examines the request for a debug parameter. If it finds one, the interceptor can present several views into the current OGNL value stack. Acceptable debug values are "xml", "console", "command", and "browser".

Using **xml** returns an XML document containing the parameters, context, session, and value stack. **Console** pops up a window where we can type OGNL expressions, which will be evaluated and displayed. **Command** is used by the console debugger and evaluates an OGNL expression, returning a string. **Browser** displays the field values of the object passed in the object parameters.

Note that if "xml" is chosen, the document returned will contain *only* the XML OGNL dump, not the actual page being requested. For this reason, it can sometimes be more useful to use the <s:debug> tag in the JSP—the OGNL dump is then included on the page being requested.

The profiling interceptor

The profiling interceptor provides minimal interceptor and action profiling information when in development mode, and the profiling request parameter is set to true.

The profiling parameter name may be changed using the profiling interceptor's profilingKey parameter. This allows us to use a different parameter (other than profiling) if, for instance, we already have a profiling parameter in our form. The interceptor removes the profiling parameter, so it won't be set on our action.

Bear in mind that only interceptors configured after the profiling interceptor will be timed. The default stack puts the profiling interceptor near the middle of the stack. This means some interceptors won't be profiled.

The profiling output appears in our console, and looks similar to the following:

```
2008-08-27 20:47:10,306 INFO  com.opensymphony.xwork2.util.profiling.
UtilTimerStack.info:31 - [102ms] - invoke:
  [102ms] - interceptor: scopedModelDriven
    [102ms] - invoke:
      [102ms] - interceptor: modelDriven
        [102ms] - invoke:
          [102ms] - interceptor: fileUpload
            [102ms] - invoke:
              [102ms] - interceptor: checkbox
 . . .
```

It's a low-resolution way to get a quick sanity-check on how long things are taking, including our action invocation.

The scopedModelDriven interceptor

The `scopedModelDriven` interceptor is closely related to the `modelDriven` interceptor discussed below, but retrieves a model object from a specified scope if the action being invoked implements the `ScopedModelDriven` interface. Because of the overlap with the `modelDriven` interceptor, we'll look at the `modelDriven` interceptor first, and then return to `scopedModelDriven`.

The modelDriven interceptor

The `modelDriven` interceptor checks to see if the action being invoked implements `ModelDriven`. If it does, this interceptor calls the action's `getModel()` method and pushes the results onto the stack.

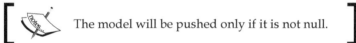

The model will be pushed only if it is not null.

This means that in our JSP, the model object, and not the action, will be the topmost object on the stack. OGNL expressions are applied against the model object first.

Consider the following example. We have a `ModelDriven` action, `getModel()` returns an instance of the `Recipe` class, and our JSP page uses the property tag to access the `name` property:

```
<s:property value="name"/>
```

We'll be calling `getName()` to the topmost stack item—the `Recipe` instance. Similarly, a form tag whose name attribute is `name` will set the value of the object returned by `getModel()`, which again is our `Recipe` instance.

This can be both useful and confusing, as accessing action properties directly becomes a bit trickier. It's particularly irritating if both the model and the action expose a property of the same name and we need the action's version. We then resort to tricky OGNL. For example, if we've implemented `ModelDriven`, and our model and action both expose a property named `hideAndSeek`, we can access the action's property in our JSP as shown here:

```
<s:property value="[1].hideAndSeek"/>
```

The [] notation provides a way to directly access the nth object on the stack. [0] would refer to the model object and [1] is our action. (What's [2]? Usually a DefaultTextProvider). Further value stack exploring is left as an exercise for the reader.

If all the properties we need are in our model object, there aren't any issues.

Getting back to the scopedModelDriven interceptor

The scopedModelDriven interceptor automatically retrieves the model object from the configured scope (it defaults to request, but session may be more appropriate). The scopedModelDriven interceptor accepts three parameters:

- className defines the class of the model object
- name defines the key under which to store the model object
- scope defines the scope

If a model object cannot be retrieved from the configured scope, one will be instantiated.

The scopedModelDriven interceptor can be very handy for creating wizard-like sequences or multi-page forms. The same caveat about accessing action properties as discussed above applies equally to scopedModelDriven.

The fileUpload interceptor

The fileUpload interceptor, as we'd expect, helps with file uploads. We may recall that when we uploaded the files, there were several file-related action properties available to us. It is the fileUpload interceptor which sets these properties.

The fileUpload interceptor takes two parameters— maximumSize and allowedTypes. The maximumSize parameter sets the maximum file size allowed (the default is approximately 2MB).

 Note that our server may set its own limit. For example, Tomcat sets a ~2MB limit. Therefore, this parameter alone may not produce the expected behavior.

The allowedTypes parameter is a comma-separated list of accepted content (MIME) types .

The `fileUplaod` interceptor uses several default error message keys:

- `struts.messages.error.uploading` indicates a general upload error
- `struts.messages.error.file.too.large` indicates a `maximumSize` violation
- `struts.messages.error.content.type.not.allowed` indicates that an unallowed type was uploaded

We can substitute our own values for these messages in our own resource files.

Recall from the chapter on form handling that the file upload interceptor deletes the file once the action is executed. We must copy the file in our action if we need it preserved.

The checkbox interceptor

The `checkbox` interceptor is responsible for submitting the value of unchecked checkboxes. If we recall the `<s:checkbox>` tag discussed earlier, we'll remember that it generated a hidden `<input>` element along with the checkbox element.

The hidden element is named by appending "__checkbox_" to the name of the related checkbox field. The `checkbox` interceptor first checks for the checkbox value itself. (Remember! Unchecked checkboxes are not submitted at all, which is just how browsers work.) If it's not checked, it's not submitted, and the `checkbox` interceptor adds the unchecked value to the request parameters.

The default unchecked value is `Boolean.FALSE.toString()`. The `checkbox` interceptor takes a `setUncheckedValue` parameter that can be used to override this default value, but it's important to note that the unchecked value is the same for all checkboxes on a page.

The staticParams interceptor

The `staticParams` interceptor sets the action parameters defined in the Struts 2 configuration file using the `<param>` elements inside of the action configurations. In addition, if the action implements the `Parameterizable` interface, a map of static parameters will be set on the action.

This doesn't mean the parameters are declared with the Java `static` keyword. They are "static" in the sense that they're defined in a configuration file.

The params interceptor

We've seen the params interceptor throughout the book, which sets the action properties from the request parameters. The default rules for what parameters may be set are somewhat complicated, but basically boil down to ensuring the parameter, and parameter value, isn't something that would cause a security issue through crafting values that are meaningful to OGNL (assignment, multiple expressions, or a context reference), aren't method executions, aren't protected Struts variables, and so on. (Looking at the interceptor parameters in the struts-default.xml file gives the exact definition.)

If the action being invoked implements ParameterNameAware, the params interceptor will query the action for a whitelist of parameters to allow or a blacklist of parameters to ignore, set using the includeParams and excludeParams respectively.

The params interceptor also accepts an ordered parameter (which is false by default) that, if set, guarantees that action properties are set **top-down**. This means subcomponent properties will be set after the top-level action properties. This would be very useful, though a bit difficult to understand without further explanation.

Finally, the params interceptor also extends MethodFilterInterceptor. So, if there's an action method for which no parameters should be set, we can configure it to exclude a set of methods.

If our action implements NoParameters, no parameters will be set on it.

Ordered parameters and ad hoc factory patterns

Ordered parameter setting using the ordered parameter allows for ad hoc factory patterns without using the Preparable interface. The nutshell version is that the number of periods (.) in a property's name determines its depth. If we have an action property named userId, it will be set before a property named user.firstName and user.firstName would be set before address.label.fullName.

Implementing a factory is as simple as having, for example, a modelClass property and instantiating an instance of that class in the setModelClass(String modelClass) method. If we then have model parameters, such as model.firstName, ordered parameter setting guarantees that they'll be set after the modelClass property (after the object has been instantiated by the setModelClass() method).

We can also use a primary key action property to retrieve a persisted object from the database. For example, if we expose a `userId` action property, the `userId` setter can retrieve an actual user object from the database. User parameters, such as `user.firstName` and `user.email`, are then set after the `userId` property that was used to retrieve the user object itself.

Using ordered parameters can be a very handy technique and provides an alternative to the `Preparable` interface.

The conversionError interceptor

The `conversionError` interceptor checks for type conversion errors. If found, the errors are then added to our action's error list, which will then be checked by the `workflow` interceptor (detailed shortly). Often, our conversion errors will also be reflected by validation errors, leading to multiple error messages for the same field (we've already seen this!).

This can be avoided by creating an interceptor stack with the `conversionError` interceptor removed, as we saw when we looked at configuring our own interceptor stacks. This may or may not be what a particular application requires. I don't recommend removing it by default, but at least now we know how to remove it.

The validation interceptor

We've already used the `validation` interceptor, which runs all appropriate validation on our action, adding field and action error messages if appropriate. However, the interceptor does not alter the request flow. The next interceptor in the default stack—`workflow`—determines what happens if there are validation errors (when appropriate).

The `validation` interceptor is also a subclass of `MethodFilterInterceptor`. As such, it accepts an `excludeMethods` parameter. This is a comma-separated list of action method names for which validation should not be run.

The default stack's default list of excluded methods (`input`, `back`, `cancel`, and `browse`) is defined in `struts-default.xml`. If we have a consistent list of methods for which validation should not be run, we can create our own interceptor stack and set the `excludeMethods` parameter, or we can configure it on a per-action basis (as seen earlier).

The workflow interceptor

The workflow interceptor just checks to see if the action being invoked implements ValidationAware and, if it does, checks for the presence of validation errors. If errors are present, the workflow interceptor does not continue normal action invocation. It returns the string "input", bringing us back to the page that caused the validation error. This interceptor modifies the application flow based on the presence of validation errors.

The result returned when there are validation errors is configured with the inputResultName parameter, the default is "input". If our action returned normally to the input form on a successful submit, we might just set inputResultName to success. However, if we do a redirect, we will lose our validation error messages (but a dispatch will always work).

The workflow interceptor is another subclass of MethodFilterInterceptor. We can configure a list of methods to be excluded from workflow processing with the excludeMethods parameter (or to include using includeMethods).

Other important interceptors and interceptor stacks

There are a few other important interceptors not included in the default interceptor stack and a predefined interceptor stack (in addition to the default stack) which are often helpful.

The token interceptor

We saw the token interceptor briefly during our discussion of the <s:token> tag. Remember, it's not included in the default interceptor stack. The token interceptor is also a subclass of MethodFilterInterceptor.

The store interceptor

The store interceptor can save (and restore) action errors and messages in session for preservation across redirects. This is useful, for example, for multiple-screen forms (such as wizards) where we need to redirect to an earlier action. Normally, action errors and messages are stored in the request (technically, they're stored in the action, which is created per-request), so they're lost across redirects.

The most common means of configuring this interceptor is by providing an operationMode parameter in the action configuration. Setting operationMode to STORE will put the action errors and messages into session. The action that needs to retrieve the messages would configure the interceptor by setting operationMode to RETRIEVE. This causes the interceptor to get the errors and messages from the session, and then set them on the action.

The roles Interceptor

The roles interceptor allows an action to configure a list of roles which are either allowed or denied to execute privileges for an action. The default implementation uses the standard HttpServletRequest.isUserInRole() method to determine the current user's roles.

This interceptor can be a handy one to subclass if, for example, our application uses roles defined in our application database. By creating our own implementation of the isAllowed(HttpServletRequest request, Object action), we could check a user object in session for a given role using our own role mechanism.

The clearSession interceptor

The clearSession interceptor does exactly what it says—it clears the session. Typically, this would be configured on a per-action basis, probably by just adding it before the application's default stack. For example, this interceptor would be one way of handling that aspect of a logout process.

The paramsPrepareParamsStack interceptor stack

The paramsPrepareParamsStack interceptor stack is similar to the default stack, but includes an additional params interceptor before the prepare interceptor. In the default stack, the params interceptor is called after the prepare interceptor calls an action's prepare() method(s) (if the action implements Preparable, of course).

With the default stack, if the prepare method requires a parameter (for example, the primary key of a persisted object used to retrieve it from a database), it will fail because the parameters are set on the action after the prepare method is called.

The paramsPrepareParamsStack sets parameters on the action before calling the prepare method(s), and then sets parameters again afterwards.

Writing our own interceptors

The interceptors included in Struts 2 are enough to write entire applications, and the default stack is often perfectly adequate for our needs. However, interceptors are a great place to put functionality required across broad sections of an application. Checking for login status, action logging (for clickstreams, audit trails, etc.), and so on, are easily implemented using interceptors.

As an example, we'll write an interceptor that trims input strings and configure it so that it runs before the `params` interceptor. This fixes an issue in the current type conversion system—a field being converted to a numeric format, for example, will end up as a conversion error if there are leading or trailing spaces entered in the form field.

Our `BigDecimal` type converter included string trimming, but they were the only types that benefitted. Other numeric conversions suffer from the same issue. A better solution is to trim all form fields (with a simple implementation to exclude properties from trimming), so the existing type converters always work with trimmed strings. This avoids an entire class of potential errors. Also, we wouldn't need to trim string properties in our action.

It is important to note that interceptors must be thread-safe. Unlike actions, which are instantiated for every request, interceptors are instantiated once per interceptor stack. Also note that when we configure interceptors on a per-action basis, we're actually creating new interceptor instances. So, the parameters we set on interceptors inside action configurations affect neither the default interceptor stack, nor the interceptor stacks of other actions.

The trim interceptor

Interceptors must implement the `Interceptor` interface:

```
public interface Interceptor extends Serializable {
    void destroy();
    void init();
    String intercept(ActionInvocation invocation)
        throws Exception;
}
```

As with many of the other interceptors, we'll subclass `MethodFilterInterceptor`, giving us the ability to turn off string trimming for specified methods (although we might never need to). `MethodFilterInterceptor` extends the `AbstractInterceptor` class, which also provides default implementations of `init()` and `destroy()`.

`MethodFilterInterceptor` expects subclasses to implement `doIntercept()`. The `intercept()` method handles the decision making of whether or not the interceptor should be invoked for the current method. If the interceptor should be invoked, the method then runs the subclass's doIntercept() method. Here's the complete implementation, imports elided:

```
package com.packt.s2wad.ch08.interceptors;
public class TrimInterceptor extends MethodFilterInterceptor {
    private List<String> excluded = new ArrayList<String>();

    public String doIntercept(ActionInvocation invocation)
                throws Exception {
        Map<String, Object> parameters =
            invocation.getInvocationContext().getParameters();
        for (String param : parameters.keySet()) {
            if (isIncluded(param)) {
                String[] vals =
                    (String[]) parameters.get(param);
                for (int i = 0; i < vals.length; i++) {
                    vals[i] = vals[i].trim();
                }
            }
        }
        return invocation.invoke();
    }

    public boolean isIncluded(String param) {
        for (String exclude : excluded) {
            if (param.startsWith(exclude)) {
                return false;
            }
        }
        return true;
    }

    public void setExcludedParams(String excludedParams) {
        for (String s : StringUtils.split(excludedParams, ",")) {
            excluded.add(s.trim());
        }
    }
}
```

We'll work our way from the bottom up.

The `setExcludedParams()` method handles the `excludedParams` configuration parameter, which is a comma-separated list of parameters to be excluded from trimming. It's there to:

- Handle cases where a field might need leading or trailing spaces
- Help prove that it works

It simply splits the string (again using Apache Commons Lang's `StringUtils`) and then puts each value into a list of excluded parameter names, which are actually prefixes (we'll get to that).

The `isIncluded()` method determines if a parameter should be trimmed or not. It simply checks to see if the parameter name starts with anything found in the excluded list. This helps us exclude something like a JavaBean by specifying just the bean name. A bean's nested and/or indexed properties, like `bean.aProperty` or `bean[0].firstName`, would also be excluded. In a production-ready version, we might lean towards a regular expression-based solution.

The `doIntercept()` method actually processes the invocation. It loops through all the parameters, checking to see if they should be included in the trimming process. If a given parameter has to be trimmed, it loops over the parameter values, trimming each. When finished, it continues with the normal program flow.

Configuring the trim interceptor

We'll set up a package just for testing this interceptor. We'll define a shortened interceptor stack which only includes the interceptors we need for the test, and inserts the new `trim` interceptor before the `params` interceptor.

We'll also configure two actions, implemented by the same class, differing only in the `trim` parameter configuration:

```
<!DOCTYPE struts PUBLIC
    "-//Apache Software Foundation//DTD Struts Configuration 2.0//EN"
    "http://struts.apache.org/dtds/struts-2.0.dtd">
<struts>
  <package name="interceptor-examples"
           namespace="/interceptors" extends="struts-default">
    <interceptors>
      <interceptor name="trim"
        class="com.packt.s2wad.ch08.interceptors.TrimInterceptor" />

      <interceptor-stack name="testTrim">
```

```xml
        <interceptor-ref name="exception" />
        <interceptor-ref name="trim"/>
        <interceptor-ref name="params">
          <param name="excludeParams">
            dojo\..*,^struts\..*
          </param>
        </interceptor-ref>
        <interceptor-ref name="conversionError" />
        <interceptor-ref name="validation">
          <param name="excludeMethods">
            input,back,cancel,browse
          </param>
        </interceptor-ref>
        <interceptor-ref name="workflow">
          <param name="excludeMethods">
            input,back,cancel,browse
          </param>
        </interceptor-ref>
      </interceptor-stack>
    </interceptors>

    <default-interceptor-ref name="testTrim"/>

    <action name="trim"
        class="com.packt.s2wad.ch08.interceptors.TrimAction">
      <result type="redirectAction">trim!input</result>
      <result name="input">
        /WEB-INF/jsps/interceptors/trim-input.jsp
      </result>
    </action>

    <action name="trim2"
        class="com.packt.s2wad.ch08.interceptors.TrimAction">
      <interceptor-ref name="testTrim">
        <param name="trim.excludedParams">excludedParam</param>
      </interceptor-ref>
      <result type="redirectAction">trim!input</result>
      <result name="input">
        /WEB-INF/jsps/interceptors/trim-input.jsp
      </result>
    </action>
  </package>
</struts>
```

Note that we wedged our new interceptor between the `exception` and the `params` interceptors. Our actions are very simple. They are identical except that "trim2" sets the "excludedParams" interceptor parameter on the new "trim" interceptor.

The Test Action

Our test action is similarly straightforward. It defines two `BigDecimal` properties. We use validation annotations to make them both required and within a double range, with no range specified — it's just to make sure they're numeric. Imports elided again.

```
package com.packt.s2wad.ch08.interceptors;
public class TrimAction extends ActionSupport {
    private BigDecimal includedParam;
    private BigDecimal excludedParam;

    public String execute() {
        System.out.println(String.format(
                "Included: %f,  Excluded: %f",
                includedParam, excludedParam));
        return SUCCESS;
    }

    @RequiredFieldValidator(message="Included is required")
    @DoubleRangeFieldValidator(message="Included BigDecimal Error")
    public void setIncludedParam(BigDecimal included) {
        includedParam = includedLong;
    }

    @RequiredFieldValidator(message="Excluded is required")
    @DoubleRangeFieldValidator(message="Excluded BigDecimal Error")
    public void setExcludedParam(BigDecimal excluded) {
        excludedParam = excluded;
    }
}
```

The `execute()` method dumps our values to the console, so that we can verify that they were converted. The form itself has just two text fields, one for each action property.

Testing the trim interceptor

When we visit `/interceptors/trim!input.action`, we see the two form fields. If we add leading and/or trailing spaces to our values, and submit the form (we use numeric values), we'll be returned to the input form.

If we visit `/interceptors/trim2!input.action` and enter a number of leading and/or trailing spaces for both values, we'll get something different on form submission — the value we excluded from trimming signals a conversion error. We see the included value returned to the form in its trimmed state while the excluded value maintains its extra spaces. It wasn't trimmed.

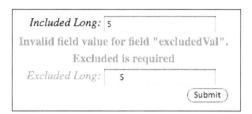

Modifying application flow with interceptors

One thing we might want to do with an interceptor is to modify the application flow (after the action executes but before the result is rendered). We might need to check the state of something at the application level that could have changed, check for a particular exception thrown by an action, and so on. This is what the `workflow` interceptor does — if there are validation errors, we're returned to our "input" result.

Our contrived use case for this functionality is that we're using Struts 2 actions written by a third-party. We don't have access to the source, and the string results they return don't match our application's naming convention. Therefore, we need to map their result values to ours. (Cut me some slack here — it could happen.)

We'll write a `ResultMappingInterceptor` to deal with the third-party's choices of values returned by the actions. The action `CrazyResultNames` has three methods: `execute()`, `input()`, and `notmapped()`. These methods return `strangeSuccess`, `irritatingInput`, and `notmapped` respectively. We'd like to have `execute()` and `input()` return `success` and `input`, and leave the `notmapped()` result alone.

Configuring the result

In this example, we'll start off by imagining how we'd like to configure the interceptor. Here, we'll configure a single action to use the interceptor:

```
<action name="mapping"
    class="com.packt.s2wad.ch08.interceptors.CrazyResultNames">
  <interceptor-ref name="defaultStack" />
  <interceptor-ref name="resultMapper">
    <param name="resultMap">
```

```
        #{"strangeSuccess" : "success", "irritatingInput" : "input"}
      </param>
    </interceptor-ref>
    <result name="input">
      /WEB-INF/jsps/interceptors/crazy-input.jsp
    </result>
    <result name="success">
      /WEB-INF/jsps/interceptors/crazy-success.jsp
    </result>
    <result name="notmapped">
      /WEB-INF/jsps/interceptors/crazy-notmapped.jsp
    </result>
  </action>
```

We're using the default stack, but adding the mapping interceptor. Here, we're just appending it to the end of the default interceptor stack. This means it will run after all the interceptors in the default stack have been executed. This may not always be what we want.

The parameter supplied to the `resultMapper` interceptor looks odd. However, the intent is clear—we want to provide a map of "from, to" pairs. The first element is the result name returned by the action, the second is what we'd want the action to return. The interceptor will then look for an occurrence of the first string and, when found, return the second string instead.

In fact, the unusual syntax is a simple OGNL. The #{} characters create an immediate map. It's not quite that simple because our interceptor will receive a string. Fortunately we can simply evaluate it ourselves. We could pass in a comma-separated list of strings, "from1, to1, from2, to2" and so on. However, in this case, we feel that the map syntax expresses our intent more clearly.

Writing the ResultMappingInterceptor

Our first stab looks like this (don't type it in yet—trust me. Imports elided):

```
package com.packt.s2wad.ch08.interceptors;
public class ResultMappingInterceptor extends AbstractInterceptor {
    private Map<String, String> mappings;

    public String intercept(ActionInvocation invocation)
                throws Exception {
        return mapResult(invocation.invoke());
    }

    public String mapResult(String from) {
```

```
        return mappings.containsKey(from)
                ? mappings.get(from) : from;
    }

    public void setResultMap(String resultMap) {
        try {
            Object o = Ognl.getValue(resultMap, null);
            if (o != null && o instanceof Map) {
                mappings = (Map) o;
            }
        } catch (OgnlException e) {
            e.printStackTrace();
        }
    }
}
```

We'll work backwards again. We use a JavaBean-style property setter to process our interceptor's parameter. In the setMap() method, we use an OGNL utility method, getValue(), to evaluate our interceptor parameter (error handling has been elided for brevity).

The mapResult() method just checks the map for the result key and, if found, returns the map value—the result that we really want the action to return. If the result isn't mapped, it just returns the original result value.

The intercept() method gets the invocation result and returns the mapped result.

But it doesn't really work. If we visit /interceptors/mapping.action, we get an error message, claiming that the result string was strangeSuccess despite the presence of our interceptor. A trip to /interceptors/mapping!input.action is met with a similar fate. Visiting /interceptors/mapping!notmapped.action, of course, works since there's a result mapping and a JSP file. But something has clearly gone wrong.

Writing the ResultMappingInterceptor and making it work

It turns out that calling invocation.invoke() actually returns *after* the result has already been rendered. This is somewhat counter-intuitive (in this case, we need to change our intuition, as that's just how it is).

There is a solution, of course—adding a `PreResultListener` to the action invocation. `PreResultListener` defines a single method, `beforeResult()`, which is run before the result is executed. The result code is provided as an argument to `beforeResult()`. We use that value to map the result, setting the mapped result on the invocation. Finally, our modified `intercept()` method ends up looking like this:

```
public String intercept(ActionInvocation invocation)
            throws Exception {
    invocation.addPreResultListener(new PreResultListener() {
        public void beforeResult(ActionInvocation invocation,
                                 String resultCode) {
            invocation.setResultCode(mapResult(resultCode));
        }
    });
    return mapResult(invocation.invoke());
}
```

Now, when we visit the previous URLs, we find that we're correctly mapping from the crazy result names of our third-party actions and are sent to the appropriate result pages.

Summary

In this chapter, we explore Struts 2 interceptors. The chapter covers most of the interceptors provided by the framework, including some of the most important ones dealing with form parameters and validation, and also how they can be configured. The chapter also tells us how we can create our own interceptors to provide application-wide functionality not provided by Struts 2, along with some ideas about the ways in which these interceptors can be applied to our own applications.

In the next chapter, we'll cover some topics relating to exception handling, application logging, and error handling in general.

References

A reader can refer to the following:

- Struts 2 Interceptors and Writing Struts 2 Interceptors:

    http://struts.apache.org/2.x/docs/interceptors.html

    http://struts.apache.org/2.x/docs/writing-interceptors.html

9
Exceptions and Logging

In the previous chapter, we were introduced to interceptors, one of the most powerful aspects of Struts 2. In this chapter, we'll cover something much more mundane, but critical—exception handling and logging. We will explore:

- The Struts 2 declarative exception handling mechanism
- Some general exception handling practices that will help us create robust applications
- Logging configuration and practices to help us take a peek inside our application's execution, and help determine what went wrong when errors occur

Handling exceptions in Struts 2

Struts 2 provides a declarative exception handling mechanism that can be configured globally (for an entire package), or for a specific action. This capability can reduce the amount of exception handling code necessary inside actions under some circumstances, most notably when underlying systems, such as our services, throw runtime exceptions (exceptions that we don't need to wrap in a try/catch or declare that a method throws).

To sum it up, we can map exception classes to Struts 2 results.

 The exception handling mechanism depends on the `exception` interceptor we saw in the previous chapter. If we modify our interceptor stack, we must keep that in mind. In general, removing the exception interceptor isn't preferred.

Global exception mappings

Setting up a global exception handler result is as easy as adding a global exception mapping element to a Struts 2 configuration file package definition and configuring its result. For example, to catch generic runtime exceptions, we could add the following:

```
<global-exception-mappings>
  <exception-mapping result="runtime"
                     exception="java.lang.RuntimeException"/>
</global-exception-mappings>
```

This means that if a `java.lang.RuntimeException` (or a subclass) is thrown, the framework will take us to the `runtime` result. The `runtime` result may be declared in a `<global-results>` element, an action configuration, or both. The most specific result will be used. This implies that an action's result configuration might take precedence over a global exception mapping.

For example, consider the global exception mapping shown in the previous code snippet. If we configure an action as follows, and a `RuntimeException` is thrown, we'll see the locally defined `runtime` result, even if there is a global `runtime` result.

```
<action name="except1"
     class="com.packt.s2wad.ch09.examples.exceptions.Except1">
  <result name="runtime">
    /WEB-INF/jsps/ch9/exceptions/except1-runtime.jsp
  </result>
  ...
```

This can occasionally lead to confusion if a result name happens to collide with a result used for an exception. However, this can happen with global results anyway (a case where a naming convention for global results can be handy).

Action-specific exception mappings

In addition to overriding the result used for an exception mapping, we can also override a global exception mapping on a per-action basis. For example, if an action needs to use a result named `runtime2` as the destination of a `RuntimeException`, we can configure an exception mapping specific to that action.

```
<action name="except2"
     class="com.packt.s2wad.ch09.examples.exceptions.Except1">
  <exception-mapping result="runtime2"
                     exception="java.lang.RuntimeException"/>
  ...
```

As with our earlier examples, the `runtime2` result may be configured either as a global result or as an action-specific result.

Accessing the exception

We have many options regarding how to handle exceptions. We can show the user a generic "Something horrible has happened!" page, we can take the user back and allow them to retry the operation or refill the input form, and so on. The appropriate course of action depends on the application and, most likely, on the type of exception.

We can display exception-specific information as well. The `exception` interceptor pushes an exception encapsulation object onto the stack with `exception` and `exceptionStack` properties. While the stack trace is probably not appropriate for user-level error pages, the exception can be used to help create a useful error message, provide I18N property keys for messages (or values used in messages), suggest possible remedies, and so on.

The simplest example of accessing the exception property from our JSP is to simply display the exception message. For example, if we threw a `RuntimeException`, we might create it as follows:

```
throw new
    RuntimeException("Runtime thrown from ThrowingAction");
```

Our exception result page, then, could access the message using the usual property tag (or JSTL, if we're taking advantage of Struts 2's custom request processor):

```
<s:property value="exception.message"/>
```

The underlying action is still available on the stack—it's the next object on the value stack. It can be accessed from the JSP as usual, as long as we're not trying to access properties named `exception` or `exceptionStack`, which would be masked by the exception holder. (We can still access an action property named `exception` using OGNL's immediate stack index notation— `[1].exception`.)

Architecting exceptions and exception handling

We have pretty good control over what is displayed for our application exceptions. It's customizable based on exception type, and may be overridden on a per-action basis. However, to make use of this flexibility, we require a well-thought-out exception policy in our application. There are some general principles we can follow to help make this easier.

Checked versus unchecked exceptions

Before we start, let's recall that Java offers two main types of exceptions—checked and unchecked. Checked exceptions are exceptions we declare with a `throws` keyword or wrapped in a `try/catch` block. Unchecked exceptions are runtime exceptions or a subclass.

It isn't always clear what type we should use when writing our code or creating our exceptions. It's been the subject of much debate over the years, but some guidelines have become apparent.

One clear thing about checked exceptions is that they aren't always worth the aggravation they cause, but may be useful when the programmer has a reasonable chance of recovering from the exception.

One issue with checked exceptions is that unless they're caught and wrapped in a more abstract exception (coming up next), we're actually circumventing some of the benefits of encapsulation. One of the benefits being circumvented is that when exceptions are declared as being thrown all the way up a call hierarchy, all of the classes involved are forced to know something about the class throwing the exception. It's relatively rare that this exposure is justifiable.

Application-specific exceptions

One of the more useful exception techniques is to create application-specific exception classes. A compelling feature of providing our own exception classes is that we can include useful diagnostic information in the exception class itself. These classes are like any other Java class. They can contain methods, properties, and constructors.

For example, let's assume a service that throws an exception when the user calling the service doesn't have access rights to the service. One way to create and throw this exception would be as follows:

```
throw new RuntimeException("User " + user.getId()
        + " does not have access to the 'update' service.");
```

However, there are some issues with this approach. It's awkward from the Struts 2's standpoint. Because it's a `RuntimeException`, we have only one option for handling the exception—mapping a `RuntimeException` to a result. Yes, we could map the exception type per-action, but that gets unwieldy. It also doesn't help if we need to map two different types of `RuntimeExceptions` to two different results.

Another potential issue would arise if we had a process that examined exceptions and did something useful with them. For example, we might send an email with user details based on the above exception. This would amount to parsing the exception message, pulling out the user ID, and using it to get user details for inclusion in the email.

This is where we'd need to create an exception class of our own, subclassed from RuntimeException. The class would have encapsulated exception related information, and a mechanism to differentiate between the different types of exceptions.

A third benefit comes when we wrap lower-level exceptions—for example, a Spring-related exception. Rather than create a Spring dependency up the entire call chain, we'd wrap it in our own exception, abstracting the lower-level exception. This allows us to change the underlying implementation and aggregate differing exception types under one (or more) application-specific exception.

One way of creating the above scenario would be to create an exception class that takes a User object and a message as its constructor arguments:

```
package com.packt.s2wad.ch09.exceptions;
public class UserAccessException extends RuntimeException {
    private User user;
    private String msg;
    public UserAccessException(User user, String msg) {
        this.user = user;
        this.msg = msg;
    }
    public String getMessage() {
        return "User " + user.getId() + " " + msg;
    }
}
```

We can now create an exception mapping for a UserAccessException (as well as a generic RuntimeException if we need it). In addition, the exception carries along with it the information needed to create useful messages:

```
throw new UserAccessException(user,
        "does not have access to the 'update' service.");
```

While we'll explore other aspects of "self-documenting" code in Chapter 14, it's worth pointing out that this could be made even safer, in the sense of ensuring that it's only used in the ways in which it is intended. We could add an enum to the class to encapsulate the reasons the exception can be thrown, including the text for each reason. We'll add the following inside our UserAccessException:

```
public enum Reason {
    NO_ROLE("does not have role"),
    NO_ACCESS("does not have access");
    private String message;
    private Reason(String message) {
        this.message = message;
    }
    public String getMessage() { return message; }
};
```

We'll also modify the constructor and getMessage() method to use the new Reason enumeration.

```
public UserAccessException(User user, Reason reason) {
    this.user = user;
    this.reason = reason;
}
public String getMessage() {
    return String.format("User %d %s.",
                user.getId(), reason.getMessage());
}
```

Now, when we throw the exception, we explicitly know that we're using the exception class correctly (at least type-wise). The string message for each of the exception reasons is encapsulated within the exception class itself.

```
throw new UserAccessException(user,
            UserAccessException.Reason.NO_ACCESS);
```

With Java 5's static imports, it might make even more sense to create static helper methods in the exception class, leading to the concise, but understandable code:

```
throw userHasNoAccess(user);
```

I've been accused of wanting my entire application to be a single line of code. What I do know is that the easier it is to read a chunk of code, the better the application is. There are limits on how far this should be taken—the static helper method may be beyond the point of usefulness, but the idea is sound.

Reading our code out loud is often a useful indicator of how "fluent" it is (this will be covered in Chapter 14). However, it can be an enlightening exercise.

Abstracting underlying exceptions

Another useful technique also involves creating application-specific exceptions whose purpose is largely to encapsulate and abstract underlying exceptions.

For example, consider a service object that may throw one of several vendor-specific checked exceptions that don't share a common subclass. Rather than configure Struts 2 to handle each exception separately (particularly when we don't care about the specifics at the application level, beyond the fact that there was a general service failure), we can configure a single application-specific exception that encapsulates both the underlying cause, and provides more contextual information as compared to the underlying exception.

We might have several implementations of a given service class. We might have an implementation that uses Hibernate to perform actual database access and another that uses hard-coded test data for testing failure modes. If the service object is designed to return a general-purpose service exception, we need to only configure that exception, leaving our application free of implementation details regarding the underlying service.

Our actual service implementation might look like the following, where SpecificDaoException is something thrown from a deeper layer, such as Hibernate:

```
public void aServiceMethod(...) {
    try {
        ourDao.daoOperation(...);
    } catch (SpecificDaoException e) {
        throw new ApplicationSpecificServiceException(
            "Exception handling the operation");
    }
}
```

On the other hand, a test service implementation, might just throw an exception while we're testing failure modes (we'll cover this further in the testing chapter):

```
public void aServiceMethod(...) {
    throw new ApplicationSpecificServiceException(
        "Testing failure mode foo");
}
```

In addition, the general-purpose, application-specific exception could provide a constructor accepting a `Throwable`. This means the underlying exception information isn't lost and can be logged for later examination. (Yes, exception chaining can lead to mile-long stack traces, and is not always appropriate.)

Handling exceptions

Have you ever seen code like this?

```
try {
    doSomething();
} catch (Exception e) {
}
```

Don't ever write that. If you see it, fix it. It's assuming several things, the worst of which is that the thrown exception is harmless. It might be harmless, but it might also be an `EndOfTheWorldException` we actually care about. It also assumes that the action taken during the catch is appropriate for all thrown exceptions—again, possible, but unlikely.

As mentioned in the earlier sections, it might make sense to convert the underlying exception to an application-specific exception. For example, if our imaginary database layer threw a `UninitializedCollectionException` while retrieving a recipe's ingredients, we might wrap it in a `RecipeServiceException`. We might even wrap it in an even more generic `DatabaseException`, making sure we pass the `UninitializedCollectionException` in its constructor to preserve the context of the original exception.

Logging

Most Struts 2 systems provide detailed logging information. Logging can be configured on several levels to control what systems are logged, and how much information each system logs.

Most of the systems use the **Commons Logging library**, a thin wrapper around various logging libraries. XWork uses its own log wrapper (and there are valid reasons not to use Commons Logging), but it is similarly configurable.

We'll take a look at how to configure Log4J, a popular logging library, and one of the logging systems Commons Logging works with. The only requirement for using Log4J is to provide the Log4J library on our classpath—Commons Logging knows how to initialize it.

Introduction to logging

There are two main things we should keep in mind about logging:

1. There are several logging levels that control logging verbosity.

2. Log types and levels are configurable for package hierarchies (including specific classes), and the most specific log configuration wins.

Log4J (and Commons Logging) defines six logging levels, ordered here by verbosity level (TRACE is the most verbose):

1. TRACE
2. DEBUG
3. INFO
4. WARN
5. ERROR
6. FATAL

Java's `java.util.logging.Level` defines its own set of standard logging levels: ALL, FINEST, FINER, FINE, CONFIG, INFO, WARNING, SEVERE, and OFF. Which level we target depends on the logging library chosen and/or our runtime environment.

Each of our log messages, then, will exist in one of these levels. For example, exceptions might be logged at the ERROR level, whereas detailed program flow might be logged at the TRACE level, which would normally be seen only during development.

Logging is configured at the package and class level. First, we'll look at how to use logging in our Java code, and then we'll look at logging configuration.

Using the loggers

In general, we'll use `Log` objects in our classes. Logs accept a Java class argument and this is probably the most common usage pattern. For example, an action class might declare a log as follows:

```
private static final Log LOG = LogFactory.getLog(ThisAction.class);
```

We can then use the logger throughout our code, calling the various methods corresponding to the logging levels we saw in the previous section. The following pseudocode shows several logging levels and how they might be used:

```
public String execute() throws Exception {
    log.trace("Enter.");
    if (StringUtils.isBlank(name)) {
        return SUCCESS;
    }
    Exception ex = null;
    try {
        log.debug("  Constructing " + name + "...");
        ex = (Exception) Class.forName(name).newInstance();
    } catch (Exception e) {
        log.error("Exception during instantiation: "
                  + e.getMessage(), e);
    }
    if (ex != null) {
        log.trace("  Throwing " + name + "...");
        throw ex;
    }
    log.debug("  Could not create instance; returning...");
    return SUCCESS;
}
```

We see three different log levels—TRACE, DEBUG, and ERROR. TRACE is used for the lowest-level diagnostic information possible, and is used for very fine-grained execution tracing. DEBUG is used for showing information useful to debugging. Finally ERROR is used for showing actual errors. Actually, it's arguable that the ERROR-level log statement above really belongs at the WARN level, which is a little less serious. INFO level messages (not used above) are for bits of information that will generally be displayed. For example, this might include configuration details.

The styles we use for the contents of our log messages are many and varied. We might indent our log messages based on the nesting inside the method and use periods at the end of statements that are complete in and of themselves. We might also use ellipses (...) for statements made before an operation occurs and also before statements that are a continuation of a chain of events. These aren't hard-and-fast rules—just conventions. Developing a consistent set of conventions can help while wading through large log files.

There are also log methods for determining if a specific log level is set. For example, if we had a collection we wanted to log if the DEBUG level was active, we would write the following:

```
if (log.isDebugEnabled()) {
    for (Object baz : bazzes) {
        log.debug(baz);
    }
}
```

It's true that we don't need the test to see if the DEBUG level is enabled. However, by wrapping the entire loop inside the check, we avoid looping through the entire collection and not printing anything out. If a debug message is unusually expensive to construct, for whatever reason, the same method can be used. For example, we might use `String.format()` to create a log message as shown here:

```
log.debug(String.format("  Throwing %s...", throwsClassname));
```

If it was an expensive format, it might be worth the extra "noise" to surround it if an `isDebugEnabled()` is called to avoid a potentially unnecessary call to `String.format()`.

Configuring the loggers

We can configure Log4J by using either XML or a properties file. We'll briefly look at the properties file configuration, and then configure various Struts 2 subsystems and our application to log at whichever level we prefer. Further configuration options can be found in the Log4J documentation or in the documentation for whatever logging implementation we decide to use.

We'll break up the properties file into chunks and discuss each one individually to help make things a bit more clear. When I refer to properties, I'll leave the `log4j` prefix as seen here:

```
log4j.rootLogger=INFO, A1
```

The `rootLogger` property defines the broadest level of logger. Any logging not specifically configured will be handled by the `rootLogger` definition. Here, we've set the log level to `INFO` and listed a single log appender `A1`.

Appenders determine how the logging occurs. For example, log statements can be directed to the console (as shown below), a file, a rolling file that is limited in size but keeps a specified number of historic log files, a database, and so on. These options are detailed in the Log4J documentation. We'll examine how to set up a console log appender. This is particularly useful when developing using an IDE with a console view, such as Eclipse, or for production servers.

```
log4j.appender.A1=org.apache.log4j.ConsoleAppender
log4j.appender.A1.layout=org.apache.log4j.PatternLayout
log4j.appender.A1.layout.ConversionPattern=%d %-5p %c.%M:%L - %m%n
```

In the example above, we define the appender as a Log4J `ConsoleAppender` class, which writes log messages to the console. Note that the appender `A1`, which we named in our `rootLogger`, is used after the `appender` property name. This lets Log4J know which appender we're defining.

We define the layout of log statements using the `layout` property, again appended to the property name. The `PatternLayout` creates a log statement template, where each character following the % character represents some specific information (for example, %d is the date).

```
log4j.logger.com.packt.s2wad=DEBUG
log4j.logger.org.apache.struts2=INFO
log4j.logger.com.opensymphony.xwork2=INFO
log4j.logger.ognl=INFO
log4j.logger.org.apache.struts2.util.StrutsTypeConverter=DEBUG
```

The remainder of our Log4J configuration file consists of setting the log level for package- and class-specific logs. The `logger` property defines the log level for whatever package (and optionally classname) follows it in the property name.

We just now configured the DEBUG level for our entire application, as all our Java classes are in the `com.packt.s2wad` package. All classes in that package will be configured to log DEBUG-level messages and higher-priority messages (such as INFO or ERROR).

We configured Struts 2 itself (and XWork and OGNL) to log only INFO-level messages (and above). However, we have configured the `StrutsTypeConverter` class at the DEBUG level. This means that everything in Struts 2, except the `StrutsTypeConverter` class, will log at the INFO level, also including other classes in the `org.apache.struts.util` package.

The ability to turn on DEBUG-level logging with this granularity can be very helpful. It allows us to keep all of our log statements in our application, but still choose the level at which to run logging in a single location. During development, we'll generally run at the TRACE or DEBUG levels. Once we move into production, it's more likely that we'd run at the INFO or WARN levels.

Turning up the logging levels can often produce gigantic log files, especially at the DEBUG and TRACE levels. Different libraries produce different amounts of logging at different levels. However, it is very instructive to crank up the log levels at regular intervals, particularly when first learning a library, system, or technology. This is required to get a feel of some of what's going on "under the hood". Turning up log levels can also help track down configuration issues, particularly at startup.

Summary

This chapter introduces us to the Struts 2 declarative exception handling mechanism, showing us how we can define both global- and action-specific exception mappings and results. The chapter also looks at ways to make our exceptions more useful by encapsulating exception-specific data in the exception class.

We also get an overview of how to configure logging for our Struts 2 application, including how to set the log levels for each of the major Struts 2 subsystems — XWork, OGNL, and Struts 2 itself.

In the next chapter, we'll move away from Struts 2 a bit and examine everybody's favorite web application language — JavaScript. Really, it's been misunderstood and abused for too long. Despite some warts, it's a capable, dynamic language that can be used to a wonderful effect, as long as it's written well. And yes, it is possible to write clean and safe JavaScript!

References

A reader can refer to the following:

- Exceptions
  http://java.sun.com/docs/books/tutorial/essential/exceptions/

- The Great Exception Debate
  http://www.ibm.com/developerworks/java/library/j-jtp05254.html
  http://www.mindview.net/Etc/Discussions/CheckedExceptions

- Commons Logging, Log4J
  http://commons.apache.org/logging/
  http://logging.apache.org/log4j/index.html

10
Getting Started with JavaScript

In the previous chapter, we covered how Struts 2 can use both application- and action-specific exception configurations to deal with application errors. We also looked at ways to enhance our exception classes by including application-specific information. Finally, we saw how to configure logging, so that we can see what's going on behind the scenes in both the framework and our own code.

In this chapter, we'll take a look at JavaScript—a common element of many web applications. Having a solid foundation in JavaScript and the **Document Object Model** (**DOM**) is critically important for developing reactive, functional web applications, and is particularly important when we start developing Ajax-based applications.

JavaScript is a much-maligned language, particularly by those without a grounding in other dynamic languages such as Lisp, Smalltalk, Self, and so on. JavaScript is an incredibly flexible and capable language when used in ways that play to its strengths. Applying non-JavaScript design patterns to JavaScript will produce inefficient code that is needlessly complex and difficult to debug.

We'll first look at some JavaScript gotchas, and will then explore some of the more advanced uses as seen in many JavaScript libraries, including a discussion of JavaScript's versions of object-oriented programming. We'll conclude by using JavaScript to create a more dynamic version of our ingredient list input fields, allowing an arbitrary number of ingredients to be entered.

Introduction to JavaScript

JavaScript has a syntax similar to C, C++, and Java. It is an object-oriented (OO) language, but not in the same way as Java. Understanding JavaScript's OO nature can bring a huge boost in productivity. While it's possible to program JavaScript in a "cookbook-style" manner (or worse, "code sample-oriented programming"), today's highly interactive applications can benefit from a deeper understanding of JavaScript.

While we won't cover the entirety of JavaScript for which there are other appropriate materials, we'll get a high-level overview of the language. We will then delve deeper into some of the more useful JavaScript and DOM patterns.

Playing with JavaScript

The easiest way to play around with JavaScript is to use Firefox combined with the Firebug plug-in. There are also some solutions for Internet Explorer if you're running on a platform that supports it. In this chapter's code, we'll sometimes assume we're in the Firebug console, allowing us to type in and execute code immediately. The rest of the code will be run inside a webpage. It will usually be obvious from the context.

Minor syntax and language notes

There are some minor syntax notes to be kept in mind, particularly some differences that can cause headaches to Java programmers.

Unicode

Modern JavaScript supports Unicode. Prior to ECMAScript v3, Unicode was allowed only in comments or string literals. Modern browsers (in theory) allow Unicode to be used anywhere, even in variable names. Personally, I'd avoid Unicode except in comments or string literals, but that may just be paranoia on my part.

Whitespace

Whitespace is ignored in JavaScript, except inside string literals. However, you can use the "\" character to continue a line, including in the middle of string literals. This will not insert a new line in the string.

```
var s = "Hello, \
world!";
alert(s); // Will alert with the string "Hello, world!".
```

Semicolons

To make JavaScript easier, it was decided that semicolons at the end of statements should be optional. This can lead to some strange issues, as they can be inserted by the JavaScript compiler in places where we don't necessarily expect. The `return`, `break`, and `continue` statements are the primary culprits. The canonical example is the following code:

```
return
    true;
```

This will be interpreted as:

```
return;
true;
```

This is almost never what we mean. The answer for this is to always use semicolons, and never rely on semicolon insertion.

Null and undefined values

JavaScript has both `null` and `undefined` values. Variables declared, but not initialized, are `undefined`, not `null`.

The equal and strict equal operators

Both `==` (equal) and `===` (strict equal), and their negated (using a prefixed `!`) counterparts may be used for equality operations. They behave differently. The equal operator does type conversion, the strict equal operator doesn't. We'll briefly examine type coercion later. In general, we'll usually want to use `===`. Equal (`==`) and strict equal (`===`) also behave differently when comparing null and undefined values. With `==`, `null` and `undefined` are equal, whereas with `===`, they are not.

The logical OR operator

The `||` (logical OR) operator can be used to ensure a variable has a value.

```
var aVariable = anotherVariable || "Default value";
```

If the value of `anotherVariable` is `null` (or `undefined`), the value of `aVariable` will be set to `"Default value"`, else it will be set to whatever there is in `anotherVariable`. This is a very common shorthand notation for the following code, and is seen a lot in good JavaScript code.

```
var aVariable;
if (anotherVariable == null) {
    aVariable = "Default value";
} else {
    aVariable = anotherVariable;
}
```

The same thing can be represented using the `?:` operator as:

```
var aVariable = (anotherVariable == null) ? "Default value"
                                          : anotherVariable;
```

We can also express this by using JavaScript's liberal notion of **truthiness**:

```
var aVariable = anotherVariable ? "Default value"
                                : anotherVariable;
```

Variables and scoping

Scoping in JavaScript is different from that in Java. One of the biggest differences is that **undeclared** variables (variables that don't use the `var` keyword) are automatically assumed to be global variables. This can cause endless headaches. Leaving off a `var` keyword inside a function can produce surprising results.

```
var i = 1;
function modifyGlobalByAccident() {
    // Re-use of global i but was
    // intended to be local to function!
    for (i = 0; i < 10; i++) {
        // ...
    }
}
modifyGlobalByAccident();
alert(i); // Now contains 10, NOT 1!
```

It can be difficult to track down interactions like this, particularly when there is a lot of code between a variable's initial declaration and its subsequent overwriting. If we intended to modify the global variable, this code is fine (we'll see how to make things more obvious later). However, it does underscore the stance that global variables are evil and can lead to difficult-to-debug code.

The other potential scoping gotcha is that in JavaScript only functions have their own scope. For example, blocks inside a `for` loop do not have their own scope, and variables declared within such a block will overwrite variables of the same name outside the block.

This is quite different from Java, where anything inside curly brackets ({ }) is its own block and enjoys a distinct variable space. In the example that follows, the initial value of `aName` will be overwritten:

```
var aName = "Dave";
var names = ["Dave", "Nick", "Omar"];
for (var i = 0; i < names.length; i++) {
    var aName = names[i];
}
alert(aName); // Alerts "Omar", NOT "Dave" (sorry, Nick).
```

Even though we used the `var` keyword, we are not creating a new variable named `aName`. It's the same one. This is at least as bad as the default global scope. Perhaps it is worse when coming from a Java background. In Java, we believe we can create unique variables wherever we want. In JavaScript, we can't. If we're not vigilant, this can cause subtle bugs that are hard to track down, particularly if we're not looking for scope-related issues.

Using, the `var` keyword inside functions does create a new variable.

```
var aName = "Dave";
var names = ["Dave", "Nick", "Omar"];
function foo() {
    for (var i = 0; i < names.length; i++) {
        var aName = names[i];
    }
    alert(aName); // Contains "Omar"; local to function.
}
foo();
alert(aName); // Contains "Dave"--the global value.
```

In the code above, notice that inside the function `foo()`, we still have access to the `aName` variable, even though we're outside the `for` loop. The `for` loop does not create its own variable scope. Only the function `foo` has its own scope. It doesn't matter where in the function we put the `var aName`.

By the same token, if we create a variable inside a function and attempt to refer to it outside of that function, it will be an error.

```
function bar() {
    var baz = "Hello";
    alert(baz); // This works.
}
alert(baz); // This doesn't.
```

JavaScript data types

JavaScript has only a few data types when compared to Java. One important difference is that variables in JavaScript are not statically typed. This implies that a variable initialized to a string in one place can be assigned a number somewhere else. Doing this is rarely a good idea, and can be a source of frustration.

Numbers

Tired of all the numeric types available in Java? JavaScript has only one—64-bit floating point. Even numbers that look like integers are actually floating point internally. This isn't always an issue, but it is something to be aware of. This should also be remembered when performing what we think is integer division—the result may not be an integer.

Floating point numbers may be represented conventionally, such as **3.14159**, or by using scientific notation, such as **6.02e23**.

JavaScript has several built-in values that may be returned from a numeric calculation, the most important being NaN and Infinity. Interestingly, Infinity can be either positive or negative.

NaN is noncomparable using the normal numeric operators, so a isNaN(obj) function is provided. Similarly, isFinite(obj) will test for positive or negative Infinity (when obj is not NaN).

JavaScript provides a Math object that has more complex mathematical operations available. A complete reference is beyond the scope of this book. The object provides many of the expected operations such as Math.sqrt(), Math.sin(), Math.cos(), and so on.

Decimal, hex, octal

Numbers can be represented in decimal, hex, or octal. Hex numbers are prefixed with a 0x, whereas octal numbers are prefixed with a 0.

Conversions

Numbers can be converted to strings with the `String(obj)` method. However, numbers created in scientific notation will not necessarily be converted to a string containing scientific notation. For example, `String(6.23e5)` will return `623000`, whereas `String(6.23e21)` will return `6.23e+21` (at least in Firefox).

Strings

JavaScript strings can be delimited with either single or double quotes. There is no functional difference between these two types of quotes. For example, if our string contains a quote of one kind, we can quote the entire string with the other quote. An alternative is to escape either type of quote with a leading backslash (\) character.

JavaScript supports many of the typical string escape sequences, such as \n, \t, and so on. Unicode characters may be embedded in a string by escaping with a \uXXXX, where XXXX is the four hexadecimal digits of the Unicode character.

Strings can be concatenated using the plus operator (+). This is similar to Java in the way memory is allocated and a new string is created. If there are a lot of string concatenations, particularly inside a loop, it can be more efficient to use the `join` method from the `Array` object:

```
aString = ["lots", " of", ..., " strings"].join("");
```

We shouldn't do this unless we're joining a lot of strings — creating the array and calling the `join()` method is more expensive when there are only a few strings.

Length and conversions

String objects have a `length` property used to determine the length of the string in Unicode characters.

String objects contain several useful methods. Again, a complete reference is beyond the scope of this book, but a few methods are worth noting. In addition to the expected `charAt`, `indexOf`, `lastIndexOf`, `substring`, `toLowerCase`, and `toUpperCase` functions, strings also have several regular expression functions (including `split`, which can take either a string separator or a regular expression to split on). The `match`, `replace`, and `search` functions all take regular expressions. As we've seen previously, a good command of regular expressions can be extremely valuable — true in the case of JavaScript as well.

JavaScript has a convenient syntax for regular expressions — we put the expression inside slashes (//). For example, the following example removes HTML `<pre>` tags from a string:

```
s = s.replace(/<pre.*>/i, "").replace(/<\/pre>/i, "");
```

Okay, I'll only make it a partial exercise for the reader. First, we're using method chaining, which we see in Java. The "i" makes it a case-insensitive regex. The purpose of the backslash in the second regex is to escape the forward slash. Otherwise, JavaScript would think our regex was done being defined, and would promptly blow up since the rest of the line wouldn't be legal JavaScript.

Conversions to other types

Strings can be converted to numbers using the `Number(obj)` method. However, `Number("010")`, despite the leading 0, will return 10 decimal, not 8 octal. So, we've been warned for all those times when we would be dealing with octal numeric data in strings.

We can also use the `parseInt(obj)` function. It defaults to base 10 numbers. The `parseInt` function takes an optional radix parameter, `parseInt(obj, radix)`. This function will stop converting as soon as it sees a character in the string that doesn't make sense in the assumed radix. This can lead to an interesting result if the string passed in contains a leading 0. If we call `parseInt("08")`, we'll actually get the number 0 back. This is because the leading zero makes `parseInt` believe it's parsing an octal number, and 8 is not a legal octal digit.

The plus (+) operator is also a unary operator that, when applied to a string, will convert it to a number. We'll look at this a bit further when we look at type coercion.

Arrays

JavaScript arrays are objects. In Java, they're sort of objects, but don't share many object semantics, and require `java.lang.reflect.Array` for direct manipulation. As in Java, they can be created with an immediate syntax, using brackets [] around the array values.

```
var array1 = [1, 2, 3, 4, 5];
```

Individual array elements can then be accessed using an array index, which starts at zero. For example, `array1[0]` will return the number 1.

Unlike Java, JavaScript arrays are actually always associative arrays, more similar to maps than arrays. When we access `array1[0]`, the index is converted to a string.

Because of this we can say things such as `array1["foo"] = "bar"`, which is more like a map than the Java arrays we're familiar with. This implies that arrays can actually be used like a structure (although objects are probably a better choice, as we'll see next).

Arrays have a length property which is used to determine the length of the array. The length property can also be used to append objects to the end of an array as shown here:

```
var a1 = [1, 2, 3];
a1[a1.length] = 4; // a1 now contains [1, 2, 3, 4].
```

We can also add elements beyond the end of an array:

```
a1[8] = 42;
```

This puts the number 42 at array index 8 (arrays are zero-based, so the 9th position). What about the values at uninitialized indices? They're filled with the `undefined` value (not `null`).

Array functions

Arrays have their own handy collection of functions (not covered in detail here). To cover in brief, the following are some methods included in the collection:

- `concat`: For concatenating one array to another
- `join`: For joining array elements, which takes an optional separator argument (the default is ",") and returns a string
- `pop` and `push`: For using arrays like a stack
- `slice`: For getting a portion of an array
- `sort`: For sorting arrays, taking an optional function as an argument (we'll look at this later)
- `splice`: Exhibits fairly complicated behavior.

Exception handling

JavaScript has exception handling similar to that of Java, but slightly different. One difference is that we can use only a single `catch` block. We still have `finally` blocks.

Throwing an exception is slightly different. We have (at least) two options. We can throw a new JavaScript `Error` object as follows:

```
function foo() {
    throw new Error("Foo threw me");
}
```

If this exception occurs outside of a `try/catch` block under Firefox with Firebug, we'll see the string we passed to the `Error` function in the JavaScript console.

We can actually throw an object of any type, not just JavaScript's `Error` object. For example, we might just create an anonymous object with the "name" and "message" properties (we'll get to anonymous objects next):

```
function foo() {
    throw { name: "FooException", message: "Foo threw me." };
}
```

If we call `foo()` outside of a `try/catch` block, the behavior is browser specific. For example, under Firefox with Firebug, we'll see a message in our console similar to this:

```
uncaught exception: [object Object]
```

This is not particularly useful. We can give our anonymous object a `toString()` method, but that starts to make our throw statement bulky. A more convenient way is to create a function that returns the exception object, complete with a `toString()` function. We'll see many ways to go about this in the next section. We create our own exception objects for the same reason we do it in Java—the ability to add exception-specific data that can be acted upon, displayed, and so on.

Introduction to JavaScript objects and OOP

Objects are at the heart of JavaScript, although functions (which are objects themselves) play a surprisingly significant role once we get more advanced. While there are a few ways to create a new object in JavaScript, the canonical method, particularly for structure-like objects, is to use the {} notation, which creates an anonymous object.

```
var o = {};
```

JavaScript objects can be thought of as a unification of objects and hash tables. An object is simply an unordered collection of name-value pairs. A name can be any string. Similarly, a value can be any value—including numbers, strings, arrays, other objects, and even functions. In a sense, every JavaScript object is a tiny database.

This is underscored by the JavaScript anonymous object syntax. By supplying a comma-separated list of name-value pairs, we can create our own data structures, which can then be accessed in an intuitive way:

```
var aDude = {
    fname: "Dave",
    lname: "Newton",
    age: Infinity // Notice no trailing comma!
};
aDude.fname; // Returns "Dave".
aDude["fname"]; // *Also* returns "Dave".
```

When we create a name-value pair, we do not need to quote the "name" string, unless it is a JavaScript reserved word. Note that there are many JavaScript reserved words that aren't actually used in the language (this is historical and somewhat confusing). Also notice that the last name-value pair does not have a trailing comma. This is significant, as not all browsers will allow a trailing comma.

Recall that we said an object can hold any value type; this includes other objects too.

```
var aDude =
    fname: "Dave",
    lname: "Newton",
    age: Infinity,
    address: {
        street: "271828 E St",
        state: "Confused",
        zip: "69042"
    }
};
```

We can access members of aDude's address object as expected — aDude.address.state. This usage of anonymous object is known as **JSON (JavaScript Object Notation)**.

Open objects and object augmentation

Values can be added to objects at any time. For example, we could add an arbitrary property to the aDude object after it's created by using either dot notation or array notation.

```
aDude.newProperty = "I'm a new property.";
aDude["anotherNewProperty"] = "Another new property.";
```

Properties may be accessed using either dot or array notation.

Object values can be functions

We'll explore this further as we go along. However, note that we can use a function as a value in an object. In other words, functions can be the value of a variable. Functions are first class objects in JavaScript.

```
aDude.toString = function() {
    return "aDude [fname=" + this.fname + ", lname="
            + this.lname + "]";
}
alert(aDude); // Alerts "aDude [fname=Dave, lname=Newton]".
```

Notice the `this` keyword used in the snippet. It is similar to Java's `this`, but significantly different depending on the situation in which it is used (we'll talk about this a bit later). A complete treatise of JavaScript OOP is well beyond the scope of this book, but we'll cover some basics.

Object maker functions

Objects can be created by dedicated creation functions. This methodology can be used to make sure objects are always created in a specific way, are assigned default values (if no specific value is specified), and so on. We'll learn more about JavaScript constructors a bit later on (they're also just functions, although not the specialized ones within a class as in Java).

```
function makeAdude(fname, lname) {
    return { fname: fname, lname: lname };
}
var aNewDude = makeAdude("Omar", "Velous");
aNewDude.fname; // Returns "Omar".
```

Here, we're simply returning an anonymous object from our function. However, the function ensures that at least the object's `fname` and `lname` values are initialized.

Functions

We've already seen that functions are first class objects. We've also seen one way in which this can be exploited—the `toString()` function in our object above was a function value. We'll cover some interesting aspects of JavaScript functions, some of which may not seem useful until we begin discussing modules and encapsulation.

When we declare a normal function in JavaScript, we're actually creating a variable that holds that function as its value—that's what the `function` keyword does. This is shorthand for the `function` operator, which takes an optional name, a parameter list, and a block of statements. The two examples given here are functionally equivalent:

```
function f1() {
    alert("Hello from f1");
}
var f2 = function () {
    alert("Hello from f2");
};
f1();
f2();
```

Function parameters

Function parameters, like all JavaScript variables, are untyped. In addition, we can call a function with fewer (or more) parameters than listed in the function definition.

```
function f1(param1, param2) {
    ...
}
f1(); // That's fine: param1 and param2 are undefined.
f1("foo", "bar", "baz", "plugh"); // That's fine too...
```

This alone can make JavaScript a bit tricky at times, but that's the nature of the beast. We can always check for a specific number of parameters. We can even check for their types to a degree. However, this is surprisingly uncommon (at least to Java programmers).

Parameters that don't receive a value from the function call are `undefined`, not `null`. Recall that using `==` (equal) will not show the difference between `undefined` and `null`, whereas using `===` (strict equal) will show the difference. For example, if we called the function with a single parameter:

```
f1("hello");
```

Inside `f1()`, the parameter `param1` would be filled with `"hello"`. `Param2`, on the other hand, would be `undefined` (not `null`). If `null` was a legitimate value for `param2`, we might need to distinguish between `null` (implying the parameter was potentially passed) and `undefined` (implying that the parameter wasn't passed in).

Using the || operator allows us to supply default parameter values if we don't receive one in the call. For example, let's assume the `param2` parameter is optional. When it's not provided, we'll supply a default value of `42` as shown here:

```
function f1(param1, param2) {
    param2 = param2 || 42;
    ...
}
```

Accessing arguments beyond those listed in the function definition resembles array access, but only in appearance. Functions receive a pseudo-parameter named `arguments`. It acts like a JavaScript array in a way that we can access its `length` property and elements using array notation's `[]` (square brackets). However, the `arguments` value does not inherit `Array`'s methods like `join`, `sort`, and so on (it's not an `Array`, but is dressed as one).

```
function f1(param1) {
    var anArg = arguments[1] || "Default value";
    ...
}
```

Some trickery

To make matters even a bit more confusing, we can actually apply `Array`'s methods on the `arguments` parameter using `Array`'s prototype (we'll cover prototypes in a little while).

```
function f1() {
    var csvArgs = Array.prototype.join.apply(arguments);
    alert(csvArgs);
}
```

While this is actually useful sometimes, it can cause headaches for those unclear about how JavaScript works. It can also cause headaches for those who do know JavaScript.

One way of testing to see if our function has received the proper number of arguments is to check against a value inside the method, such as:

```
function f1(param1, param2) {
    if (arguments.length != 2) {
        alert("Error!");
        return;
    }
    ...
}
```

This works, but requires us to remember updating the length to check against. For example, if we changed our method to require three arguments or a single argument, we'd have to remember to update our argument length check. We can automate this length checking by using the `length` property of the function objects (it used to be called `arity`).

```
function f1(param1, param2) {
    if (arguments.length != f1.length) {
        alert("Error!");
        return;
    }
    ...
}
```

The `length` property refers to how many arguments the function was created with—two in this case. Note how we refer to the function's name inside the function we're defining. The function `f1` can be referred to as `f1` inside itself (remember what we said about headaches?) We could also throw an exception rather than show an alert. Which is more appropriate depends on the application and our JavaScript architecture.

Inner functions

As a variable can hold a function, we can define a function at any place where a value is expected, including inside other functions.

```
function f1() {
    function f2() {
        alert("Meh.");
    }
    f2();
}
f1();
f2(); // Will this work? Nope.
```

Function `f2()` is not available once we've exited the `f1()` function, for two reasons:

- The equivalence of the two ways of declaring functions (including the implicit `var`)

- The scoping rules of functions we discussed earlier, which state that variables declared within a function with the `var` keyword are available only in that function

This is one way to hide functionality to avoid conflicts with our own or third-party JavaScript libraries. We'll also learn some other ways. However, this is still an important aspect of functions that comes in to play occasionally, and can always be used when a function needs to be used only locally, or we want to restrict its usage.

Closures

Closures are one of the terms often used by programming language junkies. They're an extremely powerful concept, occasionally difficult to grasp, and capable of both wondrous and terrifying behavior.

To put it briefly, **closures** are functions evaluated in a context containing other bound variables. In some ways, it sounds more complicated than it actually is.

What this actually means is that an inner function (as described in the previous section) has access to the variables from the outer function. As a simplistic example, consider the following:

```
function f1() {
    var s = "Hello";
    function f2() {
        alert(s);
    }
    f2();
}
f1();
```

Although this is not particularly useful, it illustrates the point. How can we make this useful? One key consideration is that the inner function will maintain its reference to the outer variable's value at the time of the outer function's invocation. Here's a canonical example of closures, which highlights this feature:

```
function makeAdder(x) {
    return function(n) {
        return n + x;
    };
}
```

The makeAdder() function relies on two things:

- We can use a function as a value. Here, the makeAdder() function returns a new function.

- The value of the argument x given to makeAdder() is saved across invocations. In other words, each time we call makeAdder(), the function returned maintains the value of x—the value we passed to makeAdder().

We can then call the function returned by `makeAdder()`. It will add the value of x, passed to `makeAdder()`, to the argument we pass to the function returned by `makeAdder()`. Remember what I said about headaches? This is much easier to demonstrate than to explain:

```
var add10 = makeAdder(10);
add10(1);  // Returns 11.
add10(32); // Returns 42.
```

The code above creates a function that will add the value passed to `makeAdder()`, to any value we pass to the function created, by calling `makeAdder()`. As the value x passed to `makeAdder()` is unique to each invocation, we can easily make functions that add different values to their arguments.

```
var add10 = makeAdder(10);
var add30 = makeAdder(30);
add10(32); // Returns 42.
add30(12); // Also returns 42.
```

Again, the `makeAdder()` function itself isn't particularly useful, but the idea of closures is an important concept that can be used to neatly encapsulate functionality and reduce code size in many situations (we'll see closures again in a little bit).

Introduction to JavaScript classes

JavaScript is an object oriented language, but not in the same way that Java is. The bottom line is that JavaScript doesn't have classes. JavaScript has a `new` keyword, which actually adds to the confusion.

OOP without classes can be disturbing to those of us familiar only with more typical OO languages such as Java or C++. JavaScript uses **prototypal inheritance**, where inheritance is achieved by cloning existing objects and adding new (or modifying existing) functionality. So how does the `new` keyword fit in?

Creating classes

We can model classical inheritance in JavaScript using functions and the `new` keyword. It will look different from what we're used to, and it may not be the best way to program JavaScript. However, it's used to a considerable extent, and hence it's important to understand the mechanisms.

Instead of creating a class, we'll create a function. However, to differentiate it from a normal function, we'll call it a **constructor function** and name it starting with an upper-case letter. This is a convention, not a rule. However, for Java programmers, it helps ease the transition into what is ultimately a very different programming paradigm.

Like Java, JavaScript has a `this` keyword. However, it is used differently depending upon context, and there are some restrictions regarding when it can be used (and how it will work). We'll get to one of the bigger issues with the `this` keyword in a bit. For now, we'll assume we can use it in a somewhat similar way to how we use it in Java.

```
function OurFirstClass(aParam) {
    this.aParam = aParam;
}
```

We can use this in our JavaScript code by applying the new operator to the `OurNewClass` function.

```
var inst1 = new OurFirstClass("Hello");
inst1.aParam; // "Hello"
```

Variable and function access

In Java, our classes have both data and methods. We can do something similar in JavaScript, although it looks fairly unfamiliar in its raw form. What makes it more confusing is the fact there are two ways to accomplish similar looking, but different things. Also, there are scoping rules which will add to the confusion. JavaScript has an interesting access model.

To try and pace out the confusion, we'll examine several ways of defining variables and functions in our pseudo-classes. First, we'll look at three ways of defining functions in our pseudo-classes. (Why pseudo-classes? JavaScript doesn't have classes! These are functions.) We'll try to relate JavaScript concepts to Java, wherever applicable; JavaScript purists will take (justifiable) umbrage.

```
function Pseudo1() {
    function aPrivateFunc() {
        ...
    }
    this.aPrivilegedFunc = function () {
        ...
    }
}
Pseudo1.prototype.aPublicFunc = function () {
    ...
}
```

The `aPrivateFunc()` function is as its name implies — private. It cannot be called outside of the object. It's not even available from the pseudo-class's public functions.

The `aPrivilegedFunc()` function can access private variables and functions, and is available to both public and private functions. Also note that privileged functions can be deleted or replaced from the public side, which may or may not be something we want to allow.

The `aPublicFunc()` function, defined outside our pseudo-class function, is a true public function. Adding a function to a pseudo-classes prototype is the normal way of adding public methods. Functions added to a prototype are available to objects that inherit from the prototype (which we'll examine later).

We create an instance of our pseudo-class the same way we've seen previously.

```
var inst1 = new Pseudo1();
```

We can call both the prototype function `aPublicFunc()`, and the privileged function `aPrivilegedFunc()` at our top level.

```
inst1.aPublicFunc();
inst1.aPrivilegedFunc();
```

What about accessing any of these functions from the remaining functions? (Remember what we said about headaches? Hang on.)

We cannot call the private function `aPrivateFunc()` from a reference to `inst1`.

The prototypal function `aPublicFunc()` can access `aPrivilegedFunc()`, but must use the `this` prefix.

```
Pseudo1.prototype.aPublicFunc = function () {
    alert("aPublicFunc");
    this.aPrivilegedFunc();
}
```

The privileged function `aPrivilegedFunc()` may call `aPrivateFunc()`, but must not use the `this` prefix. Also, it may call `aProtoFunc()`, but must use the `this` prefix. (The `aProtoFunc()` function is coming up in the next section — be patient!)

```
this.privilegedFunc = function () {
    alert("privilegedFunc");
    privateFunc();
    this.protoFunc();
}
```

Privileged functions may call other privileged functions, but must use the `this` prefix.

JavaScript's "this" keyword

Private functions may call neither prototypal nor privileged functions, unless we play a trick on JavaScript (which we do often). Because of the way the this operator was defined, it's a bit wrong when it comes to private functions. However, if we create a private variable (conventionally called that), we can access the instance from private methods.

```
function Pseudo1() {
    var that = this;
    function aPrivateFunc() {
        alert("aPrivateFunc");
        that.anotherPrivilegedFunc();
        that.aProtoFunc();
    }
    this.anotherPrivilegedFunc = function () {
        alert("priv2");
    }
    this.aPrivilegedFunc = function () {
        alert("aPrivilegedFunc");
        aPrivateFunc();
    }
}
Pseudo1.prototype.aProtoFunc = function () {
    alert("aProtoFunc");
}
var inst1 = new Pseudo1();
inst1.aPrivilegedFunc();
```

This and that (oh, another this pun—we've got a million of them), brings up the topic of class variables, but they're simpler than functions. They're not commonly added to the prototype. Although there's no reason they can't be, it would be like a static variable in Java, and mutable.

Private variables, such as that (covered in the above code), are accessible by private and privileged functions, but not prototypal (public) functions. Privileged variables (this.xxx variables) are accessible by public (prototypal) and privileged functions by using the this keyword, and by private functions by using the that trick, as demonstrated above.

The last thing to consider (for now) is that public members can be created at any time by adding them to the pseudo-class's prototype. Neither private nor privileged members can be added outside the constructor function.

Prototypes

We've seen some hints about the prototypal inheritance of JavaScript above, when we created a function on a class's prototype:

```
Pseudo1.prototype.aProtoFunc = function () {
    alert("aProtoFunc");
}
```

This is another way to add functions to a class. Each instance of Pseudo1 will have a aProtoFunc function. How is this used for inheritance? Let's say we want to subclass Pseudo1, a subclass named (uncreatively) Pseudo2:

```
function Pseudo2() {};
Pseudo2.prototype = new Pseudo1();
```

If we create an instance of Pseudo2, we can call aProtoFunc() on it:

```
var pseudo2 = new Pseudo2();
pseudo2.aProtoFunc(); // This works.
```

Pseudo2 may contain its own methods, defined using either its prototype or in the Pseudo2 function body (using the this keyword, as seen previously). Creating subclasses this way is a bit unwieldy. There are several ways to make this more concise. The canonical method uses a function to encapsulate creating the subclass function, setting the prototype, and returning an instance (the following is Douglas Crockford's version):

```
function object(o) {
    function F() {}
    F.prototype = o;
    return new F();
}
```

JavaScript modules and OOP

What's probably more important is how we can write JavaScript that's unlikely to conflict with other JavaScript libraries, methods, and data, (including our own) and we don't even need the package keyword.

Creating a namespace

The easiest way to isolate our JavaScript code is to just put it inside an anonymous object. This is the tactic taken by many major JavaScript libraries, and is wonderfully simple. For simply isolating functions and variables, it's a reasonable technique. It's also safer than putting all of our functions and variables into the global namespace.

As a simple example, we might create an object named MOD1 for the JavaScript specific to a given page. It doesn't matter what we call it, but it should be unique on the page.

```
var MOD1 = {
    myAlert: function (s) {
        alert(s);
    }
}
```

We'd then call the myAlert() function by prefacing it with the module name.

```
MOD1.myAlert("Hi!");
```

This way, if any other JavaScript loaded after ours has a function named myAlert(), our page's myAlert() won't be replaced by the newer definition. It's hidden inside the MOD1 object. We only need to refer to it through our module.

In the next chapter, we'll return to this methodology and see how it can be broken down depending on our requirements, and learn some additional modularization tricks.

Summary

JavaScript. Whew. Gotta love it (or not). The previous sections will, however, help us understand some of what we'll see in the wild, and start us on the path to actually enjoying JavaScript. It is, as Dr. Sobel says, a process.

This chapter looks at some of the syntactical quirks of JavaScript, particularly those that can trip up Java programmers. The chapter also gives an overview of JavaScript's version of object-oriented programming, and there's more to come.

What's next? More JavaScript! We're now going to start utilizing it in our application. In order to do that we'll start diving in to the DOM, the internal representation of our webpages, and **Cascading Style Sheets** (**CSS**), used both for styling our webpages and for identifying DOM elements of interest.

References

A reader can refer to the following:

- Firebug (its usefulness cannot be overstated):

  `http://getfirebug.com/`

- Douglas Crockford's JavaScript pages (with links to the highly recommended videos):

  `http://javascript.crockford.com/`

11
Advanced JavaScript, the DOM, and CSS

In the previous chapter, we had a crash course in some of JavaScript's more esoteric, but useful features, particularly those related to how JavaScript implements **Object-Oriented Programming (OOP)**.

JavaScript is only one aspect of the browser we need to be conversant with when developing a modern web application. We also need to be conversant in the Document Object Model (DOM). It is the internal representation of our rendered HTML and CSS, and does more than simply providing a means to design and style our pages.

There are approximately eighteen hundred million JavaScript frameworks. At the time of writing this book, Struts 2 ships Dojo 0.4.3. This is significantly different from Dojo's current 1.0 release, and relatively heavy for the type of programming we'll be doing in this chapter. For our JavaScript explorations, we'll actually use jQuery—an elegant, minimal JavaScript library that embraces JavaScript's approach to OOP. Any other JavaScript framework is likely to have similar functionality. The techniques used here are generally applicable.

 In this chapter, we'll start applying our new-found JavaScript-Fu to our application, by adding an expandable list of ingredients in our recipe entry form. Rather than limit users to a fixed number, we'll allow the addition of an arbitrary number of ingredients by dynamically adding form fields.

We'll also add some minor styling elements to help our form look a little better. A full discussion of CSS's styling abilities is beyond the scope of this book, but there are a few tricks we can use to help make our low-fidelity prototype look better than unadorned HTML. We'll also begin looking at Struts 2's internal stylesheets and discover some limitations of the default Struts 2 themes.

The importance of markup

Markup refers to both general markup languages and annotations used within the language. HTML is considered a markup language. We apply annotations to text to control how it is rendered. Markup can also refer to individual annotations within our HTML, such as putting headline tags around a headline, and so on.

It can also include markup not necessarily intended to control appearance. For example, we might surround the name of an ingredient with a span tag, giving it an "ingredient" class. This markup, which falls under the "semantic markup" definition, can often be used in unexpected ways.

It's hard to overstate the importance of comprehensive markup in our HTML. It is only by giving DOM elements an ID or CSS styles that we can refer (easily) to the elements later, whether for styling (appearance) or for the construction of semantic information. Elements without an ID or a named style are difficult to reference and may lead to fragile, order-dependent DOM manipulations.

What does this imply from a practical standpoint? We should mark up our JSP and HTML as much as is practical, paying particular attention to elements we're likely to refer to later, or that others might be interested in referring to (screen-scraping is much more enjoyable when there's known elements to scrape).

ID or style attribute?

The id attribute of DOM elements is meant to be unique per webpage. This means that an ID should be used only once on any page. Therefore, IDs are specifically for elements we know will be unique.

On the other hand, styles may appear multiple times on a page and can be used to identify elements for both styling and reference purposes. We can also apply multiple styles to a DOM element, allowing us to build up the styles and/or references we need.

Dressing up our form

Recall that the default "xhtml" theme puts our form inside a table, one row per form element, with labels for the form elements. However, our ingredient form felds needed to be handled differently, so that our quantity fields would be on the same line as the ingredient name fields. Those fields were handled manually, using the simple theme.

The `<s:head>` tag includes a CSS stylesheet on our page. The styles defined in it include:

Styles	Usage
`.wwFormTable`	The class of the table our form is contained in
`.label`	`<label>` element class
`.errorLabel`	`<label>` element class if there was a validation error
`.errorMessage`	`<span>` element's class when enclosing field errors
`.checkboxLabel`	Not used in our current form, but self-explanatory
`.checkboxErrorLabel`	Not used in our current form, but self-explanatory
`.required`	`<span>` element's class for the required indicator when the form element sets the `required` attribute to `true`
`.tdLabel`	`<td>` element's class containing the form field's label

With just a few text fields, a text area, and a submit button, our form is easy to dress up. One of the easiest form element dress-ups is creating a solid, one pixel border around form fields. This alone can take a drab, 1990's form into at least the current century. We'll load our own stylesheet after the Struts 2 head tag, in order for our styles to take precedence.

```
<%@ taglib prefix="s" uri="/struts-tags" %>
<html>
  <head>
    <title><s:text name="new.title"/></title>
    <s:head/>
    <link rel="stylesheet" type="text/css"
          href="<s:url value="/styles/main.css"/>" />
  </head>
  ...
```

In order to get the web app context, we're using Struts 2's `<s:url>` tag to create the full pathname of our CSS file. We're assuming a separate directory for our stylesheets, which we're placing in `/styles`.

We'll use this style for all our input elements and the text area. However, we would like to restrict its use to elements found inside our form's table to ensure that we don't mess up any other styling (maybe our own or of any third party) on the page. We can apply the style across the entire page, but that's not as much fun.

While we're at it, we'll add a border around the entire form. We create our own stylesheet with an entry for the `wwFormTable` class. CSS classes are indicated by putting a period (.) before the class name as shown here:

```
.wwFormTable {
  border: 1px solid #669;
  padding: 1em;
}
```

This defines a solid, one pixel, dark-bluish border. It also adds some padding to the table border, so that the border isn't too close to the text. To style input fields contained within the table, we'll style both the input elements created by the text field tags, along with the text area (although it isn't an "input" element technically like most other elements). In this case, we can style them both at the same time as shown here:

```
.wwFormTable input, .wwFormTable textarea {
  border: 1px solid #bbb;
  background: #fef;
}
```

Now, all input and text area elements within an element with the wwFormTable class will be styled as we've defined — a light blue-grey background and a grey, one-pixel border. There are two important things to be noted in this example.

The first is that we can define the style for multiple **CSS selectors** by separating the selectors with commas. The second is that we're using CSS selectors. CSS selectors are the official names for the way we select which elements to style (the stuff outside the brackets) with our style definitions (the stuff inside the brackets).

CSS selectors can be annoyingly complex and deserve more attention than we'll give them here. However, as we are striving towards rapid prototyping, for the most part, we would keep these CSS selectors mercifully simple.

Here, we use the "class" selector. The "." prefix means that we're defining a CSS class. If we used the "#" character, we'd be defining a style for a specific DOM element by ID.

We'll also create some styles for input errors and modify our form JSP to include the cssErrorClass attribute. For example, the recipe name text field tag will look like this:

```
<s:textfield key="recipe.name" cssErrorClass="inputError"/>
```

Our inputError class, defined for both input and text area elements, changes the input element color a bit and puts a dotted red line around it (not shown). Along with some other minor style changes, we'll remove most of the ingredient fields in anticipation of adding them. When we submit the form without a recipe name, we'll see something similar to the screenshot here:

New Recipe

		Name is required.			
Name:					
Description:					
Recipe Types:	☐ Main Dish	☐ Side Dish	☐ Appetizer	☐ Dessert	
Ingredient #1:					
Ingredient #2:					
Ingredient #3:					

It's still not the world's most attractive form. However, for less than 40 lines of CSS, it's not that bad. If we focus on the error message for a moment, we'll start to understand how the default "xhtml" theme can make some things difficult.

For example, if we want the text left aligned, we find the undertaking nontrivial. This is because even though the text itself is inside a span element with the class errorMessage, the span is inside of a table row with no ID or class. Subtle gotchas like this is one reason why it pays to be aware when creating DOM elements. Elements with no ID or classes are difficult (not impossible) to access and modify.

Before we get to that, we're going to drop back into the land of JavaScript for a moment.

JavaScript modules and jQuery

We ended our last chapter by looking at a simple way to hide our JavaScript, in order to protect it from being overwritten by a conflicting library. We're going to return to that conversation for a moment and show one way that particular module methodology might break down.

We'll also take a first look at jQuery, as we build an example page that adds onclick handlers to a group of links. It's another contrived example. However, the techniques used here will be utilized regularly in JavaScript-driven applications, even if we're not using jQuery.

First, we make sure that jQuery is loaded. We'll then put the reference into our HTML head section, using Struts 2's URL tag, to generate the preamble to our jQuery location.

```
<head>
  <script type="text/javascript"
          src="<s:url value="/jquery/jquery-1.2.6.js"/>" >
  </script>
</head>
```

Note that we use a `<script ...></script>` element rather than a single `<script/>`. Some browsers require the use of the first form, else our JavaScript won't work.

Our JSP will just create three links using the iterator tag. We don't really care about the content of the links, but we do care that we're adding a CSS class to each one. We'll also create another link (we'll see why in a moment) that also goes nowhere.

```
<ul>
  <s:iterator value="{'Link 1', 'Link 2', 'Link 3'}"
              var="linkText" status="stat">
    <li>
      <a href="#" class="notify">${linkText}</a>
    </li>
  </s:iterator>
  <li><a href="#">We don't care about this link.</a></li>
</ul>
```

Adding onclick handlers

To add `onclick` handlers to our links, we'll use a combination of CSS selectors, jQuery, and JavaScript. We'll build up the JavaScript one bit at a time. The following will wrap up all of our JavaScript:

```
<script type="text/javascript">
  $(function () {
      ...
  });
</script>
```

This is jQuery-speak for "run the defined function when the page's DOM is ready". The "$" is actually the name of a jQuery function, `$()`. It takes several types of arguments, and behaves differently based on the type of argument passed in. When the argument is a function, the function will be run when the DOM is ready. It's convenient shorthand, despite its mysterious appearance.

Inside that block we'll use $() again, but this time we'll pass in a string. More specifically, a CSS selector designed to return all the links on the page with a class including "notifier". When we pass a string to the `$()` function, it interprets it as a CSS selector and will query the DOM, returning an object containing the selected elements.

```
<script type="text/javascript">
  $(function () {
      $("a.notify").each(
```

```
            . . .
         );
      });
   </script>
```

The `each()` function expects another function as its argument, which takes the index of the object and the object itself as its arguments. Also, supplied as an argument inside the function, the `this` keyword refers to the current element of iteration. However, we'll use the function argument for now. Our `onclick` handler then just pops up an accusatory alert box and returns `false`, so the link won't be followed. Here's the final first iteration of our code:

```
<script type="text/javascript">
   $(function () {
       $("a.notify").each(function (i, theLink) {
           theLink.onclick = function () {
               alert("You clicked me.");
               return false;
           };
       });
   });
</script>
```

If you're not used to seeing the `function` keyword so much, this can be somewhat disturbing. Just to rehash:

- The first `function` is the function that will be run when the DOM is ready

- The second `function` is the one that will be called for each object selected by our CSS selector (it's the argument to jQuery's `each()` function)

- The final `function` is used as the `onclick` handler for each of the selected links

Using a function builder

Our next requirement is that the `onclick` handler shows the link number. We get the index in the `each()` method. We have easy access to it in the function we define as our `onclick` handler. A slight modification to the code gives us the following:

```
$("a.notify").each(function (i, el) {
   el.onclick = function () {
       alert("You clicked link " + (i+1));
       return false;
   };
});
```

Remember our discussion about closures? We're using one here, even if we didn't know it. In our `onclick` handler function, the value of `i` is retained by each of our handler functions. The handler function is created in the context of the function being called by jQuery's `each()` function.

However, we would like our `onclick` handler function to be part of a JavaScript module. (In this usage, it's not as important. However, if the handler is significantly longer, we'd probably want to abstract it away from the code that attached the handler to the links.)

Our first attempt at the modularized version looks like this:

```
var MOD = {
    linkClickHandler: function () {
        alert("You clicked link...");
    }
};
```

However, we are missing our link number. We can't just pass it to the `onclick` handler and attach it with jQuery. Consider the following code to add our handler:

```
el.onclick = MOD.linkClickHandler(i);
```

It would call the function when the DOM is ready, and not when the link is clicked! We need another layer, a layer that builds our click handler. We'll then change the code in our module to this:

```
var MOD = {
    buildClickHandler: function (i) {
        return function () {
            alert("You clicked link #" + (i+1));
        };
    }
};
```

Again, we're utilizing our new favorite term — closure. The function we're returning is enclosed by the `buildClickHandler()` function, and will retain the value of "i" we passed to `buildClickHandler()`. Now, the code that sets `onclick` handlers for our links will look like this:

```
$(function () {
    $("a.notify").each(function (i, el) {
        el.onclick = MOD.buildClickHandler(i);
    });
});
```

Each link's `onclick` handler is set to the function returned by the `MOD.buildClickHandler()` function, which receives the link index. The value of the link index is preserved in the `onclick` handler because of closures.

Of what value is this

You're probably thinking to yourself: "Man, couldn't we have just added the onclick handler to the link tag?! Why did we go through all this?" That's certainly a valid question, and in this particular case, it might have been better to do it that way.

Remember when we used to add style attributes to our elements? Remember how CSS meant we didn't have to do that anymore? The idea of removing JavaScript from our markup is very similar. In the same way, we can mark up our elements to control how they're rendered. We can also mark them up to control their behavior.

It's another layer of abstraction, but now we're making behavioral abstractions instead of rendering abstractions. By separating our behavior, we have three levels of abstraction:

- Our content (the links)
- Style (how the link is rendered)
- Behavior (what happens when we do things to the link, such as clicking it)

Although not readily apparent in this example, if we had a lot of links to add handlers to (or whatever else we're doing), we would be doing it all in one place. If our code was embedded in our HTML, changes would have to be made in many places. This way it's a matter of only a few lines of code, isolated in a single location.

Also, consider a case where the link needing a particular `onclick` handler is decided at render time—for example, when each link had a dynamically specified `style` attribute. By adding our behavior later in the game, we can save lot of noisy JSP needed to determine the `onclick` handler.

Accessing module data

We'll now add some actual functionality. Let's say our JavaScript module includes some data such as a module name, a lookup table, or something similar. It's defined in our module as we'd expect.

```
var MOD = {
    title: "Module MOD",
    ...
```

We'd like our handler to access the `title` property. Our first attempt (which I predict may fail) looks like this:

```
buildClickHandler: function (i) {
    return function () {
        alert("You clicked link #" + (i+1) + " from "+title);
    };
}
```

This won't work because `title` isn't defined in the context of the click handler function. Instead, we get a JavaScript error complaining about an undefined variable. Our second attempt (also doomed) uses the `this` keyword.

```
buildClickHandler: function (i) {
    return function () {
        alert("You clicked link #" + (i+1)
                + " from " + this.title);
    };
}
```

This doesn't give us an error, but it also doesn't give us the title in our alert box. Puzzled, we add the following:

```
buildClickHandler: function (i) {
    alert(this.title);
    return function () {
        alert("You clicked link #" + (i+1)
                + " from " + this.title);
    };
}
```

Interestingly this works, and displays the module title during the page loading process, every time `buildClickHandler()` is called. As we've seen, `this` means different things that we'd often prefer. Here, we'll use the `that` trick again:

```
buildClickHandler: function (i) {
    var that = this;
    return function () {
        alert("You clicked link #" + (i+1)
                + " from " + that.title);
    };
}
```

That gives us the result we want. The data from our module is correctly displayed when we click the links with a `notify` CSS style. Remember, in JavaScript, `this` won't always work the way we expect it to be!

The final trick

The final trick is something we'll see in the wild, although we may never use it ourselves. It's possible for us to bury our module data even further, so that it can't be accidentally overwritten and isn't visible to any other JavaScript. It's another technique for creating modules and relies on immediate function execution.

First, we'll take a quick look at what this actually means, before we start muddying the waters by making it do something. See the following JavaScript:

```
var temp = function () {
    return function (s) {
        alert(s);
}();
```

What could be the result of the execution of this JavaScript? Notice the final `()` characters. We already know that's how we invoke a function. Here, we're defining a function, and then we are invoking it. And the function we're invoking returns a function. The `temp` variable is set to the return value of our outer function, which is a function that calls `alert`.

```
temp("Wow.");
```

Now, what will this code do? It will pop up an alert box that says `"Wow."`

We can translate our existing example to this module pattern:

```
var MOD = function () {
    var title = "Module MOD";
    return {
        buildClickHandler: function (i) {
            return function () {
                alert("You clicked link #" + (i+1)
                    + " from " + title);
            };
        }
    };
}();
```

One thing to notice is that we no longer need to refer to the module title using the `that` trick. We can refer to it directly (hooray, closure). Another difference is that nothing else has access to the title, except the code inside our module. In this case, that's not a particularly useful feature. However, consider a case where a user of our module would need to be restricted to only the functionality or the data we exposed.

We could, of course, add a `getTitle()` method to our return object that returns the value, `title`. However, the `title` could not be set unless we also provided a `setTitle()` function. And they said JavaScript wasn't a real programming language!

Adding dynamic form elements

Many applications have a requirement to be able to add rows to a form at runtime. Doing so in a conventional web application requires a combination of JavaScript and DOM manipulation.

Our example will use a simple link as the trigger for adding a new recipe ingredient row. Each new row will appear above the `Add Ingredient` link, and the input focus will be set to the `quantity` field of the new row. This allows a smooth input flow when using the keyboard. To enter a quantity, the user must hit *Tab*, enter a name, and hit *Tab* again. If a new ingredient row is to be entered, the user must hit **RETURN** on the **Add Ingredient** link.

Our requirements imply several things. We must know where to add the row on the page (hence in the DOM). We must keep track of the number of ingredient rows in order to maintain the array notation used by each row's form input fields. We must be able to reference the last row added in order to set the focus on the new form field. We should also try to keep the JavaScript as small and isolated as possible.

Identifying where to add the elements

The first requirement is pretty easy as we already know that the standard Struts 2 form tags will create a row for each element in the form (by default, our form currently mixes the default "xhtml" theme with the simple theme, as we need two form elements on each row). We'll simply create a new table row with an ID. Each new ingredient row will be added immediately before the table row with the link in it.

 NOTE: We're abandoning our "unobtrusive JavaScript" for brevity. An accessible, robust site would have a real link in the `href` attribute that would re-render the page with an addition ingredient row, and we'd add the `onclick` handler after the DOM is ready. This allows the site to degrade gracefully under browsers with no JavaScript, and aids meeting accessibility requirements.

```
<tr id="addRow">
  <td> </td>
  <td>
    <a href="#" onclick="return Recipe.addRow()">
```

```
      Add Ingredient
    </a>
  </td>
</tr>
```

We haven't written our JavaScript yet, but we'll assume a `Recipe` JavaScript module with an `addRow()` function. We'll keep our JavaScript in an external file, so we won't have access to the ingredient label defined in our property file. It's obvious when we think about it. However, with so many layers involved, we sometimes forget when we can do what.

We'll also assume that our `Recipe` module has a `prepare()` function that takes the label argument and the index of the first new ingredient row. The code for loading the JavaScript and preparing our `Recipe` module for use is a boring JavaScript as seen here:

```
<script src="<s:url value="/js/recipe/recipe.js"/>"
        type="text/javascript"></script>
<script type="text/javascript">
  Recipe.prepare('<s:text name="recipe.ingredient"/>', 3);
</script>
```

The JavaScript "Recipe" module

Here comes a bunch of JavaScript. As usual, we'll work through it bit-by-bit, at least the bits that need explaining. In reality, only a few aspects of it are particularly interesting and/or problematic. Much of it is actually refactored functions that concatenate strings.

```
var Recipe = function () {
    var ingredientLabel;
    var ingredientCount;

    function getNamePrefix() {
        return "recipe.ingredients[" + ingredientCount + "]";
    };
    function createIngredientLabel() {
        return ingredientLabel+' #' + (ingredientCount+1)+':';
    };
    function createInputTag(name, size, id) {
        var s = '<input type="text" size="' + size
                + '" name="' + name + '"';
        if (id) { s += ' id="' + id + '"'; }
        return s + '/>';
    }
```

```
function createQuantityInput() {
    return createInputTag(getNamePrefix() + ".quantity",
                          5, "count_" + ingredientCount);
};

function createNameInput() {
    return createInputTag(getNamePrefix() + ".name", 30);
};

function createIngredientRow() {
    return [
        '<tr>',
        '   <td class="tdLabel">',
        '       <label class="label">',
        '           ' + createIngredientLabel(),
        '       </label>',
        '   </td>',
        '   <td>',
        '       ' + createQuantityInput(),
        '       ' + createNameInput(),
        '   </td>',
        '</tr>'
    ].join("\n");
}

return {
    prepare: function (label, count) {
               ingredientLabel = label;
               ingredientCount = count;
          },

    addRow: function (label) {
        $("#addRow").before(createIngredientRow());
        $("#count_" + ingredientCount).focus();
        ingredientCount++;
        return false;
    }
};
}();
```

Working backwards, once again we see the trailing () characters (we know this trick). This means the Recipe variable, along with our module, will be set to the results of the execution of our function—the two functions we return.

The first function, `prepare()`, is an initialization function. It sets the module's `ingredientLabel` and `ingredientCount`. We pass the results of a Struts 2 text tag. And since we manually created three ingredient rows, the next index (not count) is three.

This function, and all the rest that use the ingredient's label and count, is relying on closures. Even though we've returned the functions, they're being evaluated in the context of the `Recipe` module. As we've seen, this means that the returned methods retain their access to the ingredient's label and count. It's like magic.

The `addRow()` function is the `onclick` handler for our **Add Ingredient** link. It uses jQuery's `$()` function and a CSS selector, as we've already seen. Recall when we first discussed selectors, we defined a style for a particular ID with the "#" character. The CSS selectors work identically when accessing elements with jQuery. `$("#addRow")` will return a collection of all the DOM elements with an ID, `addRow`.

In this case, it will only return one object in the collection. However, we don't need to worry about it being in a collection because jQuery's functions are designed to work with `$()`. JQuery's `before()` function adds DOM objects immediately before (clever!) the selected DOM objects. In our case, it's a single object, our row with the **add** link.

The next statement sets the focus on the newly-created ingredient row's quantity input element. Here, we've built the CSS selector from a constant string and the current index value. We increment the ingredient count and return `false`, so the link won't be followed.

The remaining functions are "private", that is, they're accessible only from the two methods we return when we evaluate the module function. If we add a function to the `Recipe` module outside of our initial function execution, it won't have access to the private functions.

The `createIngredientRow()` function returns a string containing all the HTML for an ingredient row. JQuery's `before()` function can take an HTML string and turn it into DOM elements. Some people prefer direct DOM manipulation, for both performance and technical reasons. However, in this example, we're aiming strictly for convenience.

The `createIngrediantRow()` function, in turn, calls the remaining functions to build up the more complicated strings. None of them are particularly interesting, although `createInputTag()` does use JavaScript's ability to accept fewer (or more) parameters than the function is declared with. Here, we use it to optionally provide an `id` attribute, so that can refer to the quantity field during the `addRow()` function and set the input focus (as described earlier).

Now, when we click on the **Add Ingredient** link, we'll generate a new ingredient row, and the focus is set to its quantity field. Our JavaScript is encapsulated. It's relatively easier to modify the generated HTML if our requirements should change, and we can confuse our co-workers with our mad JavaScript skills. What more could one ask for?

The next question of how to dynamically delete a row is left as an exercise for the reader. Oh, snap! Kidding aside, deleting a row adds a considerable amount of irritation to the process. The order of ingredients is usually significant in a recipe, so we would need to either re-compute the indices or remove empty list items on the server side.

With a few minor CSS changes, we end up with the following page, showing one extra ingredient row. It won't win any beauty contests, but we're getting the basic idea.

The idea is to communicate how the application behaves to determine if it's on the right track. Obviously, there's a lot more to be done, but we nearly have enough to get the basic idea of how our application will work.

Summary

This chapter looks at CSS, which is used for both styling and adding behavior to a page. With only a very minimal amount of CSS, some clean JavaScript, and effective use of the framework, we learn to produce a partially-functional prototype quickly and easily. Bear in mind that as it stands, we're right around a thousand lines of code. For Java, that isn't all that bad.

In the next chapter, we'll look at themes and templates of Struts 2. We will focus on modifying one of the default themes to allow some currently missing functionality, focusing on enhancements that will allow us to have more fun with CSS, and exercise our mad JavaScript skills. We'll also look at FreeMarker, the template language used by Struts 2, which can also be used in place of JSP.

References

A reader can refer to the following:

- jQuery:

  `http://jquery.com/`

- CSS Selectors:

  `http://www.w3.org/TR/css3-selectors/`
  `http://css.maxdesign.com.au/selectutorial/`

- Unobtrusive JavaScript:

  `http://en.wikipedia.org/wiki/Unobtrusive_JavaScript`
  `http://www.alistapart.com/articles/behavioralseparation/`

12
Themes and Templates

We've already seen some general information regarding Struts 2's built-in themes and templates. These themes and templates define the HTML emitted by Struts 2's form tags, including the table tags around form inputs. The form tags are implemented with the FreeMarker template language.

To test the waters of defining our own theme (and its templates), we'll introduce a requirement to our recipe entry screen to have some different behavior when there is a validation error. The default behavior now is to change the style of the label and print the error message above the field. We'd like to highlight the entire row as a gentle reminder that our user has left out something important.

Extracting the templates

The first step to modifying an existing theme or creating our own is to extract the templates from the Struts 2 distribution. This actually has the advantageous performance side effect of keeping the templates in the file system (as opposed to in the library file), which allows FreeMarker to cache the templates properly. Caching the templates provides a performance boost and involves no work other than extracting the templates. The issue with caching templates contained in library files, however, will be fixed.

If we examine the Struts 2 core JAR file, we'll see a /template folder. We just need to put that in our application's classpath. The best way to do this depends on your build and deploy environment. For example, if we're using Eclipse, the easiest thing to do is put the /template folder in our source folder; Eclipse should deploy them automatically.

A maze of twisty little passages

Right now, our form has only text fields and a submit button. We'll start by looking at the template for the text field tag. For the most part, Struts 2 custom tags are named similarly to the template file that defines it. As we're using the "xhtml" theme, we'll look in our newly-created /template/xhtml folder. Templates are found in a folder with the same name as the theme.

We find the `<s:textfield>` template in /template/xhtml/text.ftl file. However, when we open it, we are disappointed to find it implemented by the following files—controlheader.ftl file retrieved from the current theme's folder, text.ftl from the simple theme, and controlfooter.ftl file from "xhtml" theme. This is curious, but satisfactory for now.

We'll assume what we need is in the controlheader.ftl file. However, upon opening that, we discover we actually need to look in controlheader-core.ftl file. Opening that file shows us the table rows that we're looking for.

Going walkabout through source code, both Java and FreeMarker, can be frustrating, but ultimately educational. Developing the habit of looking at framework source can lead to a greater mastery of that framework. It can be frustrating at times, but is a critical skill.

Even without a strong understanding of the FreeMarker template language, we can get a pretty good idea of what needs to be done by looking at the controlheader-core.ftl file. We notice that the template sets a convenience variable (hasFieldErrors) when the field being rendered has an error. We'll use that variable to control the style of the table row and cells of our text fields. This is how the class of the text field label is being set.

We notice a fair amount of work being done to support the labels being positioned on top of the form field. We're not doing that in our form, so we'll ignore that completely and will focus only on our immediate task. If we were creating our own template, we might completely remove the unused portions of the template file in order to simplify future work.

Creating our theme

To keep the template clean for the purpose of education, we'll go ahead and create a new theme. (Most of the things will be the same, but we'll strip out some unused code in the templates we modify.) While we have the possibility of extending an existing theme (see the Struts 2 documentation for details), we'll just create a new theme called s2wad by copying the xhtml templates into a folder called s2wad. We can now use the new theme by setting the theme in our <s:form> tag by specifying a theme attribute:

```
<s:form theme="s2wad" ... etc ...>
```

Subsequent form tags will now use our new s2wad theme. Because we decided not to extend the existing "xhtml" theme, as we have a lot of tags with the "xhtml" string hard coded inside. In theory, it probably wasn't necessary to hard code the theme into the templates. However, we're going to modify only a few tags for the time being, while the remaining tags will remain hard coded (although incorrectly). In an actual project, we'd either extend an existing theme or spend more time cleaning up the theme we've created (along with the "xhtml" theme, and provide corrective patches back to the Struts 2 project).

First, we'll modify controlheader.ftl to use the theme parameter to load the appropriate controlheader-core.ftl file. Arguably, this is how the template should be implemented anyway, even though we could hard code in the new s2wad theme.

Next, we'll start on controlheader-core.ftl. As our site will never use the top label position, we'll remove that. Doing this isn't necessary, but will keep it cleaner for our use. The controlheader-core.ftl template creates a table row for each field error for the field being rendered, and creates the table row containing the field label and input field itself.

We want to add a class to both the table row and table cells containing the field label and input field. By adding a class to both, the row itself and each of the two table cells, we maximize our ability to apply CSS styles. Even if we end up styling only one or the other, it's convenient to have the option.

We'll also strip out the FreeMarker code that puts the required indicator to the left of the label, once again, largely to keep things clean. Projects will normally have a unified look and feel. It's reasonable to remove unused functionality, and if we're already going through the trouble to create a new theme, then we might as well do that.

We're also going to clean up the template a little bit by consolidating how we handle the presence of field errors. Instead of putting several FreeMarker <#if> directives throughout the template, we'll create some HTML attributes at the top of the template, and use them in the table row and table cells later on.

Finally, we'll indent the template file to make it easier to read. This may not always be a viable technique in production, as the extra spaces may be rendered improperly, (particularly across browsers), possibly depending on what we end up putting in the tag. For now, imagine that we're using the default "required" indicator, an asterisk, but it's conceivable we might want to use something like an image. Whitespace is something to be aware of when dealing with HTML.

Our modified controlheader-core.ftl file now looks like this:

```
<#assign hasFieldErrors = parameters.name?exists && fieldErrors?exists
&& fieldErrors[parameters.name]?exists/>
<#if hasFieldErrors>
  <#assign labelClass = "class='errorLabel'"/>
  <#assign trClass = "class='hasErrors'"/>
  <#assign tdClass = "class='tdLabel hasErrors'"/>
<#else>
  <#assign labelClass = "class='label'"/>
  <#assign trClass = ""/>
  <#assign tdClass = "class='tdLabel'"/>
</#if>

<#if hasFieldErrors>
  <#list fieldErrors[parameters.name] as error>
    <tr errorFor="${parameters.id}" class="hasErrors">
      <td> </td>
      <td class="hasErrors"><#rt/>
        <span class="errorMessage">${error?html}</span><#t/>
      </td><#lt/>
    </tr>
  </#list>
</#if>

<tr ${trClass}>
  <td ${tdClass}>
    <#if parameters.label?exists>
      <label <#t/>
        <#if parameters.id?exists>
          for="${parameters.id?html}" <#t/>
        </#if>
        ${labelClass}
```

```
><#t/>
  ${parameters.label?html}<#t/>
  <#if parameters.required?default(false)>
    <span class="required">*</span><#t/>
  </#if>
  :<#t/>
  <#include "/${parameters.templateDir}/s2e2e/tooltip.ftl" />
</label><#t/>
</#if>
</td><#lt/>
```

It's significantly different when compared to the `controlheader-core.ftl` file of the "xhtml" theme. However, it has the same functionality for our application, with the addition of the new `hasErrors` class applied to both the table row and cells for the recipe's `name` and `description` fields. We've also slightly modified where the field errors are displayed (it is no longer centered around the entire input field row, but directly above the field itself).

We'll also modify the `controlheader.ftl` template to apply the `hasErrors` style to the table cell containing the input field. This template is much simpler and includes only our new `hasErrors` class and the original `align` code. Note that we can use the variable `hasFieldErrors`, which is defined in `controlheader-core.ftl`. This is a valuable technique, but has the potential to lead to spaghetti code. It would probably be better to define it in the `controlheader.ftl` template.

```
<#include "/${parameters.templateDir}/${parameters.theme}/
controlheader-core.ftl" />
  <td
<#if hasFieldErrors>
    class="hasErrors"<#t/>
</#if>
<#if parameters.align?exists>
    align="${parameters.align?html}"<#t/>
</#if>
><#t/>
```

We'll create a style for the table cells with the `hasErrors` class, setting the background to be just a little red. Our new template sets the `hasErrors` class on both the label and the input field table cells, and we've collapsed our table borders, so this will create a table row with a light red background.

```
.hasErrors td {
  background: #fdd;
}
```

Now, a missing **Name** or **Description** will give us a more noticeable error, as shown in the following screenshot:

This is fairly a simple example. However, it does show that it's pretty straightforward to begin customizing our own templates to match the requirements of the application. By encapsulating some of the view layer inside the form tags, our JSP files are kept significantly cleaner.

Other uses of templates

Anything we can do in a typical JSP page can be done in our templates. We don't *have* to use Struts 2's template support. We can do many similar things in a JSP custom tag file (or a Java-based tag), but we'd lose some of the functionality that's already been built.

Some potential uses of templates might include the addition of accessibility features across an entire site, allowing them to be encapsulated within concise JSP notation. Enhanced JavaScript functionality could be added to all fields, or only specific fields of a form, including things such as detailed help or informational pop ups. This overlaps somewhat with the existing tooltip support, we might have custom usage requirements or our own framework that we need to support.

Struts 2 now also ships with a Java-based theme that avoids the use of FreeMarker tags. These tags provide a noticeable speed benefit. However, only a few basic tags are supported at this time. It's bundled as a plug-in, which can be used as a launching point for our own Java-based tags.

Summary

Themes and templates provide another means of encapsulating functionality and/or appearance across an entire application. The use of existing themes can be a great benefit, particularly when doing early prototyping of a site, and are often sufficient for the finished product.

Dealing effectively with templates is largely a matter of digging through the existing template source. It also includes determining what our particular needs are, and modifying or creating our own themes, adding and removing functionality as appropriate. While this chapter only takes a brief look at templates, it covers the basics and opens the door to implementing any enhancements we may require.

In the next chapter, we'll dive into Rich Internet Applications (RIA) and the Struts 2 REST plug-in. We will also take a brief look at the legacy Dojo tags that provide some Ajax functionality out of the box.

References

A reader can refer to the following:

- FreeMarker
  `http://freemarker.org`

13
Rich Internet Applications

Remember when a website was a static HTML page with an occasional form? Remember when we wrote a low-fidelity prototype that was functional (but ugly) without much flair? The entire web used to be like that, without even the minimal we've used or our brief plunge into JavaScript treachery.

There were glimmers back in the day (do you recall **applets** — applications delivered over the web that used a platform-neutral language?). Now, instead of Java, we're using JavaScript, Flash, Silverlight, JavaFX, or a combination. Within the "browser with JavaScript" space lies another complete set of solutions. It includes lower-level solutions ssuch as Prototype and jQuery (and widget libraries built on the same), up to full-blown application environments such YUI, Dojo, GWT, and more.

What this chapter is and isn't

This chapter has changed quite a bit over its writing. Originally, there were separate RIA and Struts 2 Dojo tag chapters. However, the Struts 2 Dojo tags are based on Dojo 0.4.3, which is quite different from Dojo 1.0+. Updating the tags has become impractical, and the Dojo tags have been deprecated.

Another issue is that there are quite a few solutions for creating AJAX applications. No matter what we cover in the few pages available here, it would suit only a small number of readers and would be out-of-date more quickly as compared to the Java technologies we've been discussing.

This chapter briefly covers Struts 2 Dojo tags, along with general RIA background information, the Struts 2 REST plug-in (Struts 2.1+), and various approaches that can be of use when creating Struts 2-based RIAs.

There are a lot of applications that require only a few fancy features, and still others that depend on only a fraction of the capabilities of the libraries they use. Once we move beyond fairly simple use cases, it's generally more efficient to dive into the library we've chosen and make full use of it. Even the Struts 2 Dojo plug-in requires a good understanding of how Dojo works, once we move beyond the basics. As we get more comfortable with high-level JavaScript, it's often more convenient to just use raw Dojo or whatever JavaScript framework we're most familiar with.

Dojo tags

The Struts 2.1 Dojo Plug-in moves the AJAX tags into a plug-in and updates the AJAX tags found in Struts 2.0. The tags make simple Dojo use cases very simple. There are a few points working against the tags:

- The tags support only Dojo 0.4.3, while Dojo is in 1.x territory.
- The default Struts 2 profile creates many requests per-page for Dojo files.
- More complicated use cases require enough JavaScript and Dojo understanding that it's arguably easier to just use raw Dojo.

We must also consider that many people have strong investments in other frameworks, including Prototype, jQuery, YUI, GWT, and so on. For some people, the Struts 2 Dojo tags don't make sense (although the cleanliness is compelling for simple uses).

Simple use cases really are simple

There are many degrees to Web 2.0. Some sites may have very minor requirements—click this button, and something shows up somewhere else. Submit a form in-place and update something based on the submission. You know the drill—a little Web 2.0 pizzazz. Low-fidelity prototype? No problem—for simple use cases there will only be a minor penalty for using a different library. Nobody knows JavaScript or Dojo? That's okay. For the really easy stuff, it's not a requirement.

The Dojo <sx:head> tag

We'll cover several simple use cases using the Struts 2.1 Dojo Plug-in. Like any other custom tag library, we must use the taglib directive. The convention is to use `sx` as the Dojo tag prefix.

```
<%@ taglib prefix="sx" uri="/struts-dojo-tags" %>
```

In addition to the normal taglib directive, we must also use the `<sx:head>` tag. This is so the appropriate Dojo JavaScript libraries are included in our page. Note that the JavaScript files are served from within Struts. We do not need to have our own copy of Dojo, the plug-in has its own copy. (If we need to serve the files ourselves we can have a copy of Dojo.)

The Dojo head tag allows us to turn on Dojo debugging using the `debug` attribute. It's a good idea to keep debugging turned on during development, particularly if we're not using a tool like Firebug.

```
<sx:head debug="true" />
```

We'll occasionally need to use the non-compressed, non-cached Dojo, as shown below. Generally, the `debug` attribute gives us enough to go on, and we're less likely to forget to remove the `cache` and `compressed` attributes when we check in the production version of our code.

```
<sx:head debug="true" cache="false" compressed="false" />
```

When we look at the documentation for the head tag (we've looked, right?), we see a few other Dojo-specific attributes not discussed here. However, they serve as a reminder that the Struts 2 Dojo plug-in integrates an entirely different JavaScript-based ecosystem into our application and development environment.

Abstracting the underlying technology by generating HTML and JavaScript using custom tags can be a tremendous time- and sanity-saver. However, it's important to understand what the tags actually do. It's a good idea to examine the code emitted by the Dojo tags to get a better idea of how things work under the covers.

Make sure you're looking at the correct Dojo documentation since looking at Dojo 1.0 docs will just lead to frustration and confusion. (By the time this is published, the new jQuery plug-in might be a bit more mature—stay light on your feet!)

The Dojo <sx:a> tag

The `<sx:a>` (anchor) tag's primary purpose is to put the results of an AJAX request into an element on the calling page (typically, a `<div>` or `<span>`).

When we look at the documentation for the anchor tag, we're deluged with a number of tag attributes. We can ignore almost all of them for simple use cases. Indeed, the only attributes we really need are `href`, to define the request target, and `targets`, to define the element(s) in which to put the request result.

The `href` attribute should be built with the `<s:url>` tag. A simple example that displays two links, the results of which will be put in a `<div>`, looks like the following:

```
<%@ taglib prefix="s" uri="/struts-tags" %>
<%@ taglib prefix="sx" uri="/struts-dojo-tags" %>
<html>
  <head>
    <sx:head debug="true"/>
  </head>
  <body>
    <s:url action="simple1" var="simple1" />
    <s:url action="simple2" var="simple2" />

    <sx:a href="%{simple1}" targets="results">Simple #1</sx:a>
    <sx:a href="%{simple2}" targets="results">Simple #2</sx:a>

    <div id="results"></div>
  </body>
</html>
```

Note that even though we're creating a variable in the `<s:url>` tag, we do not use the "#" character when referencing it later in the `<sx:a>` tags (if we do, it won't work). Also note that the `targets` attribute is not plural by mistake. We can update multiple elements with the same results by supplying a comma-separated list of target IDs.

This simplistic requirement, encountered commonly in the wild, requires no hand-written JavaScript and is drop-dead simple. It may not stay that simple, but even more complicated functionality may be implemented using only tag attributes.

We can highlight and fade out the element that was updated using the `highlightColor` (no default) and `highlightDuration` (defaults to 2000 milliseconds, or two seconds). Suddenly, our application has its Web 2.0 bona fides and everybody loves it.

```
<sx:a href="%{simple2}" targets="results"
      highlightColor="#c99" highlightDuration="750">
  Simple #2
</sx:a>
```

If we're really bored, we can try clicking on the link again before the highlight has completed its color fade. We can then think about how to fix it. (Have fun with that — several other libraries suffer from the same issue!)

Do we need to show a Web 2.0-certified, spinning AJAX wheel? The `indicator` attribute defines the ID of an element to be shown while making the request—drop a spinny AJAX image into the element and we're all set. (We could buck the trend and show some text in a `<div>`, but that's not nearly as impressive.)

```
<sx:a href="%{simple2}" targets="results"
      indicator="lookHere">
  Simple #2
</sx:a>
```

Whatever is in the `lookHere` element will be shown for the duration of the AJAX request. If we're bucking the spinny AJAX image trend and using only text, and the text can be displayed in the target element(s), we can set the `showLoadingText` attribute to `true` (it defaults to `false`) to show the loading text in the target element. We can set the `loadingText` attribute (it defaults to "Loading...") to specify the text that will appear.

```
<sx:a href="%{simple1}" targets="results"
      showLoadingText="true">Simple #1</sx:a>
```

There is a specific issue with Internet Explorer when the target element is contained in the same parent as the anchor tag. In this case, it's best to use the `indicator` attribute. Setting `showLoadingText` to `false`, and using an `indicator` outside of the element containing the target element, will fix the IE issue.

We may want to use this method anyway. For example, if we want the loading text to always appear in the upper right corner or center of the browser window.

A brief side journey on topics

Dojo **topics** are a way of creating a publish/subscribe (pub/sub) model for event handling. Topics are a way of sending a message saying, "Hey! something on the page did X", defining what X is, and allowing things to happen when all those arbitrary Xs occur.

Let's examine a possible scenario where we could use the anchor tag, topics, our next tag `<sx:div>`, along with some JavaScript and Dojo, and get recipe ingredient information in one screen area and update another area of the screen with a list of recipes that also use that ingredient. (As we're still in low-fidelity prototype mode, the data itself will be fake. It will be enough to demonstrate the purpose and intent of the functionality.)

We'll capture our user story as simply as possible.

When viewing a recipe, clicking an ingredient will:

- Show the ingredient information in an information area
- Update a list of recipes containing that ingredient in a sidebar

As we've already seen, we can use the anchor tag to create the first part. The URL that we'll use is different, and we need to pass in the ingredient ID. On our recipe display page, we will then see something similar to the following:

```
<s:iterator value="recipe.ingredients" var="ring">
  <s:url action="show" namespace="/ingredients" var="ingUrl">
    <s:param name="ingredientId" value="#ring.ingredient.id"/>
  </s:url>

  <li>
    <sx:a href="%{ingUrl}"
          targets="ingredientInfo"
          highlightColor="#c99"
          highlightDuration="750"
          afterNotifyTopics="/updateRecipes"
          id="ing_%{#recIng.ingredient.id}">
      <s:property value="#ring.ingredient.name"/>
    </sx:a>
  </li>
</s:iterator>
```

Nothing new here. We click on the ingredient name and insert the results of the action into the `ingredientInfo` element.

However, the second part of our requirement is a bit more mysterious. We need to update a different element with a list of recipes that use the ingredient we clicked. We start this process by using the `afterNotifyTopics` attribute of the anchor tag. `afterNotifyTargets` accepts a comma-separated list of topic names that will be published on a successful request. For now, we assume the requests will succeed—low-fidelity prototype, remember!

Here, we publish a single topic, `/updateRecipes`, when the link is clicked. We'll use our next tag, `<sx:div>`, to "consume" this topic and update a content area after the ingredient information is displayed on the page. (I've followed the original Struts 2/Dojo convention and used a "/" prefix for topic names.)

In Dojo, a topic can be published with additional data. We'd like to use the ingredient ID as the additional data. This will allow us to request a list of recipes using that ingredient. However, there is not an immediately obvious way to bind this data to the topic using the Dojo tags. So, we're going to cheat a little bit. But first, the `<sx:div>` tag.

The Dojo <sx:div> tag

The <sx:div> tag creates an HTML <div> that loads its content using AJAX and Dojo. It can be used to automatically refresh its contents after an arbitrary time period (this can be continuous, the timer may be stopped and started, and so on). It is also used with the tabbed panel component to define the contents of each tab.

In its simplest form, the <sx:div> tag is similar to the anchor tag, but creates its own <div> for use as its target.

Finishing our user story

In our user story the requirement was to display a list of recipes using the clicked ingredient. We have an action that performs a service call and returns a list of recipes. We'll use this action as the target of our <sx:div> tag as shown next (we highlight this <div> as well, so we're aware when something happens):

```
<s:url action="recipesWithIngredient" namespace="/recipes"
        var="rwiUrl"/>
<sx:div id="recipesWithIngredient" href="%{rwiUrl}"
        preload="false" listenTopics="/updateRecipes"
        afterNotifyTopics="/resetUrl"
        highlightColor="#c99" highlightDuration="750">
</sx:div>
```

When we click an ingredient, we only get the recipe list header in our <div> tag. We're not passing in an ingredient ID because there's no way to attach the data to our topic in our <sx:a> tag. So, we don't see any recipes. This is bad.

Highlighting the need to know

This very simple usage scenario immediately highlights the need to know something about the underlying Dojo framework that makes these convenience tags possible. While it's possible to use the tags without knowing anything about Dojo, it's best to dive into Dojo if our usage moves beyond what is provided (trivially) by the tags.

Without having an understanding of what the tags are doing, it's much more difficult to add functionality or debug problems. A good working knowledge of JavaScript is also required once we move beyond the functionality included in the standard tags. (This is true with any JavaScript library, not just Dojo.)

Here's one of the difficulties of Struts 2 and the Dojo tags: since they're based on Dojo 0.4.3, the documentation is a bit sparser than we might prefer. In fact, I couldn't find (in a timely fashion) an "approved" way to implement this functionality, so I punted. This is an often unfortunate reality when developing under pressure in tight, agile release cycles.

Our implementation then consists of some JavaScript, some Dojo, and another topic. In a nutshell, when we click on an ingredient and the ingredient information request is completed (and successful), we'll change the URL of our `<sx:div>` tag to include the ingredient ID. When *that* request is done, we'll change the URL back to what it was before we added the ingredient ID in order to be ready for the next request.

To accomplish this, we'll give an ID (that includes the ingredient ID) to our first anchor tag (normally, a Dojo widget will create its own id). From our earlier `<sx:a>` tag:

```
id="ing_%{#recIng.ingredient.id}"
```

To use this embedded ID, we'll use Dojo to bind a JavaScript function to our topic, which is published upon a successful recipe information request. We also use Dojo to retrieve the original URL of our new `<sx:div>` tag—we'll use it to reset the URL in a moment.

```
var baseUrl; // A global! Don't do this in a real app.
dojo.event.topic.subscribe("/updateRecipes",
    function(data, request, widget) {
        var ingredientId = widget.widgetId.split("_")[1];
        var dest = dojo.widget.byId("recipesWithIngredient");
        baseUrl = dest.href; // Referencing a global!
        dest.href += "?ingredientId=" + ingredientId;
    });
```

This binds a JavaScript function to the `/updateRecipes` topic, published upon a successful ingredient information request (from our anchor tag, `<sx:a>`, previously). When this function executes, it receives the Dojo widget as the third parameter. From this, we can retrieve its ID (which includes our ingredient ID!), get the `<sx:div>` tag (a Dojo widget), and update its URL to include the ingredient ID.

However, as it stands, it's broken. As we click on ingredients, each ingredient ID will be appended to our `<sx:div>` URL. We defined a `afterNotifyTopics` topic on our `<sx:div>` tag as shown here:

```
afterNotifyTopics="/resetUrl"
```

We use the same Dojo/JavaScript binding to bind a function that resets the URL.

```
dojo.event.topic.subscribe("/resetUrl",
    function(data, request, widget) {
        widget.href = baseUrl; // Restore URL from global!
    });
```

To keep things simple, we didn't use our JavaScript techniques for hiding global variables and functionality. This shows how even a seemingly innocent user story can lead to much more work than anticipated. (You can tell your boss I said so.)

It also highlights why working with Dojo in its "natural state" may be a good option for anything but the simplest use cases. Not only would we get the latest Dojo, but we'd also have more recent, maintained documentation, additional functionality, and complete control.

Dojo and forms

We can submit forms using Dojo and AJAX by using the `<sx:submit>` tag. In its simplest usage, we can submit a form and update a target element with the results returned by an action as with the `<sx:a>` tag, but via a form submission. The `<sx:submit>` element can be contained in a form element, or can live outside the form by using the `formId` element.

Our user story concocted to demonstrate this is simple. We type in a string, search for recipes with that string in the title, and list the results in an HTML `<div>` on the same page.

The JSP containing the form looks like any other form, except that we use the `<sx: submit>` tag instead of the `<s:submit>` tag. The tag does all the busywork. We have almost nothing special to do.

```
<s:form action="showContainingWord">
  <s:textfield label="Recipe Word" name="recipeWord"/>
  <sx:submit targets="recipesWithWord"
      highlightColor="#ccc" highlightDuration="500"/>
</s:form>
<div id="recipesWithWord"></div>
```

Similar to the `<sx:a>` tag, we specify a target element to update with the results of the form submission. To snaz it up, we add highlight color and duration attributes. The action specified in the `<s:form>` tag is a normal Struts 2 action. Note that we do not need to set the theme to `"ajax"`. Although, as we'd expect, we need to use the `<sx:head>` tag to load the Dojo JavaScript files.

The REST plug-in

Struts 2.1's REST plug-in provides a mechanism for Struts 2 to act more REST-like, and includes convention-based URLs (think Ruby on Rails), various output formats (JSON and XML for consumption, XHTML for us humans), and so on. The REST plug-in builds on the Convention plug-in we've already covered (so a lot of knowledge is immediately useful).

REST in a nutshell

REpresentational State Transfer—now that we know why we abbreviate it, what does it really mean? In the context of a web application, it means we're exposing a set of resources (such as a "recipe" or an "ingredient" in our case) through a uniform interface (such as /recipe/1 for a recipe with an ID as 1, as expressed by a URI), and that the HTTP methods (GET, PUT, and so on) are used to indicate the type of action we're performing on the selected resource.

The REST plug-in in a nutshell

The Struts 2 REST plug-in allows a Struts 2 application to behave more RESTfully. It provides support for Ruby on Rails-like URLs (with one minor exception, which is noted below), automatically returns an appropriate result type based on the request URL, and uses convention-over-configuration to automatically determine where view-side pages (JSP, FreeMarker, Velocity, and so on) are located in the web application.

REST plug-in URLs

The REST plug-in makes several assumptions about the URL and the underlying action methods they map to. For example, if we make a GET request to the /recipe URL, the REST plug-in will call the index() method in the recipe action class, which should list recipes. A POST to the same URL will call Recipe.create(). A GET request to /recipe/1 will call the show() method and set the action's id property to "1".

The only diversion from typical REST URL/method mapping is /recipe/new, which will call editNew() (not new() as we might expect) as we can't have a new() method in Java.

The following table is adapted from the Struts 2 REST plug-in Wiki page:

HTTP Method	URI	method	Parameters
GET	/recipe	index()	
POST	/recipe	create()	
PUT	/recipe/1	update()	id=1
DELETE	/recipe/1	destroy()	id=1
GET	/recipe/1	show()	id=1
GET	/recipe/1/edit	edit()	id=1
GET	/recipe/new	editNew()	

REST plug-in results

When we use the REST plug-in, we don't configure our results using XML or annotations, yet the plug-in still returns XML, JSON, and HTML (by default, we can define other content handlers). How does the plug-in decide what to send back?

In the URL table above, we don't show any extensions. By default, the plug-in will look for and return an XHTML response, but can be configured to return XML or JSON—a serialized version of the action, similar to how the XSLT and JSON responses work. To select the return type we add an extension. For example, if we request /recipe/1.json, we'll get a JSON result back (surprise!).

The default can be changed by setting the struts.rest.defaultExtension property to any valid string, the default being xhtml. (At the time of writing this book, the documentation states the default is xml. Diving into source or library files is often a necessary skill!)

The REST plug-in also redefines the struts.action.extension configuration parameter, setting it to xhtml,,xml,json (the two commas are intentional). This allows the framework to accept these three extensions, and a fourth empty extension. The empty extension allows extension-less URLs, which will default as described above.

We'll see how to create our own result content handler in a little bit. We'll usually use one of the default handlers.

A web browser client example

Configuring our first example looks similar to the configuration used for Convention (almost no configuration at all) — because the REST plug-in builds on Convention. Our Struts 2 filter configuration is as follows:

```
<filter>
  <filter-name>struts2</filter-name>
  <filter-class>    org.apache.struts2.dispatcher.ng.filter.
StrutsPrepareAndExecuteFilter
  </filter-class>
<init-param>
    <param-name>struts.devMode</param-name>
    <param-value>true</param-value>
  </init-param>
  <init-param>
    <param-name>struts.rest.defaultExtension</param-name>
    <param-value>xml</param-value>
  </init-param>
</filter>
```

The REST controller

Controllers look like regular actions. The REST plug-in uses the name "controller" to differentiate them from regular actions. The controller below is a POJO — it doesn't extend `ActionSupport`. In our example, we're just retrieving either a single recipe or a list of all recipes and sending it back to the browser as JSON, XML, or XHTML.

```
public class RecipeController implements ModelDriven<Object> {
    private Long id;
    private Recipe recipe;
    private Collection<Recipe> recipes;
    private RecipeService recipeService =
        new FakeRecipeService();

    public HttpHeaders index() {
        modelObject = recipeService.getAll();
        return new
            DefaultHttpHeaders("index").disableCaching();
    }

    public String show() {
        modelObject = recipeService.findById(id);
        return "show";
    }

    private Object modelObject;
```

```
    public Object getModel() {
        return modelObject;
    }
    // ... Getters and setters elided
}
```

Before looking at the results of a query to this controller, there are a few things worth pointing out. Note that we're implementing `ModelDriven<Object>`. If we don't, the REST plug-in will serialize the entire controller in our response, including the service. This is almost never what we want. Implementing `ModelDriven<Object>` tells the REST plug-in to only serialize the model object.

We're using a generic `Object` as the model. This allows us to set the model to either a list of recipes or a single recipe. Yes, we lose a certain amount of type safety by going this way, but it also allows us to put related functionality into the same controller, while retaining the ability to control serialization.

Finally, notice that the `index()` method returns an `HttpHeaders` object, while the `show()` method returns a string. Returning an `HttpHeaders` object gives us fine-grained control over the headers, so that we could use Etags, control caching, and so on. The string argument is used by the XHTML response to help find the JSP (or FreeMarker, or Velocity) template to use. The string return signature skips the `HttpHeaders` control, with the string value used to look up the result as with the `HttpHeaders` constructor.

REST controller responses

When we request `/recipe`, we'll get an XML representation of the recipe list. Because of the way the REST plug-in serializes XML, we don't get a completely bare representation of the collection:

```
<java.util.Arrays_-ArrayList>
  <a class="com.packt.s2wad.models.Recipe-array">
    <com.packt.s2wad.models.Recipe>
      <id>2</id>
      <name>Water and Oil</name>
      <description>Some water and oil</description>
      <ingredients>
        <com.packt.s2wad.models.RecipeIngredient>
          <id>1</id>
          <index>1</index>
          <quantity>2 T</quantity>
          <ingredient>
            <id>4</id>
            <name>Olive oil</name>
```

```
            <description>Olive oil</description>
         </ingredient>
      </com.packt.s2wad.models.RecipeIngredient>
      <!-- ... etc ... -->
```

However, as long as we know what we're getting back, it should be okay. (We'll see how this assumption can bite us in the next section, when we look at using the XML result to populate an Ext-JS grid. There's always something!)

It begins to get interesting when we request /recipe.json. Now we get back the following:

```
[
  { "id" : 2,
    "name" : "Water and Oil",
    "description" :"Some water and oil",
    "ingredients" :
      [
        { "index" : 1,
          "ingredient" : { "description" : "Olive oil",
                           "name" : "Olive oil",
                           "id" : 4
                         },
          "quantity" : "2T",
          "id" : 1
        },
        { "index" : 2,
          "ingredient" : { "description" : "Water",
                           "name" : "Water",
                           "id" : 6
                         },
          "quantity" : "2 c",
          "id" : 2
        }
      ]
  },
  { "id" : 3,
    "name" : "Tomato Soup",
    // ... etc ...
  }
]
```

Now that we're JavaScript wizards, we know this is simply an array of anonymous objects, each with a set of properties (some of which are also anonymous objects).

If we make a request to /recipe.xhtml, the REST plug-in will find a view page using a method similar to Convention, but slightly different. The REST plug-in will look for the view file created by the controller name (recipe in this case) and the method name (index in this case), and then string them together with a hyphen in the middle. Here, it will look for a file named recipe-index.jsp.

Our JSP file can look like any other JSP file, keeping in mind that we'll be accessing the model controller property. (We could also access the recipe list from a recipes property, but since we have the model object anyway, we might as well use it.)

Accessing a single recipe is similar, and the defaults of the REST plug-in make it fairly straightforward. Remember that a request to /recipe/1 will, by default, set the controller's id property. In our default case, we'll get back an XML response. Requesting /recipe/1.json returns JSON, and /recipe/1.xhtml will look for a file named recipe-show.jsp (or .ftl and .vm, for FreeMarker and Velocity).

Note that the methods called by the REST URLs are customizable. For example, the index method name is set with the struts.mapper.indexMethodName parameter, as is the name of the id property using the struts.mapper.idParameterName parameter. See the REST plug-in documentation for further configuration parameters.

An example of a useful client

In isolation, the REST plug-in may not immediately seem useful, as we don't usually want to show the user JSON or XML (although with a style sheet, maybe we do). Ext-JS is a popular JavaScript client library that includes its own utilities and widgets, and can be a replacement for, or adjunct to, the jQuery library we've been using.

Here's the catch, at least for the time being: as of Ext-JS 2.2, XML whose elements may contain the "." character (as ours does), throws off how Ext works. Partial workarounds are available. However, I am not aware of a full solution, if one is available. The following code only works with a modified version of Ext (for those who care, it's in the DomQuery code), and doesn't quite work all the way at that.

 A better way around the issue would be to change the way the REST plug-in serializes our action's mode. For example, by eliminating the package prefix and including only the actual class name. Hacking Ext is an incomplete and fragile solution.

The following code, in the `recipe-index.jsp`, includes the JavaScript in the JSP file. In this case, we are breaking away from the best practices, but we'll let it go for the sake of simplicity.

```
<%@ taglib prefix="s" uri="/struts-tags" %>

<html>
  <head>
    <link rel="stylesheet" type="text/css"
href="<s:url value='/ext-2.2/resources/css/ext-all.css' />"/>
    <script type="text/javascript"
      src="<s:url value='/ext-2.2/adapter/ext/ext-base.js'/>">
    </script>
    <script type="text/javascript"
      src="<s:url value='/ext-2.2/ext-all-debug.js'/>">
    </script>
  </head>

  <body>
    <div id="example-grid"></div>

    <script type="text/javascript">
      Ext.onReady(function() {
          var store = new Ext.data.Store({
              url: '<s:url value="/recipe"/>',
              reader: new Ext.data.XmlReader({
                  record: "com.packt.s2wad.models.Recipe",
                  id: 'id'
                  }, [ 'name', 'description' ])
          });
          var grid = new Ext.grid.GridPanel({
              store: store,
              columns: [
                  { header: "Name",
                    width: 110,
                    dataIndex: 'name',
                    sortable: true },
                  { header: "Description",
                    width: 410,
                    dataIndex: 'description',
                    sortable: true }
              ],
              renderTo: 'example-grid',
              width: 540,
              height: 200,
              frame:true,
```

```
            title:'Recipe List'
        });

        store.load();
    });
</script>
</body>
</html>
```

It's not our goal to learn Ext (that's a subject for a different book). The key lines to note are where we set the `store` variable's `url` property to our recipe controller's index method. We then tell our Ext `XmlReader` that the recipe records are contained in the `com.packt.s2wad.models.Recipe` elements. We would also want to pay attention to the ID, name, and description elements contained as child elements of each.

With the code above, when we visit `/recipe.xhtml`, we'll get the following page, which is complete with sortable **Name** and **Description** columns.

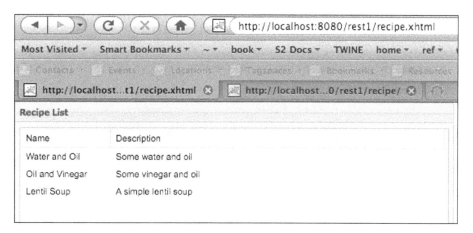

A command-line example

Some of us still use the command line! It's a useful tool for testing and running quick-and-dirty functionality. It's often faster than firing up a browser and clicking our way through a task. REST gives us a convenient way to access web applications without having to drive a browser.

For a simple example, we'll create a Ruby script that retrieves a recipe by ID and displays it in a human-readable format. We'll get the recipe in an XML format and use Ruby's REXML to pull out the information we want to see. In this case, we'll display just the title and description. By using Ruby's `rest_client` library, the code for displaying the list of recipes from the command line is quite short (the following code is located in the code bundle for Chapter 13). For those of us who only use Java, it will seem too short.

```ruby
require 'rest_client'
require 'rexml/document'

begin
    url = "http://localhost:8080/recipe"
    r = RestClient::Resource.new(url)
    doc = REXML::Document.new(r.send("get"))

    recipes = []
    doc.elements.each("java.util.Arrays_-ArrayList/a/com.packt.s2wad.
        models.Recipe") do |el|
        recipes << [el.elements['id'].text.to_i,
                    el.elements['name'].text]
    end

    recipes.sort! {| a,b | a[0] <=> b[0] }

    recipes.each do |r|
        puts "ID #{r[0]}: #{r[1]}"
    end
rescue RestClient::Exception => e
    puts e.response.body if e.respond_to? :response
    raise
end
```

While this isn't a particularly useful example, it does show how a very small amount of code can be used to create useful tools and utilities. One of the advantages of RESTful web applications is that they're accessible from arbitrary clients. Browsers, command-line utilities, Swing applications, Lisp applications, and so on. Anything that can make web requests, and without the complexities of a full-blown SOAP-style interface

Custom content handler example

We can also create our own content handlers, in case the default REST plug-in handlers either don't do precisely what we need, or if we need to emit a content type that is not supported out of the box. For example, we might provide our own XML handler tailored to our client library that doesn't use the "." character as the package name separator to support Ext-JS better.

In the spirit of moving away from XML, we might want to create YAML output when we request a resource with the .yaml extension. YAML is a lightweight syntax for representing data. It is similar to XML, but uses indentation rather than closing tags to separate elements. It's more human-readable than XML, and is sufficient in a wide variety of situations.

YAML in a nutshell

YAML stands for **YAML Ain't a Markup Language.** (At least it does now. This is a retronym, as it was originally called **Yet Another Markup Language**) It uses indentation to indicate structure (whereas XML uses opening and closing tags). It can represent lists, hashes, and maps. It can refer to previously-defined elements and copy them, optionally overriding properties, and so on.

For example, a shopping list in YAML might look like this:

```
--- # Shopping list
date: 2008-01-24
user:
  fname: Dave
  lname: Newton
items:
  - name: tomato paste
    quantity: 8oz
  - name: garlic
    quantity: 4 cloves
  - name: salt
    quantity: 1t
```

For the most part, this should be self-explanatory. The list items are marked with a "-" and hash entries get a "key: value" pair. The leading "---" is optional, but allows us to have multiple documents in the same file. See the references at the end of the chapter for additional YAML information.

Writing our YAML handler

We'll look only at the interface we need to implement where we will add our own content type handler and the code necessary to create YAML output. Our YAML handler will implement `org.apache.struts2.rest.handler.ContentTypeHandler`, which defines four methods:

- `getExtension()`: Returns the extension handled by the YAML handler
- `getContentType()`: Does as we'd expect
- `toObject()`: To handle conversion to and from YAML
- `fromObject()`: Same as toObject()

We'll only look at the `fromObject()` method, which ends up being only a few lines long thanks to the JYaml library. The `fromObject()` method takes an object and serializes it to YAML. The REST plug-in itself determines if the content handler needs to serialize the entire action, or just the model, by checking to see if the action implements `ModelDriven`, as we had already seen.

```
public class YamlHandler implements ContentTypeHandler {
    public String fromObject(Object o, String s,
                             Writer writer)
                throws IOException {
        if (o == null) {
            log.debug("Not serializing null object.");
            return null;
        }
        writer.write(Yaml.dump(o));
        return null;
    }
    // ... etc ...
}
```

Now that's pretty simple code. Thanks, JYaml!

Configuring our YAML handler

We must also configure the REST plug-in, and let it know that our new YAML handler exists. This is done in a `struts.xml` file, for both the bean definition and some constants. The constants could be moved to our `web.xml` file, as we've done with other constants. In this case, as the bean and constants are so closely related, I prefer to keep them in the `struts.xml` file. However, there's probably no good reason for this other than preference. The `struts.xml` file for this example consists of the following:

```
<struts>
  <bean name="yaml"
    type="org.apache.struts2.rest.handler.ContentTypeHandler"
    class="com.packt.s2wad.yaml.YamlHandler" />
  <constant name="struts.rest.handlerOverride.yaml"
            value="yaml"/>
  <constant name="struts.action.extension"
            value="xhtml,,xml,json,yaml" />
</struts>
```

The `<bean>` element defines our content handler. The `handlerOverride` constant registers the YAML content handler bean and provides the file extension. The `struts.action.extension` constant tells Struts 2 that actions with a `.yaml` extension should map to an action.

Handling our YAML

Once our YAML is handled, we can make a request to `/recipe.yaml` and receive a YAML representation of our recipe list. We can also request `/recipe/1.yaml` and retrieve the YAML representation of the recipe with an `id` of 1. The following is the recipe's YAML representation:

```
--- !com.packt.s2wad.models.Recipe
name: Lentil Soup
description: A simple lentil soup
id: &1 !java.lang.Long 1
ingredients:
  - !com.packt.s2wad.models.RecipeIngredient
    id: *1
    index: 1
    ingredient: !com.packt.s2wad.models.Ingredient
      description: Basic red lentils
      id: *1
      name: Lentils
    quantity: 1 c
  - !com.packt.s2wad.models.RecipeIngredient
    id: !java.lang.Long 2
    index: 2
    ingredient: !com.packt.s2wad.models.Ingredient
      description: Water
      id: !java.lang.Long 6
      name: Water
    quantity: 2 c
  - !com.packt.s2wad.models.RecipeIngredient
    id: !java.lang.Long 3
```

```
index: 3
ingredient: !com.packt.s2wad.models.Ingredient
  description: Vinegar
  id: !java.lang.Long 5
  name: Vinegar
quantity: 1 T
```

Notice that JYaml also includes some Java type information used for deserializing from a YAML stream.

Arguably, not many clients consume YAML directly (and that's a fair point). However, this short example does show how the REST plug-in can be extended to handle custom content types. We could just as easily serve CSV using the same techniques by adding an appropriate content handler.

Summary

This chapter takes a look at some of Struts 2's support for Ajax through the Dojo tags. It also highlights that some use-cases require in-depth knowledge of Dojo, even though the tags make the easiest tasks very easy. However, as many of our applications will require custom behavior, this isn't necessarily the "worst thing" in the world.

The chapter also covers the Struts 2 REST plug-in that furthers our "convention over configuration" path. The REST plug-in returns data in several formats, including XHTML, JSON, and XML, which can be consumed by client-side libraries. We also see that it's easy to produce our own content type handlers in case the default content types aren't enough.

In the next chapter, we'll look at how we can test our application using different types of testing, including unit testing and functional testing, and by driving a browser to test our application in its native habitat.

References

A reader can refer to the following:

- Dojo:

  http://www.dojotoolkit.org

- REST:

  http://en.wikipedia.org/wiki/Representational_State_Transfer

- REST Plug-in:

  http://struts.apache.org/2.x/docs/rest-plugin.html

- JSON:

  http://www.json.org

- rest_client (for Ruby):

  http://rest-client.heroku.com/rdoc

- YAML:

  http://www.yaml.org

  http://en.wikipedia.org/wiki/YAML

- JYaml

  http://jyaml.sourceforge.net

14
Comprehensive Testing

In the previous chapter, we looked at the aspects of Struts 2 related to **Rich Internet Application** (**RIA**) development. We'll now move into testing, a key component of robust deliverables.

"Testing is for the weak! We are strong!", "QA does our testing", "It's so simple, it doesn't need testing", or "It takes too long to write tests!", and so on. There are plenty of excuses. However, having a comprehensive suite of application tests of various types, frees our minds so that we can worry about more important things such as application functionality and resilience to change.

Instead of worrying if our latest refactoring broke the application, or wondering if the junior (or senior!) developer's awesome new functor library she/he found on the Internet broke the entire application or a rarely-used (but critical) portion of it, we can make changes both small and large with (relative) impunity. It's difficult to oversell the beauty and comfort of never having to say: "I don't want to touch that because I'm not sure what will happen."

Tests can also be used as a part of the acceptance process. By creating tests that follow user stories, it's easier to know when we're done, easier to prove to our clients we're done, easier to understand how the application should behave under various circumstances, and so on.

In this chapter, we'll take a look at the various ways we can test our application, ways that Struts 2 aids in our testing endeavors, and how tests can be used as a part of our application's documentation and deliverables.

Test-driven development

In simple words, **Test-driven development** (**TDD**) means that we first write the tests and then the code that makes them pass. Pure TDD states that we write code only to fix a failing test, meaning we must first verify that our test has failed. It sounds obvious, but without knowing when we fail, we can't know if we've done something right.

In a very real sense, by writing the tests first, we are designing our application as we go. Rather than using **Big Design Up Front (BDUF)** — a waterfall-style method — we use our tests as a way to refine our system even as we code. It provides us with live feedback on our API, as well as a way to verify that it works as intended. Think of it as another use case of our API besides the application itself. The more usage data points we have, the happier we are!

Pay as we go

Writing tests does take time — like any investment, the returns may not be seen immediately (although sometimes there are immediate benefits, particularly when writing tests expose use cases we hadn't thought of, flaws in design, and so on). As we go into the details of testing, we'll see some reasons why the initial investment is worth the effort, and generally ends up saving time and aggravation down the road.

Unit testing

Unit testing is probably the most familiar aspect of TDD. Even if we're not using pure TDD, it's easy to add unit tests to new codebases. Simply put, unit testing is supposed to exercise and validate a small area (a unit) of code functionality. Unit tests provide a repeatable way to prove our code works (or doesn't work). Adding unit tests to existing code is more difficult, particularly if the code was not written with testability in mind.

Unit tests focus code intent

In addition to providing executable documentation of our code, which in itself is probably worth the initial test-writing overhead, unit testing can help focus the intent of our code. As unit tests are, according to definition, focused on testing small bits of functionality, it helps remind us to keep our code small and contained. Rather than writing a large, monolithic method that scatters its focus across concerns, we're more likely to divide that method into smaller, more focused, and more easily testable units of work.

Keep tests small

As unit tests are targeted at small, focused units of work, most should run quite quickly. Tests that take too long to run, won't be run, thus negating any benefit. However, sometimes long-running tests are required. When this occurs, it's reasonable to break long-running tests into a separate test suite. The tests should still be run. However, both the application and its tests can be segmented in such a way that the small and fast tests can be run frequently, while the long-running tests would be required to run only after major changes.

An example of long-running tests that may be required to run only under specific circumstances are tests that access an actual database. Because of the communication overhead, possible initialization delays, and query performance, some groups of tests might take several minutes, or even hours, to run, rather than the desired several seconds.

In this case, we can break the database tests into a separate suite and run them only when the database access code changes, as a part of acceptance testing on code checking, as part of a continuous integration process, and so on.

Test, code, refactor—the "heartbeat" of TDD

In *Test Driven*, Lasse Koskela refers to the process of test, code, and refactor as the "heartbeat" of TDD. The sequence becomes automatic after consistent implementation. Write failing tests. Write the code that makes them pass. Refactor, lather, rinse, repeat as necessary. It's an iterative process—the stronger the heartbeat, the stronger the code.

JUnit

JUnit was one of the first comprehensive Java unit testing frameworks. There are resources available by way of its website, books, articles, and so on. It is supported by Ant, Maven, and essentially every common Java IDE.

We'll now take a quick look at using JUnit as a part of TDD, by specifying some functionality, writing the initial tests, and then implementing the functionality itself. We'll create the tests using JUnit and then TestNG (another unit testing framework). We will again use JUnit to create tests for a Struts 2 action. Finally, we'll return to TestNG to show how we can test a Struts 2 interceptor.

Revisiting our iterator filter

Let's take another look at our iterator filter from Chapter 5, where our (gleefully contrived) requirement was to create an iterator filter that removed strings without vowels when using a view-side iterator tag. It's actually a pretty simple requirement, and complete testing might involve the interaction of the iterator itself. However, some testing can be done in isolation.

The code for our `SubsetIteratorFilter.Decider` consisted of the implementation of the `decide()` method defined by the `Decider` interface. Let's pretend we didn't already write the code and that we're creating it using the TDD mindset—write tests that fail, and then create the code that makes them pass.

Our requirements for the decider are the following:

- Allow only strings to be compared. Throw an exception if we get a non string.

- If a string has a vowel, return true, otherwise, return false.

Pretty simple! We may argue that something this simple doesn't require testing. TDD states that *nothing* is so simple it doesn't require testing. Note that our original version of the filter was for a single-character string. Now we're assuming that the string can be of any length.

The test environment

There are several ways to create and run our tests. Full coverage is beyond the scope of this book. We can run our tests from the command line, using a build process, through an IDE, as part of a continuous integration process, and so on.

For the example in the following section, we'll use the Eclipse JUnit test creation for JUnit 4.x and not delve into the intricacies of all the possibilities. There are several books, along with a multitude of articles and tutorials available, that discuss various ways of integrating tests into the development process. The following test will be runnable with a few clicks in nearly any IDE.

The initial test stub

Eclipse will create an initial test stub for testing our `decide()` method. By default, it simply fails—recall that when following the pure TDD paradigm, we always want to start with failing tests. If we run the following stub class as a JUnit test, it fails. Mission accomplished!

```
package com.packt.s2wad.ch14.examples;

import static org.junit.Assert.*;
import org.junit.Test;

public class TestVowelDecider {
    @Test public void testDecide() {
        fail("Not yet implemented");
    }
}
```

As seems common with the phrase "Mission accomplished!", we're not finished just yet.

Testing vowel recognition

First, we'll create a test to make sure we get back the right Boolean value for various string values. Recall that we want a `true` for strings with vowels and `false` otherwise. Again, we write the test first.

Our test is simple—we pass in some strings and make sure we get the right value back.

```
@Test public void testVowelRecognition() throws Exception {
    VowelDecider vd = new VowelDecider();
    assertTrue("Has vowels", vd.decide("has vowels"));
    assertFalse("Has no vowels", vd.decide("hsnvwls"));
}
```

The string arguments to `assertTrue/False()` are human-readable strings that describe the test being run. The second argument is expected to return a boolean. In this case, the `decide()` method returns a boolean, so no antics are required to manipulate the results of the class under test.

When writing our test, as it is focused very tightly on vowel recognition, we immediately see a hole in our specification. We haven't explicitly specified what happens if there's an empty string. Of course, empty strings don't contain vowels, so technically it should fail the test. However, our use case might demand otherwise. This is a specification ambiguity that should be cleared up and stated explicitly, either in the specification or in the test. In this case, we'll assume that an empty string should return `false` and should add the appropriate assertion (seen below), as it has no vowels. (We'll handle a null check in the next test case, don't panic.)

```
assertFalse("Empty string has no vowels", vd.decide(""));
```

We'll also assume that we created a default implementation of `VowelDecider.decide()` using Eclipse. Normally, `boolean` methods will return `false` by default, which is just fine for now. Our primary goal is to ensure that our tests can fail—we'll make them pass soon enough.

When we run our test against our new default implementation, we should get an immediate failure. Our first test checks for vowels, and the stub implementation returns `false`. For example, using the Eclipse JUnit integration, we'll see something similar to the following when we attempt the test:

We add our first stab at implementation using the `String`'s `matches()` method, which should work for us.

```
public boolean decide(Object o) throws Exception {
    String s = (String) o;
    return s.matches(".*[aeiouy]+.*");
}
```

The regular expression says to accept any number of occurrences (including none) of any character, followed by at least one vowel, followed again by any number of occurrences (including none) of any character. We'll also add some sanity check tests to make sure single-character strings work for both a vowel and a non-vowel (which could help identify a broken regular expression).

Testing non-string parameter exceptions

We probably would have written this test in parallel, or in the same method as our first test. We've broken it out to keep things simple. Moreover, this test checks for a very different error.

Now we'll check that we get an exception if we pass `decide()` a `null` or non-`String` parameter. Again, our goal is to write failing tests first, before implementing the code that makes the test pass. If we can't verify that our tests can fail, we can't trust the test when it passes.

The desired behavior is to throw an `IllegalArgumentException` for both `null` and non-`String` parameters. JUnit 4's `@Test` annotation optionally accepts a `Throwable`, with the exception expected to be thrown. In order to test both nulls and non-strings, it's easier to just write two tests, although we could forgo the convenience of the annotations and wrap the separate tests in `try/catch` blocks.

It's a matter of taste, but the annotation method is more concise and arguably expresses our intent more clearly. In addition, the annotation allows documentation generation tools to pull out more information programmatically.

Our illegal argument tests now look like the following. Remember that we haven't yet implemented the argument-checking functionality in our class under test—we must have failing tests.

```
@Test(expected=IllegalArgumentException.class)
public void testNonStringArgument() throws Exception {
    VowelDecider vd = new VowelDecider();
    vd.decide(1);
}

@Test(expected=IllegalArgumentException.class)
```

```
public void testNullArgument() throws Exception {
    VowelDecider vd = new VowelDecider();
    vd.decide(null);
}
```

Now, when we run our test, it fails because we have no code implementing the parameter type checking shown below. To get our test to pass, we add the highlighted code to our filter implementation. It's as simple as you would expect:

```
public boolean decide(Object o) throws Exception {
    if ((null == o) || !(o instanceof String)) {
        throw new
          IllegalArgumentException(
            "Expects non-null String");
    }
    String s = (String) o;
    return s.matches(".*[aeiouy]+.*");
}
```

Now our tests pass and, in theory, we have specification-compliant code. Any changes to the code earn a run of the unit tests to make sure we didn't accidentally break something. The tests are run before the code is checked into our source control system.

It's important to note that this method of checking exceptions only ensures we're throwing the appropriate class. It can't be used to check for things such as custom exception values. If we need to test the returned exception for anything other than the type, we need to wrap our class under test in a try/catch block and perform our asserts manually.

Test granularity and test setup

One consequence of how we structured our tests is that the first test failure in a test method will stop the test execution immediately. This may not be the desired behavior. We might want to run each test individually and have more granularity over our test successes and failures.

We can also posit that we may not want to construct a new test object (VowelDecider, in this case) for every test. In this case, it doesn't matter. However, if the test setup is particularly time consuming (as we'll see a bit later when we fire up a browser to run client-based tests via Selenium), we'll want to initialize our test harness only once per set of tests.

We first create a test method for each of our asserts (and exception checking) from above, giving us the following collection of methods (code not shown to save space, you're welcome)

```
@Test public void testSingleVowel() throws Exception {...}
@Test public void testWordsWithVowels() throws Exception {...}
@Test public void testSingleConsonant() throws Exception {...}
@Test public void testNoVowels() throws Exception {...}
@Test public void testEmptyString() throws Exception {...}
{...}
```

If we want to use the same instance of the `VowelDecider` for each test, we can create a test class property to hold the filter and instantiate it in a setup method. In JUnit, we annotate a test setup method with the `@BeforeClass` annotation. This method will be run when the test class is instantiated.

```
private VowelDecider vd;
@BeforeClass public static void setup() {
    vd = new TddVowelDecider();
}
```

As we would expect, there is a corresponding `@AfterClass` annotation we can use when we need to perform cleanup on anything used in our test fixture.

JUnit also provides `@Before` and `@After` annotations—methods annotated with these will be run before (or after) every test in the class. For example, if the class under test held some internal state that needed to be cleared before every test, the code could be put in a `@Before` method.

TestNG

TestNG is a JUnit alternative that may suit some people. It was created to address some of the perceived shortcomings in JUnit, particularly before JUnit 4.x was released. The underlying basics are very similar and it shares support similar to that of JUnit. However, I'd guess it's not as popular due to the name recognition JUnit enjoys.

A TestNG conversion of our `TestVowelDecider`, `NgTestVowelDecider`, looks nearly identical, and by statically importing TestNG's JUnit assertion methods, it looks even more identical.

TestNG also provides `@BeforeClass` and `@AfterClass` annotations. The basic `@Test` annotation is the same. Tests can use a Java `assert` for the actual test, or with the JUnit-compatibility static imports, use JUnit-like `assertTrue`, `assertFalse`, and so on. Testing for exceptions is also similar, but we can use an array of expected exception types. An equivalent TestNG test class would look similar to our JUnit test:

```
package com.packt.s2wad.ch14.examples;

import static org.testng.AssertJUnit.assertFalse;
import static org.testng.AssertJUnit.assertTrue;
import org.testng.annotations.BeforeClass;
import org.testng.annotations.Test;

public class NgTestVowelDecider {

    private VowelDecider vd;

    @BeforeClass public void setup() {
        vd = new VowelDecider();
    }

    @Test public void testDecide() throws Exception {
        assertTrue("Has vowels", vd.decide("has vowels"));
        assertFalse("Has no vowels", vd.decide("hsnvwls"));
        assertFalse("Empty string has no vowels",
                    vd.decide(""));
    }

    @Test(expectedExceptions=IllegalArgumentException.class)
    public void testNonStringArgument() throws Exception {
        vd.decide(1);
    }

    @Test(expectedExceptions=IllegalArgumentException.class)
    public void testNullArgument() throws Exception {
        vd.decide(null);
    }
}
```

TestNG's capabilities go far beyond this limited example. One of my favorite features is the ability to group tests using a simple string name. Rather than grouping tests by package or creating suites manually, we can tag tests with a string and run just those tests. A canonical example is to group tests on the basis of their execution speed. In our current example, they're all pretty fast. So, I'll create an exception-handling group by annotating the two tests that check the exception handling.

```
@Test(groups="exceptions",
      expectedExceptions=IllegalArgumentException.class)
public void testNullArgument() throws Exception {
    vd.decide(null);
}
@Test(groups="exceptions",
      expectedExceptions=IllegalArgumentException.class)
public void testNonStringArgument() throws Exception {
    vd.decide(1);
}
```

No matter how we're running the tests, we can choose to run only those tests belonging to the exceptions group. For example, the Eclipse TestNG plug-in integrates with the Run dialog allowing us to define a configuration to include only specific test groups. It can often be more convenient to run some tests from our IDE than using an Ant or Maven process. Test groups are cool and can help avoid manual test grouping.

However, when we try to run the exceptions group, it fails. This is because our @BeforeClass setup method is not assigned to a group. We must either assign it to the exceptions group (this is a bad idea, because we need to for all the groups) or add a alwaysRun parameter to the @BeforeClass annotation. Now, our setup method looks like this:

```
@BeforeClass(alwaysRun=true)
public void setup() {
    vd = new VowelDecider();
}
```

We can also specify that an entire test class belongs to a given group (while still allowing individual methods to belong to additional groups).

There is a lot more we can do with TestNG's annotations—we can specify test ordering dependencies using @Test's dependsOnGroups or dependsOnMethods parameters. We can supply data to test methods using the @DataProvider or @Parameters annotations, or we can supply parameters to the @Test annotation (these are very powerful and allow a variety of ways to parameterize test data). We can specify the number of times to invoke the test method. There's a lot more—spending some time with the TestNG documentation will most likely get us at least a little bit more excited about unit testing.

TestNG is a powerful testing framework that deserves a look if we're not already tied to JUnit. Either framework provides a tremendous amount of functionality and peace of mind when used as part of a comprehensive testing practice.

Legacy code and unit testing

Adding unit tests to legacy code provides several benefits. For poorly-documented codebases, it is a method of documentation. It increases a developer's understanding of the existing code. It provides a basis against which to refactor and prove the correctness of the refactoring.

Retroactive unit testing might not be as easy as doing it up-front, but can provide a way to reduce existing design debt, and adds value beyond the cost of writing and verifying the tests.

Simple action testing

Struts 2's actions can also be unit tested. Some testing requires a fair amount of setup. We won't cover that here, saving it for an advanced Struts 2 book. However, we can easily test a large amount of action functionality using techniques we've seen so far.

Remember when we hinted that we would look at Dependency Injection, otherwise known as Inversion of Control (IoC), again? We're here!

Detour: Dependency Injection (Inversion of Control)

Dependency Injection (DI) is a common technique for deciding which implementation of an interface is used. In order to use DI effectively, we think in terms of using interfaces rather than implementations—this is a good idea anyway. For example, when we use an ArrayList, we almost always declare the type of the variable as List, rather than ArrayList as shown here:

```
List aList = new ArrayList();
```

We're doing the same thing in our action used to view recipes. Our FakeRecipeService implements the RecipeService interface:

```
public class View extends ActionSupport {
    private RecipeService recipeService =
        new FakeRecipeService();
    public String execute() throws Exception {
        recipe = recipeService.findById(recipe.getId());
        return SUCCESS;
    }
...
```

One implication is that when we use our recipe service we care only about its RecipeService-ness, not that we're using the FakeRecipeService implementation.

Another implication is that if we create another RecipeService implementation, HibernateRecipeService (that uses Hibernate), the code in the execute() method doesn't need to change. We only need to change recipeService's initialization.

In this code, the `View` class chooses the `RecipeService` implementation to use. DI turns this on its head by letting something else determine the implementation we'll use for our `recipeService`. There are several options for defining which implementation to use. Most options depend on some combination of configuration files, publicly-accessible setter methods, or annotations. We'll look at using Spring and a configuration file in a moment.

```java
public class View extends ActionSupport {
    private Recipe recipe;
    private RecipeService recipeService;
    public String execute() throws Exception {
        recipe = recipeService.findById(recipe.getId());
        return SUCCESS;
    }
    public void setRecipeService(RecipeService
                                 recipeService) {
        this.recipeService = recipeService;
    }
    public void setRecipe(Recipe recipe) {
        this.recipe = recipe;
    }
}
```

Note that our above code could still choose the `RecipeService` implementation, but we also allow external forces to set the `RecipeService` implementation for the class. In fact, we could just instantiate this class, set all the appropriate values, and call `execute()`:

```java
View view = new View();
view.setRecipeService(new FakeRecipeService());
Recipe recipe = new Recipe();
recipe.setId(1);
view.setRecipe(recipe);
String result = view.execute();
```

Assuming no exception is thrown, we should get the string `success` in `result`.

For now, just remember that DI means that the implementation of an interface can be set outside of the class that uses the implementation.

Dependency Injection helps us test

Our current recipe view action returns success no matter what. It might be better if we return a different result depending on whether or not the recipe in question was found. We'll add a requirement (only partially contrived!) that if the service doesn't find a recipe for the supplied recipe ID, we'll return a notFound message. This would allow us to create a result for our action that might show an error page, a page with a search box, and so on.

Then our mini-user story for this is as follows:

- Users may search for a recipe by recipe ID

With the following mini stories by way of clarification:

- Show an error page if no recipe is found
- Otherwise, show the recipe

We can test part of this functionality by making sure our view action returns the appropriate value, notFound or success, under the appropriate conditions.

We already have a FakeRecipeService containing a known set of recipes. It's easy to write a test that will exercise our action (recalling that we must first write a failing test). Our test class is very straightforward and utilizes our new-found love of DI.

```
package com.packt.s2wad.ch14.test.actions;
...
public class TestRecipeViewAction {
    private View view;
    private Recipe recipe;
    @BeforeClass public void setup() {
        view = new View();
        view.setRecipeService(new FakeRecipeService());
    }
    @Test(groups="actions")
    void testRecipeFoundResult() throws Exception {
        recipe = new Recipe(1, null);
        view.setRecipe(recipe);
        assertTrue(view.execute().equals("success"),
                "Recipe found returns 'success'");
    }
    @Test(groups="actions")
    void testRecipeNotFoundResult() throws Exception {
        recipe = new Recipe(42, null);
        view.setRecipe(recipe);
        assertTrue(view.execute().equals("notFound"),
                "Recipe found returns 'success'");
    }
}
```

As we can set the `RecipeService` implementation used by our recipe viewing action, we can tell it to use our `FakeRecipeService`. We know the `FakeRecipeService` has a recipe with `ID == 1`, and doesn't have one for `ID == 42`, we'll use those as our tests. (In a real system, we might define known IDs in the fake recipe service.)

The `testRecipeFoundResult()` test passes, as our action always returns `success` at the moment. Our other test fails, so that we've at least partially satisfied our "tests must fail" requirement. We then tweak our action slightly:

```
public String execute() throws Exception {
    recipe = recipeService.findById(recipe.getId());
    if (recipe.notFound()) {
        return "notFound";
    }
    return SUCCESS;
}
```

The `Recipe`'s `notFound()` method is a convenient method to check if the recipe instance is equal to a static `Recipe` instance we used to indicate a recipe wasn't found. This helps us get rid of the process of null checking of recipes returned by our services, eliminating one class of possible application errors. It's a matter of some debate as to which method is best—scattering null-checks throughout an entire codebase, or creating "empty" objects to represent non existence.

Our tests now pass. We've exercised one portion of our recipe view tests.

This is nice, but how can we configure our Struts 2 application to use a particular implementation of `RecipeService` across the entire application—not just in test fixtures?

Detour: Struts and Spring in a nutshell

Spring, among a great many other things, is a Dependency Injection container. This means that we can use Spring to manage our DI. For example, we can configure our application to always use our `FakeRecipeService` implementation via a configuration file.

Struts 2 integrates with Spring with the Struts 2 Spring plug-in. We still need the Spring library—the plug-in provides only the Spring integration, not Spring itself. We'll take a quick look at how to configure our application to use our `FakeRecipeService` for its `RecipeService` needs.

Spring web.xml configuration

We use Spring's `ContextLoaderListener` to load our Spring configuration files. This is configured in our `web.xml` file. We will also define a context parameter to tell Spring where to find our Spring configuration files. Here, we'll define them to lie anywhere on our classpath and be named `applicationContext*.xml`, giving us the option of breaking up our Spring configuration in whatever way seems reasonable.

```
<context-param>
  <param-name>contextConfigLocation</param-name>
  <param-value>
    classpath*:applicationContext*.xml
  </param-value>
</context-param>

<listener>
  <listener-class>
    org.springframework.web.context.ContextLoaderListener
  </listener-class>
</listener>
```

At the time of writing this book, it was also necessary to set a Struts 2 configuration variable relating to Spring autowiring (it may not be necessary by the time you're reading this). We add the following `<init-param>` element to our Struts 2 filter definition:

```
<init-param>
  <param-name>
    struts.objectFactory.spring.autoWire.alwaysRespect
  </param-name>
  <param-value>true</param-value>
</init-param>
```

Spring context configuration file

We'll put an `applicationContext.xml` file at the root of our classpath, using the XSD-based configuration introduced in Spring 2.0. The outline looks like this:

```
<?xml version="1.0" encoding="UTF-8"?>
<beans xmlns="http://www.springframework.org/schema/beans"
       xmlns:xsi="http://www.w3.org/2001/XMLSchema-instance"
       xsi:schemaLocation="
         http://www.springframework.org/schema/beans
         http://www.springframework.org/schema/beans/
                 spring-beans-2.5.xsd">
  ...
</beans>
```

We can define a recipe service bean in our Spring context file with the following short XML fragment:

```
<bean name="recipeService"
      class="com.packt.s2wad.ch14.recipe.FakeRecipeService"/>
```

Now, something scary happens: if we visit our view-by-id action, even though we don't define a recipe service in the action, we get a recipe back on a valid ID. The magic here is "autowiring by name". The default behavior is that when a class managed by Spring (as our actions are under the Spring plug-in) contains a public property with the same name as a bean defined in a Spring configuration file, that bean will be injected into the class.

In this case, our recipe view action has a public setter method `setRecipeService()`, and our `FakeRecipeService` Spring bean is named `recipeService`. This means when the action class is instantiated, the action's `setRecipeService()` method will be called and will be given a new instance of `FakeRecipeService`.

If we need to use a different `RecipeService` implementation, we just update our Spring configuration file, and any Spring-managed objects (like our actions) that have a `setRecipeService()` method will get an instance of the recipeService's type. Rather than changing all the classes that need a `RecipeService` implementation, we can change the behavior of the entire application through Spring. This is handy (and I am the King of Understatements).

However, we shouldn't forget that when we rely on magic, particularly name-based magic, it can turn around and bite us in uncomfortable places. If our bean names happen to match a property expected elsewhere, it can lead to spectacular stack traces, mysterious class cast exceptions, and much cursing. Actions can also be configured explicitly. Some people prefer this methodology, and it can often eliminate mysterious problems.

Testing Struts 2 in context

Earlier, we tested a Struts 2 action by calling its `execute()` method. This is helpful, and may be sufficient in many cases. However, it would be more robust to call action methods in the context of things such as a particular interceptor stack configuration.

It's the same with interceptors. We might be able to abstract the bulk of an interceptor's code and test it independently. However, ideally we'd like to call the interceptor's `intercept()` method (or `doIntercept()`, and so on, depending on the interceptor's superclass) with an action invocation. This is particularly true if the interceptor is supposed to act only on actions implementing a specific marker interface.

Testing a Struts interceptor

Here, we'll test our `trim` interceptor with an action invocation. For the most part, things look like a regular unit test. The main difference is that we need to set up some framework objects in order to create a mock action invocation.

We'll use TestNG's `@BeforeClass` annotation to create a `TrimInterceptor` instance and set its excluded parameters list. We'll also set up some XWork configuration objects which we can use to generate action invocations. The test class's imports and setup method looks like this:

```
package com.packt.s2wad.ch14.test.interceptors;

import static org.testng.Assert.assertFalse;
import static org.testng.Assert.assertTrue;

import java.util.HashMap;
import java.util.Map;

import org.testng.annotations.BeforeClass;
import org.testng.annotations.Test;

import com.opensymphony.xwork2.ActionContext;
import com.opensymphony.xwork2.ActionProxyFactory;
import com.opensymphony.xwork2.config.Configuration;
import com.opensymphony.xwork2.config.ConfigurationManager;
import com.opensymphony.xwork2.inject.Container;
import com.opensymphony.xwork2.mock.MockActionInvocation;
import com.opensymphony.xwork2.util.XWorkTestCaseHelper;
import com.packt.s2wad.ch14.interceptors.TrimInterceptor;

public class TestTrimInterceptor {

    private TrimInterceptor trim;
    protected ConfigurationManager configurationManager;
    protected Configuration configuration;
    protected Container container;
    protected ActionProxyFactory actionProxyFactory;

    @BeforeClass
    public void setup() throws Exception {
        trim = new TrimInterceptor();
        trim.setExcludedParams(
            "simple, nested.simple, indexed, complex.foo");

        configurationManager = XWorkTestCaseHelper.setUp();
        configuration =
            configurationManager.getConfiguration();
        container = configuration.getContainer();
```

```
            actionProxyFactory =
                container.getInstance(ActionProxyFactory.class);
        }
        ...
    }
```

Our test is simple since all the work is done in the helper method. The `testTrimming()` method takes three arguments—the name of the request parameter, its value, and the value we expect after running through the interceptor.

The request parameter would be the name of the parameter found in a form submission. The `trim` interceptor uses its `excludedParams` property to determine whether a particular request parameter should be trimmed.

```
    @Test(groups="interceptors")
    public void testTrimming() {
        testTrimming("foo", " hello ", "hello");
        testTrimming("complex.nar", " hello ", "hello");
        testTrimming("simple", " hello ", " hello ");
        testTrimming("complex.foo[1]", " hello ", " hello ");
    }
```

For example, based on the `excludedParams` we set in the `setup()` method, we would expect a request parameter named `foo` to be trimmed. Therefore, our first test passes our test helper the untrimmed form submission value, along with the trimmed value we expect the interceptor to pass on to our actions. (There are better ways to consolidate the `excludedParams` value and the parameter/expected value pairs than what we're using here.)

The `testTrimming()` method creates the action invocation, runs the interceptor's `doIntercept()` method, and makes sure we're getting the value we want back.

```
    private void testTrimming(final String param,
                              final String val,
                              final String expected) {
        MockActionInvocation i = setupInvocation(param, val);
        try {
            trim.doIntercept(i);
            Map<String, Object> params =
                i.getInvocationContext().getParameters();
            assertTrue(params.containsKey(param),
                    "Parameters contains param key");
            String newVal = ((String[]) params.get(param))[0];
            assertTrue(newVal.equals(expected),
                    "Trim operation correct.");
```

```
    } catch (Exception e) {
        assertTrue(false, "Should not have gotten exception");
    }
}
```

 For simplicity, this test assumes that each request parameter name contains a single value, and it's true in our tests. A comprehensive test would also test multiple values.

The `setupInvocation()` method accepts a parameter name and value, and sets the request parameter. It then creates a mock action invocation, to which we attach the action context containing the request parameters.

```
private MockActionInvocation setupInvocation(
        final String param,
        final String val) {
    Map<String, Object> params =
        new HashMap<String, Object>() {{
            put(param, new String[] { val });
        }};
    MockActionInvocation i = new MockActionInvocation();
    ActionContext c = ActionContext.getContext();
    c.setParameters(params);
    i.setInvocationContext(c);
    return i;
}
```

 If we were testing an interceptor that required a specific action (for example, to test an interceptor that acted only on actions that implemented a specific interface), we could provide the action invocation with an instance of the action being invoked.

These techniques allow us to test an interceptor in the context of an action invocation.

Client-side (functional) testing

Testing our Java code is obviously very important, but it's equally (or maybe even more) important to test the application in its native habitat, that is, in the browser. In some ways, this is among the most important means of testing our application, as the application itself (which lives in the browser) is the deliverable seen by the application's user.

Selenium

Selenium allows us to test web applications by running a browser. We can use it to click links, check for DOM elements and their contents, submit forms, and so on. Basically, anything that a user can do with our web application can be done using Selenium.

Selenium can drive several browsers, including Internet Explorer, Firefox, and Safari. These examples were tested using Firefox, but they're simple and should work across browsers. Note that as of IE 6 there were, as seems typical, the occasional gotcha. When possible, it's often easier to test using Firefox.

Selenium RC

In order to integrate our Selenium tests into our unit testing, we'll use **Selenium RC** (**Remove Control**) and the Java client driver. In a nutshell, our tests use the client driver to communicate with the Selenium RC server, which in turn drives the browser.

For our purposes, we're just going to run the server from the command line, which is as easy as starting up the server jar:

```
$ java -jar selenium-server.jar
```

The test scenario

For our tests, we'll look at a quick iteration of a login screen and make sure that what we expect to see on the screen actually shows up under various scenarios. The login screen is a typical login, containing both email and password fields. There's a message for failed logins, and we're taken to a welcome page on a successful login.

For this example, we'll keep things simple and contained to a single class. Not all of the source will be presented here. It's quite likely you'll find your own set of convenience classes, methods, suites, and so on. This is just an overview of the process.

Our first Selenium test

The first sanity check is to make sure the appropriate form fields are displayed in the browser. We can use Selenium to check for DOM elements with given IDs, so this is not a problem. Following the TDD methodology, we write our test first, before creating the page. In this case, we actually created the page stub first. In pure TDD, we'd first test for the presence of the page, and it would probably be a valuable test to add.

Our test class needs to perform some Selenium housekeeping. We'll use TestNG's @ BeforeClass and @AfterClass annotations to do this for us. We're simply starting up a browser at the beginning of all the tests in the class and closing it afterwards. If we had a lot more test classes, we'd probably want to create the browser before all the tests ran. This will help avoid the additional overhead of browser startups.

Remember that tests must be as fast as is practically possible, but shouldn't be much faster. The functional tests we're showing here might live in their own TestNG group, giving us the ability to run them separately from other groups:

```
private static String LOGIN_INPUT_URL =
    "http://localhost:8080/user/login!input.action";
private Selenium selenium;

@BeforeClass public void setup() {
    selenium = new DefaultSelenium(
        "localhost", 4444, "*firefox", LOGIN_INPUT_URL);
    selenium.start();
}


@AfterClass public void tearDown() {
    selenium.stop();
}
```

We'll add a convenience method to test for the presence of an element in the DOM, taking an explanatory message and a Selenium selector. (See the Selenium documentation for a complete explanation of querying the DOM. There are many ways we can query elements, including CSS selectors.)

```
public void assertElementPresent(final String msg,
                                 final String selector) {
    assertTrue(msg + ": '" + selector + "'",
            selenium.isElementPresent(selector));
}
```

We'll then write our first simple test (designed to fail) that tests the presence of the form, the two form text inputs, and a login button with the text Login.

```
@Test(groups="functional")
public void testLoginFormFields() {
    selenium.open(LOGIN_INPUT_URL);
    assertElementPresent("login form", "id=loginForm");
    assertElementPresent("userName field", "id=email");
    assertElementPresent("password field", "id=password");
    assertElementPresent("Login button",
                        "//input[@value='Login']");
}
```

The test will fail because the form doesn't exist. We create the login form as a normal Struts 2 form, nothing terribly exciting here:

```
<s:form id="loginForm" action="login" method="post">
  <s:textfield id="email" name="email" label="Email"/>
  <s:password id="password" name="password" label="Password"/>
  <s:submit value="Login"/>
</s:form>
```

Running the test again confirms that the form fields we expect to exist are now present. We continue writing our tests to verify proper validation behavior. If either field is missing, we should get an error message to that effect. Shown below is the email validation test. Password validation is essentially identical. (The `typeOrClear()` method is a helper that enters text into text fields.)

```
@Test public void testEmailValidation() {
    testLoginFormFields();

    typeOrClear("email", null);
    typeOrClear("password", "ohai");

    selenium.click("//input[@value='Login']");
    selenium.waitForPageToLoad("10000");

    // Should not have moved to /welcome.action.
    assertUrlEndsWith("/login.action");
    assertElementPresent("An error message span",
                         "css=span[class~='errorMessage']");
    String text =
        selenium.getText("css=span[class~='errorMessage']");
    assertTrue(text.equals("Email is required."));
}
```

Note that if both fields are omitted, there will be two `errorMessage` spans. It becomes more difficult to get the text in that case. However, as any CSS selector may be used, it's simple enough to build up the appropriate selector. At the same time, we probably don't want to do that. It's much cleaner to appropriately assign an ID to the span, table row, or similar objects. This is another great opportunity to further customize our FreeMarker tag templates to mark up our HTML in order to make testing easier (and hopefully, much more likely to be done).

Our next test is to make sure a failed login puts an action error in the JSP. We'll specify that action errors will appear in a `<div>` with an `id` of `flash` and a class of `error`. The important consideration is that we're specifying how we'll identify page elements much earlier. As we've seen, the more we can mark things up, the better off we are.

The relevant portion of the test looks like following:

```
assertUrlEndsWith("/login.action");
assertElementPresent("The flash span",
                     "css=div[id=flash][class~='error']");
String text =
    selenium.getText("css=div[id=flash][class~='error']");
assertTrue(text.indexOf("Login failed") > -1);
```

Our initial run will fail. Our action doesn't set an action error, and our JSP doesn't do anything with action errors that don't exist. Remember, TDD says write failing tests first. Tests that cannot fail are useless.

In our JSP, we test for the presence of action errors. If there are any, we render a `<div>` with our expected ID and class, using the standard Struts 2 `<s:actionerror/>` tag inside, at least for now.

The last test we'll look at is the results of a successful login. This is little more than checking the subsequent URL, although in the actual system we might check to make sure that user-specific information was on the page, and so on. We've configured a "welcome" action in our default package, and we know its URL.

```
assertUrlEndsWith("/welcome.action");
```

A real test system might process any Struts 2 configuration files to avoid needing to know the actual URL. We could also check for the URL. However, we prefer using configuration information to determine the action suffix, and so on.

The tests might also be prototyped using the Selenium IDE. This is a Firefox plug-in that can record browser sessions. This tool can be used by the developer, or with a good testing or QA department. These tests may be manipulated by a developer to create the unit tests (it can output Java code directly, but it usually needs work), or used to test from within the browser.

Client-side testing can become very complex, particularly with the addition of AJAX and other rich client behavior. With today's heavy use of JavaScript and DOM manipulation, the ability to mechanically verify behavior is very important, even if it's not practical to verify every bit of HTML or behavior on a page.

Other forms of testing

There are many other forms of testing and development methodologies, and ways of integrating them into the process. We'll take a very brief look at other test tools in our arsenal. There are essentially an unlimited number of ways any of these methods fit into our development process. It is often dependent on the type of application, the nature of the client relationship, and so on.

It's possible to develop every application with some level of the following practices in place. The peace of mind they can provide is generally worth the additional effort, and when automated, they provide free benefits for the rest of the life of the project.

Acceptance testing

The client-focused Selenium testing discussed earlier may be used as a part of an acceptance testing process. Acceptance testing can be used to verify the correct operation of our user stories (remember those?)

When we unit-tested our Struts 2 action for listing recipes, we had a couple of "mini stories" accompanying it. They wouldn't necessarily belong in a user story, but might belong in an acceptance test.

Acceptance testing is a mechanism for determining the correct application behavior. It provides a metric for knowing the system is as the client requires. Therefore, acceptance tests are best-owned by our client, as they're the ones to whom the tests will be delivered and they should be most interested in knowing when the application is done.

Acceptance tests should preferably be written by the client *with* us (the developer), in a non-technical language (the language should match the domain of the application). The tests should be focused, precise, and clear. They should focus on underlying functionality and not bring in too much detail of how that functionality is being implemented.

By focusing on "what" and not "how", we get a verifiable snapshot of the system's behavior. For web applications, this looks a lot like the client-side testing we've already discussed. Indeed, a subset of the client-side tests may very well be used as a part of an acceptance test suite. By driving a browser, we're testing our deliverable from the standpoint of a user.

Acceptance testing might also include various database processes such as batch jobs, complicated queries, actions across systems, and similarly complex tasks. My admittedly simplistic take on this is that they're a subset of unit and client-side tests. However, they may exist as a separate documentation (or however they're being expressed), and hence are different, even if only in intent.

Load testing

Load testing the system should be done fairly early in the process, and not as an afterthought. Integrating an automated load test into a continuous build system can provide much needed input towards identifying problems early in the process—it's easier to confront issues immediately upon noticing them. Load testing can help point out configuration errors, database bottlenecks, scalability issues, shared data abuse, and more. Even a small amount of load testing can be valuable.

Load testing with JMeter

JMeter is a Java-based desktop application that performs functional load testing. It can simulate any number of users making variably-timed requests, including ramping up usage over time. JMeter is designed primarily as a load tester and not as a functional tester (for which we've used Selenium). Its main purpose is to make requests, rather than examining the results of those requests, and to time the requests.

JMeter includes a GUI for creating and running the test plans. Test plans are saved in an easy-to-understand XML format, allowing simple and automated test plan generation through any language that can manipulate XML.

JMeter provides many ways to vary the requests being made, including timing differences, request parameter variation, normal and Ajax requests, GET and POST requests, request interleaving, and more (see the JMeter documentation for further details).

As a simple example, we'll configure a load test of an ingredient list page, simulating 25 users, ramping up over a period of 30 seconds, each requesting the ingredient list page, in HTML format, four times, with a delay of 0.5-1.5 seconds between each request. This sounds complicated, but it only scratches the surface of what JMeter and similar tools are capable of.

It might sound like JMeter provides more than what is necessary, but understanding how our application works under various types of loads can be critically important. Not all applications are used constantly throughout the day. Some might experience a heavy load early in the morning, or during end-of-the-week reporting, and so on.

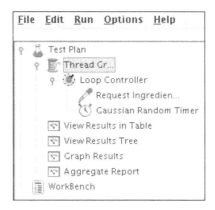

The JMeter GUI screenshot shown above shows a tree on the left, which represents the test plan and its nested elements. Each thread group (represented by a spool of thread) represents a certain number of users. Here, we see a single thread group, each containing a simple loop controller that repeats itself a specified number of times. We'll request our ingredient list, wait a variable amount of time, and repeat. We've also specified various views of our requests, which we'll cover in a moment.

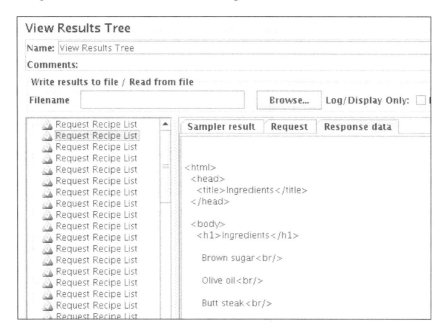

The thread group contains 25 users, ramping up their requests over 30 seconds, which will loop twice (we won't show a picture of this here, but we'll see it when we look at the XML test plan). The request is simply a GET request to our HTML ingredient list page. The Gaussian Random Timer element allows us to choose a constant offset, which specifies the minimum time delay, and a random component.

When we run this test plan, we can examine the results in several ways. The **View Results Tree** element provides a view of each request, including the response data. On the previous screen, we see the basic HTML returned by our test ingredient listing.

We can also get an aggregate report of our test plan, which will return the number of samples, the average time-per-request, the minimum and maximum times, and so on. This provides a high-level view of the load test results.

Our test plans are saved in an XML format. The test plan shown above creates around 200 lines of XML code. We'd never create these XML test plans by hand—we'd either use the GUI or generate them programmatically. One feature not discussed here allows our test plans to use data sets to generate requests, form parameters, and so on. These data sets could also be generated automatically from actual system data.

Recovery testing

Recovery testing is not so much an issue of application testing, but of process testing, on several levels. It includes making sure that the source control system is set up properly. It includes ensuring the build processes is repeatable, including across build machines, along with deployment and configuration scripts, and so on—basically anything that is involved throughout the entire life of application development.

How much recoverability testing is required is closely related to the deliverables. If we're just delivering a WAR file, we may not feel the need to test our local backup system (but we have a working one, right?) or other well-known processes. If the deliverable includes a turn-key, source- and design-included application along with training, then a higher standard needs to be followed and be integrated into the client's preferred mechanisms if possible.

Summary

Testing provides a huge amount of freedom. It can reduce the amount of written documentation and provide an executable specification. Testing covers a wide range of topics, from the smallest unit of code to the behavior of the system as a whole, under various scenarios.

In the next chapter, we'll continue looking at application documentation (remember, tests are documentations!), but from a more traditional standpoint, that is, documenting our code the old-fashioned way. We will also discover some tools and methodologies that go beyond simple Javadocs.

References

A reader can refer to the following:

- Test-driven development

  http://en.wikipedia.org/wiki/Test-driven_development
  http://c2.com/cgi/wiki?TestDrivenDevelopment

- JUnit

  http://www.junit.org

- TestNG

  http://testng.org

- Dependency Injection/Inversion of Control

  http://en.wikipedia.org/wiki/Dependency_injection

- Spring

  http://www.springsource.org/

- Struts 2 Spring Plugin

  http://struts.apache.org/2.x/docs/spring-plugin.html

- Selenium

  http://seleniumhq.org/

- JMeter

  http://jakarta.apache.org/jmeter/

15

Documenting our Application

Every developer's favorite task is documenting their application (or so I've heard). As irritating as documentation can be, delivering a complete solution implies comprehensive, usable documentation. This goes beyond (but includes) typical Javadocs. However, more is required in order to understand how a particular application works, how its parts fit together, where dependencies lie, and so on. Even us, the developers, benefit from having a wide variety of documentation available.

In this chapter, we'll look at the ways in which we can document our applications, coding styles that can aid in understanding, tools and techniques for creating documentation from application artifacts, different types of documentation for different parties, and so on.

Documenting Java

Everybody knows the basics of documenting Java, so we won't go into much detail. We'll talk a bit about ways of writing code whose intention is clear, mention some Javadoc tricks we can use, and highlight some tools that can help keep our code clean. Clean code is one of the most important ways we can document our application. Anything we can do to increase readability will reduce confusion later (including our own).

Self-documenting code

We've all heard the myth of self-documenting code. In theory, code is always clear enough to be easily understood. In reality, this isn't always the case. However, we should try to write code that is as self-documenting as possible.

Keeping non-code artifacts in sync with the actual code is difficult. The only artifact that survives a project is the executable, which is created from code, not comments. This is one of the reasons for writing self-documenting code. (Well, annotations, XDoclet, and so on, make that somewhat less true. You know what I mean.)

There are little things we can do throughout our code to make our code read as much like our intent as possible and make extraneous comments just that: extraneous.

Document why, not what

Over-commenting wastes everybody's time. Time is wasted in writing a comment, reading it, keeping that comment in sync with the code, and, most importantly, a *lot* of time is wasted when a comment is not accurate.

Ever seen this?

```
a += 1; // increment a
```

This is the most useless comment in the world.

Firstly, it's really obvious we're incrementing something, regardless of what that something is. If the person reading our code doesn't know what += is, then we have more serious problems than them not knowing that we're incrementing, say, an array index.

Secondly, if a is an array index, we should probably use either a more common array index or make it obvious that it's an array index. Using i and j is common for array indices, while idx or index is less common. It may make sense to be very explicit in variable naming under some circumstances. Generally, it's nice to avoid names such as indexOfOuterArrayOfFoobars. However, with a large loop body it might make sense to use something such as num or currentIndex, depending on the circumstances.

With Java 1.5 and its support for collection iteration, it's often possible to do away with the index altogether, but not always.

Make your code read like the problem

Buzzphrases like **Domain Specific Languages (DSLs)** and **Fluent Interfaces** are often heard when discussing how to make our code look like our problem. We don't necessarily hear about them as much in the Java world because other languages support their creation in more "literate" ways. The recent interest in Ruby, Groovy, Scala, and other dynamic languages have brought the concept back into the mainstream.

A DSL, in essence, is a computer language targeted at a very specific problem. Java is an example of a general-purpose language. YACC and regular expressions are examples of DSLs that are targeted at creating parsers and recognizing strings of interest respectively.

DSLs may be **external**, where the implementing language processes the DSL appropriately, as well as **internal**, where the DSL is written in the implementing language itself. An internal DSL can also be thought of as an API or library, but one that reads more like a "little language".

Fluent interfaces are slightly more difficult to define, but can be thought of as an internal DSL that "flows" when read aloud. This is a very informal definition, but will work for our purposes.

Java can actually be downright hostile to some common DSL and fluent techniques for various reasons, including the expectations of the JavaBean specification. However, it's still possible to use some of the techniques to good effect. One typical practice of fluent API techniques is simply returning the object instance in object methods. For example, following the JavaBean specification, an object will have a `setter` for the object's properties. For example, a `User` class might include the following:

```
public class User {
    private String fname;
    private String lname;
    public void setFname(String fname) { this.fname = fname; }
    public void setLname(String lname) { this.lname = lname; }
}
```

Using the class is as simple as we'd expect it to be:

```
User u = new User();
u.setFname("James");
u.setLname("Gosling");
```

Naturally, we might also supply a constructor that accepts the same parameters. However, it's easy to think of a class that has many properties making a full constructor impractical. It also seems like the code is a bit wordy, but we're used to this in Java. Another way of creating the same functionality is to include setter methods that return the current instance. If we want to maintain JavaBean compatibility, and there are reasons to do so, we would still need to include normal setters, but can still include "fluent" setters as shown here:

```java
public User fname(String fname) {
    this.fname = fname;
    return this;
}
public User lname(String lname) {
    this.lname = lname;
    return this;
}
```

This creates (what some people believe is) more readable code. It's certainly shorter:

```java
User u = new User().fname("James").lname("Gosling");
```

There is one potential "gotcha" with this technique. Moving initialization into methods has the potential to create an object in an invalid state. Depending on the object this may not always be a usable solution for object initialization.

Users of Hibernate will recognize the "fluent" style, where method chaining is used to create criteria. Joshua Flanagan wrote a fluent regular expression interface, turning regular expressions (already a domain-specific language) into a series of chained method calls:

```java
Regex socialSecurityNumberCheck =
    new Regex(Pattern.With.AtBeginning
                .Digit.Repeat.Exactly(3)
                .Literal("-").Repeat.Optional
                .Digit.Repeat.Exactly(2)
                .Literal("-").Repeat.Optional
                .Digit.Repeat.Exactly(4)
                .AtEnd);
```

Whether or not this particular usage is an improvement is debatable, but it's certainly easier to read for the non-regex folks.

Ultimately, the use of fluent interfaces can increase readability (by quite a bit in most cases), may introduce some extra work (or completely duplicate work, like in the case of setters, but code generation and/or IDE support can help mitigate that), and may occasionally be more verbose (but with the benefit of enhanced clarity and IDE completion support).

Personally, I'm of the opinion that regular expressions are so incredibly important that it's worth learning them in their native form, as they can be used in many environments, including the IDEs so loved by Java developers. Large expressions can be broken down into components and created by concatenating strings. But the point here is more about the style of fluent programming, rather than this specific example.

Contract-oriented programming

Aspect-oriented programming (AOP) is a way of encapsulating cross-cutting functionality outside of the mainline code. That's a mouthful, but essentially it means is that we can remove common code that is found across our application and consolidate it in one place. The canonical examples are logging and transactions, but AOP can be used in other ways as well.

Design by Contract (DbC) is a software methodology that states our interfaces should define and enforce precise specifications regarding operation.

"Design by Contract" is a registered trademark of Interactive Software Engineering Inc. Other terms include **Programming by Contract (PbC)**, or my personal favorite, **Contract Oriented Programming (COP)**, which is how I'll refer to it from now on. I have a lot of respect for Eiffel and its creator, but this type of trademarking bothers me. Maybe I'll trademark "Singleton"?!

How does COP help create self-documenting code? Consider the following portion of a stack implementation:

```
public void push(final Object o) {
    stack.add(o);
}
```

This seems simple enough. The information available to us is that we can push an object, whatever pushing means.

What happens if we attempt to push a null? Let's assume that for this implementation, we don't want to allow pushing a null onto the stack.

```
/**
 * Pushes non-null objects on to stack.
 */
public void push(final Object o) {
    if (o == null) return;
    stack.add(o);
}
```

Once again, this is simple enough. We'll add the comment to the Javadocs stating that null objects will not be pushed (and that the call will fail/return silently). This will become the "contract" of the push method — captured in code and documented in Javadocs.

The contract is specified twice — once in the code (the ultimate arbiter) and again in the documentation. However, the user of the class does not have proof that the underlying implementation actually honors that contract. There's no guarantee that if we pass in a null, it will return silently without pushing anything.

The implied contract can change. We might decide to allow pushing nulls. We might throw an `IllegalArgumentException` or a `NullPointerException` on a null argument. We're not required to add a `throws` clause to the method declaration when throwing runtime exceptions. This means further information may be lost in both the code and the documentation.

As hinted, Eiffel has language-level support for COP with the `require/do/ensure/end` construct. It goes beyond the simple null check in the above code. It actively encourages detailed pre- and post-condition contracts. An implementation's `push()` method might check the remaining stack capacity before pushing. It might throw exceptions for specific conditions. In pseudo-Eiffel, we'd represent the `push()` method in the following way:

```
push (o: Object)
    require
        o /= null
    do
        -- push
    end
```

A stack also has an implied contract. We assume (sometimes naively) that once we call the `push` method, the stack will contain whatever we pushed. The size of the stack will have increased by one, or whatever other conditions our stack implementation requires.

One aim of COP is to formalize the nature of contracts. Languages such as Eiffel have one solution to that problem, and having it built-in at the language level provides a consistent means of expressing contracts.

Java, of course, doesn't have built-in contracts. However, it does contain a mechanism that can be used to get some of the benefits for a conceptually-simple price. The mechanism is not as complete, or as integrated, as Eiffel's version. However, it removes contract enforcement from the mainline code, and provides a way for both sides of the software to specify, accept, and document the contracts themselves.

Removing the contract information from the mainline code keeps the implementation clean and makes the implementation code easier to understand. Having programmatic access to the contract means that the contract could be documented automatically rather than having to maintain a disconnected chunk of Javadoc.

SpringContracts

SpringContracts is a beta-level Java COP implementation based on Spring's AOP facilities, using annotations to state pre- and post-contract conditions. It formalizes the nature of a contract, which can ease development.

Let's consider our `VowelDecider` that was developed through TDD. We can also use COP to express its contract (particularly the entry condition). This is a method that doesn't alter state, so post conditions don't apply here.

Our implementation of `VowelDecider` ended up looking (more or less) like this:

```
public boolean decide(final Object o) throws Exception {
    if ((o == null) || (!(o instanceof String))) {
        throw new IllegalArgumentException(
            "Argument must be a non-null String.");
    }
    String s = (String) o;
    return s.matches(".*[aeiouy]+.*");
}
```

Once we remove the original contract enforcement code, which was mixed with the mainline code, our SpringContracts `@Precondition` annotation looks like the following:

```
@Precondition(condition="arg1 != null && arg1.class.name == 'java.
lang.String'",
            message="Argument must be a non-null String")
public boolean decide(Object o) throws Exception {
    String s = (String) o;
    return s.matches(".*[aeiouy]+.*");
}
```

The pre-condition is that the argument must not be null and must be (precisely) a string. (Because of SpringContracts' Expression Language, we can't just say `instanceof String` in case we want to allow string subclasses.)

We can unit-test this class in the same way we tested the TDD version. In fact, we can copy the tests directly. Running them should trigger test failures on the null and non-string argument tests, as we originally expected an `IllegalArgumentException`. We'll now get a contract violation exception from SpringContracts.

One difference here is that we need to initialize the Spring context in our test. One way to do this is with JUnit's `@BeforeClass` annotation, along with a method that loads the Spring configuration file from the classpath and instantiates the decider as a Spring bean. Our class setup now looks like this:

```
@BeforeClass public static void setup() {
    appContext = new ClassPathXmlApplicationContext(
                "/com/packt/s2wad/applicationContext.xml");
    decider = (VowelDecider)
                appContext.getBean("vowelDecider");
}
```

We also need to configure SpringContracts in our Spring configuration file. Those unfamiliar with Spring's (or AspectJ's) AOP will be a bit confused. However, in the end, it's reasonably straightforward, with a potential "gotcha" regarding how Spring does proxying.

```
<aop:aspectj-autoproxy proxy-target-class="true"/>

<aop:config>
  <aop:aspect ref="contractValidationAspect">
    <aop:pointcut id="contractValidatingMethods"
          expression="execution(*
            com.packt.s2wad.example.CopVowelDecider.*(..))"/>
    <aop:around pointcut-ref="contractValidatingMethods"
                method="validateMethodCall"/>
  </aop:aspect>
</aop:config>

<bean id="contractValidationAspect"
class="org.springcontracts.dbc.interceptor.
ContractValidationInterceptor"/>

<bean id="vowelDecider"
      class="com.packt.s2wad.example.CopVowelDecider" />
```

If most of this seems like a mystery, that's fine. The SpringContracts documentation goes into it a bit more and the Spring documentation contains a wealth of information regarding how AOP works in Spring. The main difference between this and the simplest AOP setup is that our autoproxy target must be a class, which requires CGLib. This could also potentially affect operation.

The only other modification is to change the exception we're expecting to SpringContract's `ContractViolationCollectionException`, and our test starts passing. These pre- and post-condition annotations use the `@Documented` meta-annotation, so the SpringContracts COP annotations will appear in the Javadocs. It would also be possible to use various other means to extract and document contract information.

Getting into details

This mechanism, or its implementation, may not be a good fit for every situation. Runtime performance is a potential issue. As it's just some Spring magic, it can be turned off by a simple configuration change. However, if we do, we'll lose the value of the on-all-the-time contract management.

On the other hand, under certain circumstances, it may be enough to say that once the contracts are consistently honored under all of the test conditions, the system is correct enough to run without them. This view holds the contracts more as an acceptance test, rather than as run-time checking. Indeed, there is an overlap between COP and unit testing as the way to keep code honest. As unit tests aren't run all the time, it may be reasonable to use COP as a temporary runtime unit test or acceptance test.

Javadocs

We'll cover only a few things regarding Javadocs. I'm sure we're all very familiar with them, but there are a few tips that might be helpful occasionally.

Always write Javadocs!

The first bit of advice is to always write Javadocs, except when they're not really needed. Getters and setters that have no additional functionality really don't need them. However, as soon as a getter or setter does more than just get or set its value, it may deserve documentation. Even minor functionality that's trivial to understand when looking at the code may deserve Javadocs. We may not have access to the source or we may only want to look at the API documentation.

The first sentence

The first sentence of a Javadoc comment is used as the summary documentation. It isn't necessary to encapsulate every nuance of the member being documented in the first sentence, but it's important to give a very clear and concise overview of the member. By default, the first sentence is everything up to the first "." (period). Some tools will complain if the first sentence is not properly terminated.

The proper way to describe the grammar of the first sentence is something along the lines of: "use a verb phrase in the third person declarative form." What does that mean in real life?

```
/**
 * Builds and returns the current list of ingredients.
 *
 * @return List of ingredients.
 */
public List<Ingredient> buildIngredientList() { ... }
```

In the case of methods, the Javadoc summary should answer the question: "What does this member do?" One answer could be: "`buildIngredientList()` builds and returns the list of ingredients." This is opposed to saying something such as "Build and return list of ingredients", which doesn't work as an answer to the question. This is the "verb phrase" part.

The "third person declarative" part (informally) means that we answer the question as directly as possible. Sentence fragments are okay here. Additional exposition harms clarity. For example, we probably would not want to write the following:

```
/**
 * This method builds and returns the current list
 * of ingredients.
 */
```

That's not a direct answer to the question "What does `buildIngredientList()` do?". Therefore, this probably is not the best style of documentation.

This method is simple enough. Therefore, we may not need the `@return` Javadoc tag. What it returns is already specified in the first sentence. However, some tools may complain about missing Javadoc tags.

For variables, a simple descriptive sentence such as the following is usually fine:

```
/** Pre-built recipe summary. */
private String summary;
```

Is it okay to have member variables without Javadocs? The answer is yes, if the purpose is self-evident from the name. However, if our build process includes a tool that enforces Javadoc requirements, we'll either get irritating warnings or we'll need to specify what to exclude from checking.

If there aren't any Javadoc requirements, then all bets are off. However, bear in mind that Javadocs are also used by the IDE to provide information in various forms such as roll-over Javadoc pop-ups. It often boils down to whether or not we are able to come up with a good variable or method name. If we can, then the benefits of essentially repeating the same information in a Javadoc comment are very low and are probably not worth it.

Add information beyond the API name

In our `buildIngredientList()` example seen earlier, our first sentence really doesn't tell us much more than the name of the method does. This is good because it means that our method name (the API name) is probably correct and sufficient. However, let's assume that the method actually does something interesting during the construction of the ingredient list. That information should then be added to the Javadocs.

The information does not (necessarily) belong in the summary. Therefore, we can simply continue with another sentence (this is a bit contrived, since it could be merged into the first sentence quite easily).

```
/**
 * Builds and returns the current list of ingredients.
 * Initializes ingredient information if necessary.
 */
```

The summary information will consist of only the first sentence, but both sentences will be in the complete Javadocs. Note that in this case, it might make more sense to use a single sentence similar to the following:

```
/**
 * Builds and returns the current list of ingredients,
 * initializing ingredient info when necessary.
 */
```

The trick is to consistently make good decisions regarding what the most essential information is, and communicating it cleanly and concisely.

Write for multiple formats

Javadocs should be written with the thought that they might be read in several formats. Some common ways of viewing Javadocs include embedded in source code, using an IDE or an IDE popup/hover, the results of a `grep`, and so on. They may also be viewed as HTML, such as after they've been processed with the Javadoc tool. Javadoc comments may even be included in a wiki, through some sort of snippet mechanism or by including it in various forms of documentation.

In our example above, we have two sentences in a row. Let's say that we need to highlight the fact that the ingredient information will be initialized if necessary. Our first attempt just adds a bold `Note` to the second sentence.

```
/**
 * Builds and returns the current list of ingredients.
 *
 * <b>Note:</b> Initializes ingredient information if
 * necessary.
 */
```

The word `Note:` will stand out in the HTML output, but will appear connected to the opening sentence. Javadoc doesn't honor text-based line breaks. We must use HTML to format our Javadocs. Creating separate paragraphs requires the use of paragraph tags.

By formatting our Javadoc as indented HTML, we can create documentation that reads reasonably well in both text and HTML formats. Additionally, with judicious use of HTML tags, we can use doclets that create printable PDF documentation (or other printable formats).

```
/**
 * Builds and returns the current list of ingredients.
 *
 * <p>
 *   <b>Note:</b> Initializes ingredient information
 *   if necessary.
 * </p>
 */
```

As usual, this example is a bit contrived. We'd probably just want to put it all in the first sentence.

Generating targeted Javadocs

One reason people give for not writing Javadocs for a particular method is that the method isn't necessarily designed to be used by others, or that exposing even the documentation isn't a good idea. The Javadoc tool gives us a few ways to restrict what documentation is generated.

Visibility

The most obvious way to restrict what documentation is generated is based on visibility. By default, Javadoc will generate documentation for all of the public and protected classes. By using the -public, -protected, -package, and -private flags, we can control the level of visibility for which documentation will be generated. Note that we need to specify only one flag—any member with equal or greater visibility will have documentation generated for it.

For example, running Javadoc with the -public flag will generate documentation for only public members, creating Javadocs suitable for the users of an API. Running with the -private flag will generate documentation for all of the members, making the documentation suitable for the developers of the same API.

The -exclude argument

The -exclude argument allows us to supply package names that will be excluded from Javadoc generation. For example, if we want to create documentation that specifically excludes an "internal-use only" package (security through obscurity?), we can use the -exclude argument to provide a ":" (colon) separated list of packages for which no Javadocs will be generated.

```
javadoc -exclude com.packt.s2wad.internal {...}
```

No classes in the com.packt.s2wad.internal package will be documented.

The -use argument

The -use argument will generate a "Use" page for each class C being documented. The "Use" page will contain an entry for each package, class, method, and fields "using" class C. Uses include subclasses, methods that use the class as a parameter, and methods that return an instance of the class.

This page may not be as useful as a graphical representation of the class interdependencies, but it's an option that's available out of the box. Creating various diagrams is possible with add-on Javadoc doclets such as yDoc or UmlGraph, as well as with non-Javadoc-oriented tools.

Creating new Javadoc tags with the -tag argument

One Javadoc capability that's trivial to take advantage of is creating our own Javadoc tags. These tags are similar to the `@param` and `@return` tags that Javadoc recognizes by default. This capability may or may not fit into your organization or coding style, but it's simple enough to use that it's worth an introduction. Another potential issue is that our IDE or build process probably won't be capable of validating the information contained in the tag, unlike the default tags. For example, Eclipse can flag a warning if a method's parameters don't have corresponding `@param` tags.

We could document an action that puts a variable into session by creating a `@session` Javadoc tag. By telling the Javadoc tool to pay attention to that tag, we can create output for it just like the built-in `@param` tag. An action's Javadocs might look like this:

```
/**
 * Retrieves recipe, creating session parameters as needed.
 *
 * @session CONSTANTS.LAST_RECIPE The last recipe accessed.
 *
 * @returns SUCCESS or ERROR if retrieval fails.
 */
```

We instruct the `javadoc` tool to pay attention to our new tag by giving it `-tag` arguments. The easiest method is to just add `-tag session` to the `javadoc` command. How this is done depends on your build environment. It can be done using an Ant script, via an IDE `javadoc` frontend, and so on.

Adding the `-tag session` argument instructs `javadoc` to create output for `@session` tags similar to `@param` and `@returns` tags. The generated output will appear after the standard tags. If we want to change the order in the HTML we must supply a complete list of `-tag arguments` including the built-in tags as well. Each tag's output is generated in the order specified on the command line. If we wanted to see the `@session` documentation before the `@return` tag's documentation, then we'd specify both documentations on the command line as follows:

-tag session -tag return

We can also specify the header for a custom Javadoc tag. To set a header for the session tag we use colon-separated values (ignoring the a for now):

```
-tag session:a:"Session attributes accessed:"
```

Note that the header label for built-in tags can be modified in the same way, provided we have a good reason to do so. However, we will probably never have a good reason to do so.

The "a" we snuck in there determines where in the source code we can use the tag, with "a" meaning anywhere we want. A complete list of determinants is found in the `javadoc` tool documentation, but includes "t" for types (classes and interfaces), "m" for methods, "f" for fields, and so on. These may be combined, so a tag to identify injected entities for both types and fields could be specified as follows:

```
-tag injected:tf:"Injected entities:"
```

If we now try to use our new `@injected` tag in a method declaration, the Javadoc tool will signal an error, as it's been specified as being valid only for types and fields.

Note that this functionality of `javadoc` may overlap some use of annotations. For example, assume we're using an interceptor that loads and saves an annotated variable from and to the JEE session. It would make more sense to use a doclet that included this information from the annotation, rather than writing (and worse, maintaining) the Javadoc manually—the more we can do automatically, the better.

Never write Javadocs!

I know what you're thinking—but as soon as we write Javadocs, we've entered into an implicit contract to always keep them up-to-date, in perpetuity, over the life of the program. If we can't do that, it may be better not to write any. Remember, wrong documentation is worse than having no documentation.

There are many cases where it makes sense to write detailed Javadocs, describing a complicated or non-obvious algorithm being chief among them. However, it's arguable whether such documentation belongs in the application's non-code documentation or in a wiki.

Never write inline Java comments!

If we find ourselves writing chunks of comments inside methods to explain each section of a method, we might be better off refactoring the chunk into its own method. Of course, some code lends itself to this more readily than others, which might be impractical for a variety of reasons. There's always a trade-off. However, there is always a cost associated with non-code documentation, as it is ultimately maintained separately from the code itself.

Using UML

UML (Unified Markup Language) can handle a wide range of documentation duties, much more than will be covered here. Even UML-like diagrams can be of great assistance in many aspects of documentation. It's not necessary to follow all of the UML notation or diagrams completely, purchase an expensive enterprise UML tool, and so on. However, a basic understanding of UML is very handy when documenting our own application, or reading the documentation of other projects that use UML.

There are many ways to integrate UML into the development and documentation process. It might be used to generate source code, it can be included in both developer and end-user documentation (where appropriate), and so on. Two of the more common UML diagrams related directly to Java code are the **package** and **class** diagrams, which most of us are already familiar with.

Package diagrams

Package diagrams are similar to class diagrams, but provide a very high-level overview of an application's package and package dependencies. We saw a portion of a package diagram back in Chapter 3 when we looked at a portion of the XWork 2 packages. There, we only looked at the XWork interfaces and did not highlight package coupling.

Class diagrams

One of the most useful and commonplace UML diagrams is probably the class diagram. The class diagram is used to show the relationship between different classes in a system. Class diagrams can be created at various levels of detail to provide very high-level overviews or extremely detailed information, including all of a class's properties.

For example, a portion of our `com.packt.s2wad.recipe` package's class diagram can be represented by the following UML class diagram. Note that this is an incomplete diagram and doesn't show our implementation of `RecipeService`. It's also fairly high-level, and doesn't show any class properties or methods.

However, it's still useful because it's obvious that we have two classes that use a `RecipeService`, and two classes that have a relationship to the `Recipe` class. This type of high-level overview is particularly important when first learning an application, identifying high-level class-coupling issues, and so on.

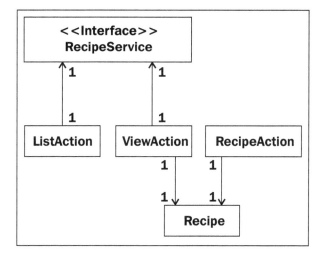

A class diagram for an entire application can be a bit overwhelming, and isn't always useful due to the sheer amount of information. Restricting what is visible at both the class and package level can be very useful allowing usable documentation to be generated.

The previous image was generated with ArgoUML, an open source UML tool from application source. It was then edited by hand to improve the layout, to remove class members and operations, and so on.

Java source can also be generated from UML models. Several IDEs and modeling tools supply this functionality. The direction of generation, whether generating UML from source or source from UML, is largely a matter of preference, culture, and how well the available tools work for our style (or the style of our client).

Sequence diagrams

Another popular and useful UML diagram, which is relatively lightweight, is the sequence diagram. These diagrams are used to document interactions between entities. These entities are normally classes. However, it's not unreasonable to extend the sequence diagram metaphor beyond the official definition when necessary, such as adding user interactions, browser functionality, and so on.

As a quick example, we can take a look at the typical Struts 2 form validation processing sequence, compressing the non-related interceptors into a single entity:

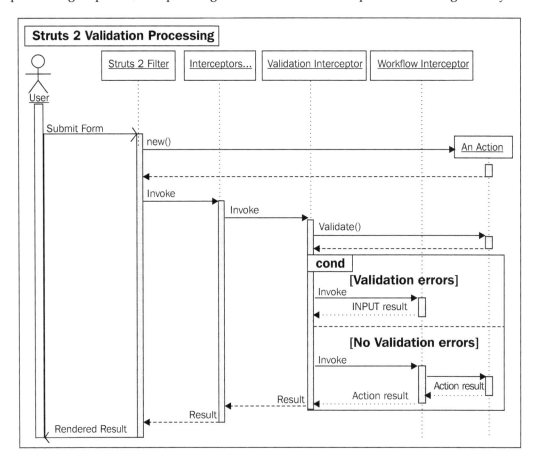

Here, we're representing the user action of submitting a form in the sequence diagram. This (in simplified form) causes the Struts 2 filter to instantiate the appropriate action class, indicated by the **new()** message. The rest is (I'd imagine) largely self-explanatory.

Sequence diagrams are often easier to comprehend than plain text and can be more convenient than the code itself, as they aggregate as many classes as needed. As usual, they can suffer from decay, as the code continues to be modified and the diagrams aren't being generated automatically or being actively maintained.

This diagram was created using the Quick Sequence Diagram Editor, which creates an exportable diagram using simple text-based input (I was tempted to call it a DSL, but managed to stop myself). The input for this diagram is relatively short.

```
#![Struts 2 Validation Processing]
user:Actor "User"
s2f: "Struts 2 Filter"
etc: "Interceptors..."
val: "Validation Interceptor"
workflow: "Workflow Interceptor"
/action: "An Action"
user:s2f.Submit form
s2f:action.new()

s2f:Result=etc.Invoke
etc:Result=val.Invoke

val:action.validate()

[c:cond Validation errors]
  val:INPUT result=workflow.Invoke
--[No validation errors]
  val:Action result=workflow.Invoke
  workflow:Action result=action.Invoke
[/c]
s2f:user.Rendered Result
```

Personally, I think the send/receive messages are defined backwards. It's pretty easy to create our own DSL (for example, in Ruby) that corrects this error. It's also relatively straightforward to create a log format that could be parsed to create diagrams from actual code. Therefore, running unit tests could also be a part of the documentation process.

Documenting web applications

Documenting an entire web application can be surprisingly tricky because of the many different layers involved. Some web application frameworks support automatic documentation generation better than others. It's preferable to have fewer disparate parts. For example, Lisp, Smalltalk, and some Ruby frameworks are little more than internal DSLs that can be trivially redefined to produce documentation from the actual application code.

In general, Java frameworks are more difficult to limit to a single layer. Instead, we are confronted with HTML, JSP, JavaScript, Java, the framework itself, its configuration methodologies (XML, annotations, scripting languages, etc.), the service layers, business logic, persistence layers, and so on—feeling sleepy? Complete documentation generally means aggregating information from many disparate sources and presenting them in a way that is meaningful to the intended audience.

High-level overviews

The site map is obviously a reasonable overview of a web application. A site map may look like a simple hierarchy chart, showing a simple view of a site's pages without showing all of the possible links between pages, how a page is implemented, and so on.

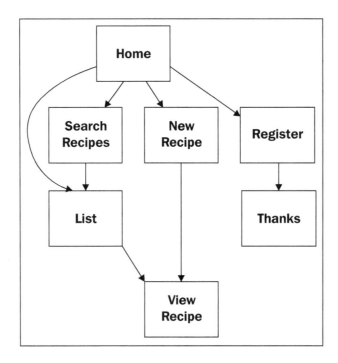

This diagram was created by hand and shows only the basic outline of the application flow. It represents minor maintenance overhead since it would need to be updated when there are any changes to the application.

Documenting JSPs

There doesn't seem to be any general-purpose JSP documentation methodology. It's relatively trivial to create comments inside a JSP page using JSP comments or a regular Javadoc comment inside a scriptlet. Pulling these comments out is then a matter of some simple parsing. This may be done by using one of our favorite tools, regular expressions, or using more HTML-specific parsing and subsequent massaging.

Where it gets tricky is when we want to start generating documentation that includes elements such as JSP pages, which may be included using many different mechanisms—static includes, `<jsp:include.../>` tags, Tiles, SiteMesh, inserted via Ajax, and so on. Similarly, generating connections between pages is fraught with custom cases. We might use general-purpose HTML links, Struts 2 link tags, attach a link to a page element with JavaScript, ad infinitum/nauseum.

When we throw in the (perhaps perverse) ability to generate HTML using Java, we have a situation where creating a perfectly general-purpose tool is a major undertaking. However, we can fairly easily create a reasonable set of documentation that is specific to our framework by parsing configuration files (or scanning a classpath for annotations), understanding how we're linking the server-side to our presentation views, and performing (at least limited) HTML/JSP parsing to pull out presentation-side dependencies, links, and anything that we want documented.

Documenting JavaScript

If only there was a tool such as Javadoc for JavaScript. Fortunately, I was not the only one that had that desire! The JsDoc Toolkit provides Javadoc-like functionality for JavaScript, with additional features to help handle the dynamic nature of JavaScript code. Because of the dynamic nature, we (as developers) must remain diligent in both in how we write our JavaScript and how we document it.

Fortunately, the JsDoc Toolkit is good at recognizing current JavaScript programming paradigms (within reason), and when it can't, provides Javadoc-like tags we can use to give it hints.

For example, consider our JavaScript `Recipe` module where we create several private functions intended for use only by the module, and return a map of functions for use on the webpage. The returned map itself contains a map of validation functions. Ideally, we'd like to be able to document all of the different components.

Because of the dynamic nature of JavaScript, it's more difficult for tools to figure out the context things should belong to. Java is much simpler in this regard (which is both a blessing and a curse), so we need to give JsDoc hints to help it understand our code's layout and purpose.

A high-level flyby of the `Recipe` module shows a layout similar to the following:

```
var Recipe = function () {
    var ingredientLabel;
    var ingredientCount;
    // ...
    function trim(s) {
        return s.replace(/^\s+|\s+$/g, "");
```

```
    }
    function msgParams(msg, params) {
        // ...
    }
    return {
        loadMessages: function (msgMap) {
            // ...
        },
        prepare: function (label, count) {
            // ...
        },
        pageValidators: {
            validateIngredientNameRequired: function (form) {
                // ...
            },
            // ...
        }
    };
}();
```

We see several documentable elements: the `Recipe` module itself, private variables, private functions, and the return map which contains both functions and a map of validation functions. JsDoc accepts a number of Javadoc-like document annotations that allow us to control how it decides to document the JavaScript elements.

The JavaScript module pattern, exemplified by an immediately-executed function, is understood by JsDoc through the use of the `@namespace` annotation.

```
/**
 * @namespace
 * Recipe module.
 */
var Recipe = function () {
    // ...
}();
```

(Yes, this is one of those instances where eliminating the comment itself would be perfectly acceptable!) We'll look at the JsDoc output momentarily after covering a few more high-level JsDoc annotations.

We can mark private functions with the `@private` annotation as shown next:

```
/**
 * @private
 * Trims leading/trailing space.
 */
function trim(s) {
    return s.replace(/^\s+|\s+$/g, "");
}
```

(Again the JsDoc comment could be replaced by creating a better function name. Really—I named it poorly so that I could bring up the documentation issues.)

It gets interesting when we look at the map returned by the `Recipe` module:

```
return /** @lends Recipe */ {
    /**
     * Loads message map.
     *
     * <p>
     *   This is generally used to pass in text resources
     *   retrieved via <s:text.../> or <s:property
     *   value="getText(...)"/> tags on a JSP page in lieu
     *   of a normalized way for JS to get Java I18N resources
     * </p>
     */
    loadMessages: function (msgMap) {
        _msgMap = msgMap;
    },
    // ...
```

The `@lends` annotation indicates that the functions returned by the `Recipe` module belong to the `Recipe` module. Without the `@lends` annotation, JsDoc doesn't know how to interpret the JavaScript in the way we probably intend the JavaScript to be used, so we provide a little prodding.

The `loadMessages()` function itself is documented as we would document a Java method, including the use of embedded HTML.

The other interesting bit is the map of validation functions. Once again, we apply the `@namespace` annotation, creating a separate set of documentation for the validation functions, as they're used by our validation template hack and not directly by our page code.

```
/**
 * @namespace
 * Client-side page validators used by our template hack.
 * ...
 */
pageValidators: {
    /**
     * Insures each ingredient with a quantity
     * also has a name.
     *
     * @param {Form object} form
     * @type boolean
     */
    validateIngredientNameRequired: function (form) {
        // ...
```

Note also that we can annotate the type of our JavaScript parameters inside curly brackets. Obviously, JavaScript doesn't have typed parameters. We need to tell it what the function is expecting. The `@type` annotation is used to document what the function is expected to return. It gets a little trickier if the function returns different types based on arbitrary criteria. However, we never do that because it's hard to maintain—right?

 Overloading JavaScript return values is typical because JavaScript has a wider range of truthiness and falseness than Java. This is okay, even though it gives Java programmers conniptions. That's okay too, and can be mildly entertaining to boot.

JsDoc has the typical plethora of command-line options, and requires the specification of the application itself (written in JavaScript, and run using Rhino) and the templates defining the output format. An alias to run JsDoc might look like the following, assuming the JsDoc installation is being pointed at by the `${JSDOC}` shell variable:

```
alias jsdoc='java -jar ${JSDOC}/jsrun.jar
              ${JSDOC}/app/run.js -t=${JSDOC}/templates/jsdoc'
```

The command line to document our `Recipe` module (including private functions using the `-p` options) and to write the output to the `jsdoc-out` folder, will now look like the following:

```
jsdoc -p -d=jsdoc-out recipe.js
```

The homepage looks similar to a typical JavaDoc page, but more JavaScript-like:

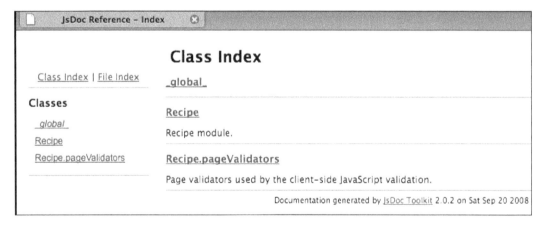

A portion of the `Recipe` module's validators, marked by a `@namespace` annotation inside the `@lends` annotation of the return map, looks like the one shown in the next image (the left-side navigation has been removed):

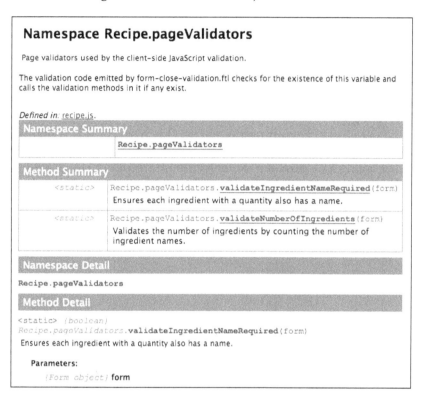

We can get a pretty decent and accurate JavaScript documentation using JsDoc, with only a minimal amount of prodding to help with the dynamic aspects of JavaScript, which is difficult to figure out automatically.

Documenting interaction

Documenting interaction can be surprisingly complicated, particularly in today's highly-interactive Web 2.0 applications. There are many different levels of interactivity taking place, and the implementation may live in several different layers, from the JavaScript browser to HTML generated deep within a server-side framework.

UML sequence diagrams may be able to capture much of that interactivity, but fall somewhat short when there are activities happening in parallel. AJAX, in particular, ends up being a largely concurrent activity. We might send the AJAX request, and then do various things on the browser in anticipation of the result.

More UML and the power of scribbling

The UML activity diagram is able to capture this kind of interactivity reasonably well, as it allows a single process to be split into multiple streams and then joined up again later. As we look at a simple activity diagram, we'll also take a quick look at scribbling, paper, whiteboards, and the humble digital camera.

Don't spend so much time making pretty pictures

One of the hallmarks of lightweight, agile development is that we don't spend all of our time creating the World's Most Perfect Diagram™. Instead, we create just enough documentation to get our points across. One result of this is that we might not use a $1,000 diagramming package to create all of our diagrams. Believe it or not, sometimes just taking a picture of a sketched diagram from paper or a whiteboard is more than adequate to convey our intent, and is usually much quicker than creating a perfectly-rendered software-driven diagram.

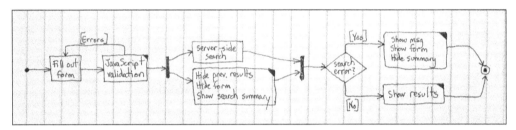

Yes, the image above is a digital camera picture of a piece of notebook paper with a rough activity diagram. The black bars here are used to indicate a small section of parallel functionality, a server-side search and some activity on the browser. I've also created an informal means of indicating browser programming, indicated by the black triangles. In this case, it might not even be worth sketching out. However, for moderately more complicated usage cases, particularly when there is a lot of both server- and client-side activity, a high-level overview is often worth the minimal effort.

The same digital camera technique is also very helpful in meetings where various documentation might be captured on a whiteboard. The resulting images can be posted to a company wiki, used in informal specifications, and so on.

User documentation

Development would be substantially easier if we didn't have to worry about those pesky users, always wanting features, asking questions, and having problems using the applications we've developed. Tragically, users also drive our paycheck. Therefore, at some point, it can be beneficial to acknowledge their presence and throw them the occasional bone, in the form of user documentation.

Developing user documentation is a subject unto itself, but deserves to be brought up here. We can generally assume that it will not include any implementation details, and will focus primarily on the user interface and the processes our applications use.

When writing user documentation, it's often sufficient to take the user stories, decorate them with screenshots and extra expository text, and leave it at that. It really depends on the client's requirements how much (if any) user-specific documentation is needed. If it's an application which will be used inside the client's business, it may be sufficient to provide one or more onsite training sessions.

One thing worth mentioning is that a screenshot can often save oodles of writing effort, communicate ideas more clearly, and remain easily deliverable through the application itself, in a training environment, and so on.

[Screenshots can be a valuable documentation tool at many levels, including communications with our client when we're trying to illustrate a point difficult to communicate via text or still images alone.]

Documenting development

The last form of documentation we'll look at is development documentation. This goes beyond our UML diagrams, user manual, functional specification, and so on. Development documentation includes the source control and issue tracking systems, the reasoning behind design decisions, and more. We'll take a quick look at some information we can use from each of these systems to create a path through the development itself.

Source code control systems

A **Source Code Control System** (**SCCS**) is an important part of the development process. Our SCCS is more than just a place to dump our source code—it's an opportunity to give a high-level overview of system changes.

The best ways to use our SCCS are dependent on which SCCS we use. However, there are a few quick ideas we can adopt across any SCCS and use them to extract a variety of information about our development streams.

Most clients will have their preferred SCCS already in place. If our deliverable includes source, it's nice if we can provide it in a way that preserves our work history.

Code and mental history

The history of change can be used on several levels, in several ways. There are products available that can help analyze our SCCS, or we can analyze it ourselves depending on what kind of information we're looking for.

For example, the number of non-trivial changes made to a file provides information in itself—for whatever reason, this file gets changed a lot. It's either an important document, a catchall, a candidate for parameterization, and so on. If two files are always modified together, then there's a chance of an unnecessarily tight coupling between them.

Sometimes, we just need to know what we were working on a for a particular date(s). We can retrieve all of our SCCS interaction for auditing purposes, to help determine what we were doing on a particular date, as part of a comprehensive change and time tracking system, and so on.

Commit comment commitment

We should view our commit comments as an important part of development documentation. One way to normalize commit comments is to create them as Javadoc-like comments, but different. Mostly, this just means that the first sentence is a succinct summary of the unit of work done, and the remaining sentences describe what was actually done.

What that first sentence includes is somewhat dependent on the rest of the development infrastructure. It's reasonable to put an issue tracking reference (see next section) as the most prominent part of that comment, perhaps followed by the same summary sentence as the issue item, or a summary if that's too long.

The rest of the commit comment should include any information deemed useful, and might include general change information, algorithm changes, new tests, and so on. This is the section for comments such as "Aaaaaaaaarg!", which aren't useful summaries, although it's often the most accurate.

Having a summary commit comment sentence also allows tools to get the output of history or log commands, and create a new view of existing information when necessary. For example, getting a list of files we changed between certain dates, along with a summary of why the files were changed. These can be used as a part of release notes, high-level summaries, and so on.

When (and what) do we commit

We should tend to commit more rather than less. The more recently a change was made, the easier it is to remember why and what was modified. Update the spelling in a single comment? Sure, might as well commit. When that file is changed later, and you're code-reviewing the changes, it's easier to look at only significant changes, and not at some trivial changes such as a punctuation change made the day before.

Also, while combining related commits, strive to keep them as granular as possible. For example, let's say we've updated some functionality in an action. As we were doing that, we corrected a couple of spelling errors in some other files. In an ideal world, even minor non-code changes would get their own commit, rather than being lumped in with changes to the code itself. If we see a commit message of "corrected spelling", we can probably ignore it. If it's lumped in to an issue-specific commit, we need to check the file itself to know if it's really part of the issue, and we'll be disappointed to find out it was to fix a misspelled Javadoc.

However, in the real world, we're not always so disciplined. In that case, the commit would be commented with information about the actual issue being addressed. However, in the comments, we might note that some spelling changes were included in the commit.

Note that some SCCSs make the task of breaking up our commits easier than others.

Branching

Even relatively simple changes in application functionality might warrant an experimental branch in which we could play with reckless abandon. By indicating the start of a unit of work in our SCCS, we allow all of the changes related to that unit of work to be easily reproduced.

It also creates a mini repository within which we can keep revision control of our development spike. It keeps the experimental code and its changes out of our mainline code and isolates the changes based on a distinct unit of work, which makes us feel better about life in general.

If the experimental branch lasts a long time, it should be updated with the current trunk (the head revision) as the mainline development proceeds. This will ease integration of the experimental patch when it's completed and merged back into the mainline code.

Branching discipline

Just as commits should be as granular as possible, any branches we create should be tied as closely as possible to the underlying work being done. For example, if we're working on refactoring in an experimental branch, we shouldn't begin making unrelated changes to another system in the same branch. Instead, hold off on making those changes, or make them in the parent revision and update our revision against the mainline code.

Branches of branches? Perhaps, but the management of multiple branches gets very irritating very quickly and is rarely worth the effort.

Issue and bug management

It's equally important to maintain a list of defects, enhancements, and so on. Ideally, everyone involved in a project will use the same system. This will allow developers, QA, the the client, or anybody else involved, to create help tickets, address deficiencies, and so on.

Note that the structure for doing this varies wildly across organizations. It will not always possible or appropriate to use our client's system. In cases like this, it's still a good idea to keep an internal issue management system in place for development purposes.

Using an issue tracking system can consolidate the location of our high-level to-do list, our immediate task list, our defect tracking, and so on. In a perfect world, we can enter all issues into our system and categorize them in a way meaningful to us and/or our clients. A "bug" is different from an "enhancement" and should be treated as such. An **enhancement** might require authorization to implement, it could have hidden implications, and so on. On the other hand, a **bug** is something that is not working as expected (whether it's an implementation or specification issue), and should be treated with appropriate urgency.

The categories chosen for issue tracking also depend on the application environment, client, and so on. There are a few that are safe, such as bug, enhancement, and so on. We can also have labels such as "tweak" "refactoring" and so on. These are primarily intended for internal and developmental use in order to indicate that it's a development-oriented issue and not necessarily client driven.

Issue priorities can be used to derive work lists. (And sometimes it's nice to knock off a few easy, low-priority issues to make it seem like something was accomplished.) A set of defined and maintained issue priorities can be used as part of an acceptance specification. One requirement might be that the application shouldn't contain any "bug"-level issues with a priority higher than three, meaning all priority one and priority two bugs must be resolved before the client accepts the deliverable.

This can also lead to endless, wildly entertaining discussions between us and the client, covering the ultimate meaning of "priority" and debating the relative importance of various definitions of "urgent", and so on. It's important to have an ongoing dialog with the client, in order to avoid running into these discussions late in the game. Always get discrepancies dealt with early in the process, and always document them.

Linking to the SCCS

Some environments will enjoy a tight coupling between their SCCS and issue tracking systems. This allows change sets for a specific issue to be tracked and understood more easily.

When no such integration is available, it's still relatively easy to link the SCCS to the issue tracking system. The two easiest ways to implement this are providing issue tracking information prominently in the SCCS commit comment (as discussed in an earlier section) or by including change set information in the issue tracking system (for example, when an issue is resolved, include a complete change set list).

Note that by following a convention in commit comments, it's usually possible to extract a complete list of relevant source changes by looking for a known token in the complete history output. For example, if we always referenced issue tracking items by an ID such as (say) "ID #42: Fix login validation issue", we could create a regular expression that matches this, and then get information about each commit that referenced this issue.

Wikis

We all know what a wiki is, but I'd like to advocate a moment to highlight their use as a way to create documentation and why they're well-suited to an agile environment.

Wikis lower the cost of information production and management in many ways, particularly when it's not clear upfront all that will be required or generated. By making it easy to enter, edit, and link to information, we can create an organic set of documentation covering all facets of the project. This may include processes used, design decisions, links to various reports and artifacts—anything we need and want.

The collaborative nature of wikis makes them a great way for everyone involved in a project to extend and organize everything related to the project. Developers, managers, clients, testers, deployers, anybody and everybody related to the project may be involved in the care and upkeep of the project's documentation.

Developers might keep detailed instructions on a project's build process, release notes, design documents (or at least links to them), server and data source information, and so on. Some wikis even allow the inclusion of code snippets from the repository, making it possible to create a "literate programming" environment. This can be a great way to give a high-level architectural overview of an application to a developer, who may be unfamiliar with the project.

Many wikis also provide a means of exporting their content, allowing all or part of the wiki to be saved in a PDF format suitable for printed documentation. Other export possibilities exist including various help formats, and so on.

Lowering the barrier to collaborative documentation generation enables wide-scale participation in the creation of various documentation artifacts.

RSS and IRC/chat systems

RSS allows us quick, normalized access to (generally) time-based activities. For example, developers can keep an RSS feed detailing their development activities. The feed creation can come from an internal company blog, a wiki, or other means. The RSS feed can also be captured as a part of the development process documentation.

Particularly in distributed development environments, a chat system can be invaluable for handling ad hoc meetings and conversations. Compared to email, more diligence is required in making sure that decisions are captured and recorded in an appropriate location.

Both RSS and IRC/chat can be used by our application itself to report on various issues, status updates, and so on, in addition to more traditional logging and email systems. Another advantage is that there are many RSS and chat clients we can keep on our desktops to keep us updated on the status of our application.

And let's face it, watching people log in to our system and trailing them around the website can be addictive.

Word processor documents

Personally, I'm not in favor of creating extensive word processor documents as the main documentation format. There are quite a few reasons for that: it can be more difficult to share in their creation, more difficult to extract portions of documents for inclusion in other documents, some word processors will only produce proprietary formats, and so on.

It's substantially more flexible to write in a format that allows collaborative participation such as a Wiki, or a text-based format such as DocBook that can be kept in our SCCS and exported to a wide variety of formats and allow linking in to, and out of, other sections or documents.

When proprietary formats must be used, we should take advantage of whatever functionality they offer in terms of version management, annotations, and so on. When a section changes, adding a footnote with the date and rationalization for the change can help track accountability.

Note that some wikis can be edited in and/or exported to various formats, which may help them fit in to an established corporate structure more readily. There are also a number of services popping up these days that help manage projects in a more lightweight manner than has been typically available.

Summary

We've examined the many ways of creating documentation throughout the entire development process. In particular, we've tried to highlight ways in which we can use existing tools, artifacts, and processes in order to help generate a wide variety of information.

We've also learned that documentation can be a project in itself. We have also seen that a lot of documentation, while potentially invaluable, may also represent a liability if we are forced to maintain it manually. This leads us to assume that documentation generated from the code itself (or as a by-product of running that code) is easier to sell to both ourselves and our management.

References

A reader can refer to the following:

- Fluent Interfaces:

  http://www.martinfowler.com/bliki/FluentInterface.html

- Aspect Oriented Programming:

  http://en.wikipedia.org/wiki/Aspect-oriented_programming

- Design by Contract:

  http://en.wikipedia.org/wiki/Design_by_contract

- SpringContracts:

  http://springcontracts.sourceforge.net

- yDoc:

  http://www.yworks.com/en/products_ydoc.html

- UmlGraph:

  http://www.umlgraph.org

- ArgoUML:

  http://argouml.tigris.org

- Quick Sequence Diagram Editor:

  http://sdedit.sourceforge.net/

- JsDoc Toolkit:

  http://code.google.com/p/jsdoc-toolkit/

Index

Thank you for buying

Apache Struts 2
Web Application Development

Packt Open Source Project Royalties

When we sell a book written on an Open Source project, we pay a royalty directly to that project. Therefore by purchasing Apache Struts 2 Web Application Development, Packt will have given some of the money received to the Apache Struts project.

In the long term, we see ourselves and you—customers and readers of our books—as part of the Open Source ecosystem, providing sustainable revenue for the projects we publish on. Our aim at Packt is to establish publishing royalties as an essential part of the service and support a business model that sustains Open Source.

If you're working with an Open Source project that you would like us to publish on, and subsequently pay royalties to, please get in touch with us.

Writing for Packt

We welcome all inquiries from people who are interested in authoring. Book proposals should be sent to author@packtpub.com. If your book idea is still at an early stage and you would like to discuss it first before writing a formal book proposal, contact us; one of our commissioning editors will get in touch with you.

We're not just looking for published authors; if you have strong technical skills but no writing experience, our experienced editors can help you develop a writing career, or simply get some additional reward for your expertise.

About Packt Publishing

Packt, pronounced 'packed', published its first book "Mastering phpMyAdmin for Effective MySQL Management" in April 2004 and subsequently continued to specialize in publishing highly focused books on specific technologies and solutions.

Our books and publications share the experiences of your fellow IT professionals in adapting and customizing today's systems, applications, and frameworks. Our solution-based books give you the knowledge and power to customize the software and technologies you're using to get the job done. Packt books are more specific and less general than the IT books you have seen in the past. Our unique business model allows us to bring you more focused information, giving you more of what you need to know, and less of what you don't.

Packt is a modern, yet unique publishing company, which focuses on producing quality, cutting-edge books for communities of developers, administrators, and newbies alike. For more information, please visit our website: www.PacktPub.com.

JasperReports for Java Developers

ISBN: 1-904811-90-6   Paperback: 344 pages

Create, Design, Format and Export Reports with the world's most popular Java reporting library

1. Get started with JasperReports, and develop the skills to get the most from it

2. Generate report data from a wide range of datasources

3. Integrate Jasper Reports with Spring, Hibernate, Java Server Faces, or Struts

JBoss Tools 3 Developers Guide

ISBN: 978-1-847196-14-9   Paperback: 408 pages

Develop JSF, Struts, Seam, Hibernate, jBPM, ESB, web services, and portal applications faster than ever using JBoss Tools for Eclipse and the JBoss Application Server

1. Develop complete JSF, Struts, Seam, Hibernate, jBPM, ESB, web service, and portlet applications using JBoss Tools

2. Tools covered in separate chapters so you can dive into the one you want to learn

3. Manage JBoss Application Server through JBoss AS Tools

4. Explore Hibernate Tools including reverse engineering and code generation techniques

Please check **www.PacktPub.com** for information on our titles

Liferay Portal 5.2 Systems Development

ISBN: 978-1-847194-70-1 Paperback: 420 pages

Build Java-based custom intranet systems on top of Liferay portal

1. Learn to use Liferay tools to create your own applications as a Java developer, with hands-on examples

2. Customize Liferay portal using the JSR-286 portlet, extension environment, and Struts framework

3. Build your own Social Office with portlets, hooks, and themes and manage your own community

4. The only Liferay book aimed at Java developers

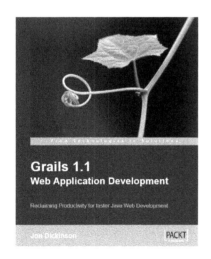

Grails 1.1 Web Application Development

ISBN: 978-1-847196-68-2 Paperback: 250 pages

Reclaiming Productivity for faster Java Web Development

1. Ideal for Java developers new to Groovy and Grails — this book will teach you all you need to create web applications with Grails

2. Create, develop, test, and deploy a web application in Grails

3. Take a step further into Web 2.0 using AJAX and the RichUI plug-in in Grails

4. Packed with examples and clear instructions to lead you through the development and deployment of a Grails web application

Please check **www.PacktPub.com** for information on our titles

www.ingramcontent.com/pod-product-compliance
Lightning Source LLC
Chambersburg PA
CBHW062046050326
40690CB00016B/2995